THE HISTORICAL LITERATURE OF MORI ŌGAI

SAIKI KŌI AND OTHER STORIES

SAIKI KŌI
and other stories

VOLUME 2 OF THE HISTORICAL LITERATURE OF MORI ŌGAI

edited by
  DAVID DILWORTH
  J. THOMAS RIMER

additional contributions by
  EDMUND R. SKRZYPCZAK
  WILLIAM R. WILSON

Ж THE UNIVERSITY PRESS OF HAWAII · HONOLULU

UNESCO COLLECTION OF REPRESENTATIVE WORKS
Japanese Series

ENGLISH TRANSLATION: © UNESCO 1977

MANUFACTURED IN THE UNITED STATES OF AMERICA

BOOK DESIGN BY ROGER J. EGGERS

Library of Congress Cataloging in Publication Data

Mori, Ōgai, 1862–1922.
　Saiki Kōi and other stories.

　(The historical literature of Mori Ōgai ; v. 2)
(UNESCO collection of representative works : Japanese
series)
　Includes bibliographical references.
　1. Japan—History—Tokugawa period, 1600–1868—
Fiction. I. Title. II. Series: UNESCO collection
of representative works : Japanese series.
PL811.07A23　1977　vol. 2　895.6'3'4s　[895.6'3'4]
ISBN 0-8248-0454-6　　　77-4455

"Suginohara Shina" was previously published in *Monumenta Nipponica* 26, nos. 1 & 2, 1971, and is reprinted here by courtesy of
Monumenta Nipponica. "Yasui fujin" was previously published in
Mori Ōgai zenshū (Tokyo: Chikuma Shōbō, 1971), and is reprinted
here by courtesy of the Mori Ōgai kinenkai.

The jacket illustration is adapted from the print "Seiro no nikai,"
from the James A. Michener Collection, Honolulu Academy of
Arts.

CONTENTS

PREFACE

THE PRESENT TWO VOLUMES make available in translation a representative portion of Mori Ōgai's "historical literature." This body of writings consists of a mixed genre of historical novellas and short stories (*rekishi shōsetsu*), and of historical biographies (*shiden*). Ōgai wrote almost exclusively in this genre after the ritual suicide of General Nogi Maresuke following the death of the Emperor Meiji in 1912.

In preparing the present volumes, we have grouped the more "literary" pieces (*rekishi shōsetsu*) in volume one, and the more "biographical" pieces in volume two. In the case of each volume, however, the chronological order in which the stories and biographies were written has been preserved.

We have followed current Japanese usage in classifying Ōgai's historical literature according to the rubrics of *rekishi shōsetsu* and *shiden*. But it should be noted that Ōgai repeatedly emphasized that it was his aesthetic intent to minimize the distinction between literary and historical elements. This was part of his declared war against contemporary "naturalism," exemplified in the practice of the self-confessional "I novel," which he felt was a vehicle unsuited to the purposes of expressing the higher moral and aesthetic qualities of human life. As for "nature," he wrote, this must include the whole reservoir of hunan values and aspirations of which "history" is a mirror.

To Ōgai, all history is contemporary history, and its imaginative recreation in contemporary literary forms involves the writer in a process of creative cultural hermeneutic. His detailed repossession of significant aspects of the Japanese character, especially as reflected in the cultural life of the Tokugawa period (the chief source of subject matter for his historical literature), appears to be unparalleled among modern Japanese writers down to the present generation.

A closer reading of the "biographies" (*shiden*) in terms of Ōgai's overall aesthetic intention will yield a number of specific dividends. It is often in the biographies that Ōgai's mature reformulation of his philosophical ideas and conception of the beautiful can be found. His earlier aesthetic theory, forged in controversy over three decades of literary criticism, and his many literary portraits of himself as a writer of Apollonian temperament, as "eternal malcontent," "onlooker," and so on, are often given final expression in the themes and dialogue of the biographical pieces.

As has been pointed out in reference to *Shibue Chūsai* and other full-length biographical studies, Ōgai finally turned to the historical biography as a vehicle of pursuing an oblique literary autobiography. Just as often he used the biographical form to ring new changes on the characters and themes of his earlier fictional writings. The result was that the biographies became a unique personal activity through which Ōgai continued to weave the complex tapestry of personal reminiscence, self-reflection, and social commentary that motivated his entire literary career.

In addition to the many acknowledgments of debts of gratitude to friends and colleagues noted in the Preface to the first volume, we should like here to especially reiterate our thanks to Edmund R. Skrzypczak for his contribution of the translation of "Tsuge Shirōzaemon," and to William R. Wilson for his translation of "Saiki Kōi," in the present volume. We should also like to reiterate our expression of gratitude to Mr. Milton Rosenthal of the Division of Cultural Affairs, UNESCO, Paris, who sponsored our work, and arranged the contractual terms with The University Press of Hawaii.

THE SIGNIFICANCE
OF ŌGAI'S HISTORICAL LITERATURE

INSTITUTIONALLY, modern Japanese history is dated from the Meiji Restoration of 1868. While the deeper currents of this phase of Japan's historical process must be traced to the Tokugawa period (1600–1867), the forty-four years named for the Meiji emperor were clearly a watershed. To be sure, the cultural dynamics of this recent chapter in Japanese history can be compared with earlier periods, for it is obvious that the Nara, Heian, Kamakura, Muromachi, and Tokugawa periods of Japanese history were each a "modern" age in their time. In the Meiji period, however, Japan embarked upon a course of immense consequences. Responding to external and internal pressures after centuries of virtual seclusion, she began a wholesale assimilation of Western civilization.

The thinker Fukuzawa Yukichi (1835–1901) observed at the beginning of the Meiji era that social variables were then being set in motion within Japan only comparable in scope to the large-scale importation of Chinese institutions and Buddhism in the sixth century A.D.[1] Fukuzawa was only one of many Japanese intellectuals of the day who urged their countrymen to set themselves the task of catching up with, and even surpassing, the civilization of the Western world. And these were not merely rhetorical flourishes. Many of these early Meiji figures lived to see the basic accomplishment of this national project by the time of the death of the Meiji emperor in 1912.

By whatever measure, the political, economic, and cultural transformation of Meiji Japan bids fair to consideration as one of the major chapters in Japanese history. Heidegger has spoken of a "sense of destiny" and "shared co-historicizing" of a people who resolutely shape the givenness of their existence into their own authentic project.[2] It is difficult to deny such a self-conscious effort, and accomplishment, to the people of Meiji, for read in both general and particular terms, that is precisely what the historical record tells us. The Meiji legacy continues in the powerful economic and cultural momentum of present-day Japan.

But given the subsequent evolution of Japanese history, it is now possible to go further than Fukuzawa's generation and contend that the Meiji era appears to have been one of the outstanding matrices of cultural productivity in world history. It would be instructive to compare the Meiji achievement, for example, with that of Athens of the fifth century B.C., of China of the T'ang dynasty, or of the fifteenth-century Italian Renaissance. The Meiji era has at least a special claim to attention for having been one of the first successful points of integration of contemporary world culture.

Our present two volumes, consisting of the "historical literature" of Mori Ōgai (1862–1922), present a conspicuous—perhaps paradigmatic—instance of how Japanese cultural modernization worked in bridging the civilizations of the East and the West. By Japanese standards, Mori Ōgai was one of the more important figures of the modern Japanese cultural transformation. If this is indeed true, then Ōgai can be ranked as having contributed a share to the unfolding of contemporary world culture. Our aim in providing access to his "historical literature" through translation has been to make available to a wider reading public the essential dimensions of his thought in his final, most mature phase of writing.

Heretofore Ōgai has remained one of the more neglected figures in modern Japanese cultural history. This has been due presumably to the complexity of his life and works, which defies routine analysis. The stature of his genius and his place in Japan's cultural modernization is only now slowly coming into focus as we have gained competence in viewing Japan's modern cultural dynamics in international terms. Our decision to translate a representative selection of the final works of Ōgai's literary career has been motivated by the hope of contributing to a wider appreciation of Ōgai's exemplary role in the cultural modernization of the Meiji and Taishō (1912–1926) periods.

The fact is uncontrovertible that Ōgai was a major figure in his day. As the Japanese novelist and Marxist critic, Nakano Shigeharu, has observed, the Meiji era produced many great men in various walks of public life; yet Mori Ōgai and his contemporary, Natsume Sōseki (1867–1916), towered over their own society as the truly outstanding figures of their time. Their contemporaries looked up to Ōgai and Sōseki as articulators of the important responses to the problems of their day, as well as of deep attitudes toward life in general. For this reason their major writings became classics in their own time.[3]

Confining ourselves to Ōgai, Nakano Shigeharu has written, in another context, that Ōgai remains the most important "historical symbol" in the last century of Japanese history. He contends that the basic concerns and accomplishments of Japanese society are mirrored in Ōgai's career to a greater degree than in that of any other single figure in the first one hundred years since the Meiji Restoration.[4] As extravagant as this assessment appears to be, the specialist will be hard-pressed to refute it, for by every conceivable measure—even that of Sōseki—Ōgai exerted a major impact upon his times and reflected, par excellence, the spiritual forces at work in Japan's modernization process.

I have suggested that one reason for the neglect Ōgai has heretofore received from Western scholars is probably this protean career of Ōgai itself. He was in the vanguard of Western studies in his day. He combined a medical career with distinguished government service, culminating in his elevation to the rank of Surgeon General of the Japanese army, and in his participation in the advisory council to Yamagata Aritomo, the senior statesman of the time. For all this, Ōgai also dominated the literary world. His intellectual process as a serious student of Japanese, Chinese, and Western literary traditions, and as perhaps the peerless translator of foreign literature in modern times, suggests comparison with the outstanding Renaissance Humanists of the West and the greatest literati of China. Yet Ōgai's was an essentially modern mind. His double career as army medical doctor, teacher, and bureaucrat, on the one hand, and as translator, literary critic, essayist, novelist, poet, short-story writer, and biographer, on the other, helped shape powerful cultural dynamisms at the crucial juncture of late Meiji when international values were being internalized and integrated with their own indigenous culture by the Japanese people.[5]

There is the constant danger that the specialist in one aspect of Japanese culture will underestimate Ōgai simply for the want of a broad enough measure to deal with the versatility and productivity of his accomplishments. Ōgai himself, as we shall see below, was acutely aware of the strains to which his many-sided nature subjected him. A careful study of his career will show that he used the medium of his own literary creations as the chief means to integrate these tensions, and to probe their deeper ground in his own genius.

Japanese critics usually point to the last phase of Ōgai's writing as the time in which he most creatively integrated the dimensions of his career. This was a period of exceptional intellectual vitality during which Ōgai, between 1912 and 1918, reformulated his philosophical and aesthetic ideas in the genre of "historical literature." After the death of the Meiji emperor and the *junshi* of General Nogi and his wife in 1912, Ōgai chose to write almost exclusively in this vehicle of "historical literature"—a term inclusive of fictional (*rekishi shōsetsu*) and biographical (*shiden*) pieces. Here again specialists will find it difficult to sort out the two literary forms, since Ōgai himself did not care to make the distinction. Yet Ōgai's "historical literature" as a whole remains the most praised of his total literary output, and the primary source material for the student of his philosophical ideas.

Our present task, then, is the difficult one of endeavoring to understand Ōgai as a creative figure in the context of Japanese modernization. The center point of his own creativity was his literary output, which reached its most adequate form of expression in the "historical literature" of his last phase of writing. But we then need an appropriate conceptual model for probing the intellectual and aesthetic dimensions of Ōgai's "historical literature."

In this regard I would suggest that the philosopher Watsuji Tetsurō (1889–1960) has provided us with a productive heuristic model for probing the complexities of Ōgai's life and works. In his essay, "The Synchronistic Character of Japanese Culture," Watsuji has focused attention upon a repeated pattern of Japanese civilization, which consists of vigorous assimilation of waves of foreign civilization without the displacement of indigenous elements. According to Watsuji, the coexistence of various sediments of value traditions in a variety of integrative contexts allows for a distinctive kind of cultural dynamics. To borrow a metaphor from contemporary physics, the quantum-lattice of Japanese culture provides for a complex pattern of interflow between valuational levels and their potential energies in a given matrix of integration. Thus the creative process in the Japanese case—as exemplified in representative religious, philosophical, literary, and aesthetic forms—entails an internalization of the sedimented cultural tradition, on the one hand, and its crystallization into a new historical mode of disclosure, on the other.[6]

The mix of continuous and discontinuous cultural elements in the Meiji era clearly illustrates this conceptual model. But I would argue that the exceptional symbiosis of premodern and modern, Japanese and foreign dimensions in Ōgai's "historical literature" is a specific instance of the same phenomenon.

For example, the overlapping forms of historical novel and historical biography that became the chief vehicles of Ōgai's final phase of creative writing reflect the legacy of historiography, historical fiction, and literary biography, which has been a prevailing element in Japanese and Chinese civilizations. Noteworthy in reference to Ōgai's work is the tradition of the Japanese historical chronicles such as the *Heike monogatari*, the *Taiheiki*, and the *Gikeiki*, which have gained their permanent places in the mainstream of Japanese literature and philosophy. Ōgai's "historical literature" cannot fail to impress the thoughtful reader as having repossessed this ancient genre. But the same genre was transformed under Ōgai's pen into a personal vehicle of modern literature expressive of his mature philosophical outlook.

Again, Ōgai's aesthetic intention in working with historical materials grew out of his long-standing polemic against the self-confessional genre of contemporary "realistic" and "naturalistic" literature.[7] But while the very problematic of this debate grew out of the importation of Western forms of literature and aesthetic theory in his day, Ōgai's use of the genre of "historical literature" to illustrate his own aesthetic ideals resulted in his repossession of concepts of "reality" and "nature" deeply rooted in Oriental civilization. In such representative pieces as "Sakai jiken," "Jiisan baasan," "Tsuge Shirōzaemon," or "Saiki Kōi," for example, the reader is left with a distinct philosophical impression. In these and other such stories or biographies, Ōgai's meticulous attention to detail was guided by his aesthetic intention of creating a typology of ideal human qualities set in relief by the ineluctable working of historical and natural forces. Ōgai's characteristic touch, which takes the historical particular as expressive of the wider universal, clearly links his "historical literature" with the Buddhist and Confucian sensibilities discoverable in such works as the *Heike monogatari*, the *Taiheiki*, and the *Gikeiki* of medieval Japan, or the *Chūshingura* of the Tokugawa period.

The stylistic excellence of Ōgai's "historical literature" has been noted by Japanese novelists and critics as well.[8] Both in masterpieces of literary merit such as "Abe ichizoku" and "Sanshō dayū," and in outstanding biographical works such as "Kuriyama Daizen" and "Shibue Chūsai," Ōgai is said to have achieved a creative fusion of personal, historical, philosophical, and aesthetic dimensions through the medium of an impeccable prose narrative. However, the same kind of "synchronistic" phenomenon reappears here. After establishing himself as a leading exponent of modern Japanese prose style in his pre-1912 literary works, Ōgai combined modern colloquial Japanese with a masterful use of classical Chinese to produce the historical tone of these writings.

In a word, the significance of Ōgai's "historical literature" consists in the fact that it became the final expression of Ōgai's protean genius. At the same time, it functioned as an important vector of Japanese cultural modernization. To understand this process of conceptual and symbolic transformation that took place in Ōgai's "historical literature," and to lay the groundwork for a greater appreciation of the personal dimension in the same works, let us now consider in more detail the phenomenon of Ōgai's "double career." We will then be in a position to consider some of the leading themes of Ōgai's pre-1912 novellas and short stories. Finally we shall conclude with an analysis of the "spiritual naturalism" of Ōgai's final literary output.

Ōgai's Double Career

We have said above that the historical genre to which Ōgai turned after 1912 can be understood as the final stage of integration of the many facets of his career. Even in speaking below of his "double career"—as army medical doctor and man of letters—I am risking the danger of oversimplifying Ōgai's long struggle to hold together the many dimensions of his private and public selves. John Dower has touched upon this aspect of Ōgai's career in the following words:

> "Tsuina" is one of Ōgai's more curious, and curiously revealing, pieces—a tired composition about tiredness and the difficulties of maintaining a literary reputation when one is called upon to fulfil other obligations. As an Army medical doctor, Ōgai occupied at this time a high position in the Japanese military bureaucracy; indeed, . . . for most of his life the greater part of his time and energies were devoted to concerns other than the literary and intellectual contributions upon which his reputation now rests. The extent to which his writings were influenced by this relentless everyday fact is impossible to calculate. Certainly Ōgai himself was acutely conscious of conflicting demands, and in 1910, . . . he attempted to address (and rationalize) this dilemma in an interesting story entitled *Asobi* (Play) in which the protagonist, a clear shadow of Ōgai himself, was a minor government official who had achieved a small reputation as a writer.[9]

Ōgai's works as a whole are a record of this continuing struggle with time and circumstance to realize his literary and intellectual gifts. The sometimes rough-hewn, highly condensed, and apparently unfinished character of many of his writings undoubtedly reflect this "relentless everyday fact." On the other hand, his works have the stamp of personal authenticity which this struggle helped produce. We can go further and note that the "unfinished" and "unexpressed" qualities of his stories became an element in his own self-consciousness as an "eternal malcontent" in his middle years, and are a function of his romanticism and idealism in general. His career-long struggle to be creative in the cultural sphere can in fact be found as one symbolic motif in the late historical fiction and biographies.

Let us take note of some of the elements in Ōgai's career. Ōgai graduated from the medical school of the newly established Tokyo University in 1881 at the age of nineteen. He was among the first wave of graduates of the Meiji university system to be sent abroad, and therefore, together with such other graduates of the 1880s as Inoue Tetsujirō, Okakura Kakuzō, Uchimura Kanzō, Nitobe Inazō, Miyake Yūjirō, Tsubouchi Yuzō, and Inoue Enryō, was destined to influence the new faces who graduated from the universities in the 1890s. By the time these latter figures graduated in the 1890s—including such outstanding names as Kiyozawa Manshi, Ōnishi Hajime, Natsume Sōseki, and Nishida Kitarō—Ōgai had already sojourned four years in Germany and had begun to have an impact upon the intellectual life of the times.

Ōgai's sojourn in Germany between 1885 and 1888 was primarily devoted to advanced training in the medical field at the Universities of Leipzig, Munich, Dresden, and Berlin. Yet we have evidence of the double career he had commenced even at this demanding time. According to his "Doitsu nikki," one of the four diaries he kept during these years, Ōgai had amassed a collection of one hundred seventy volumes of Western books during the first year alone of his sojourn.[10] These included German translations of Aeschylus, Sophocles, Euripides, and Dante, as well as works of Goethe, and anthologies of German and world literatures. Concerning the influence of this reading on Ōgai's development as a man of letters, Hasegawa Izumi has observed:

> The Chinese marginalia in the books which Ōgai read in Germany often include references to passages from Takizawa Bakin and Tamenaga Shunsui as well as to Chinese classics such as the *Suikōden*. This suggests that Ōgai began to cultivate himself as a writer by reading extensively in Chinese and Japanese fiction and proceeded from there to a comparative study of Oriental and Western literatures, a method that enabled him to cover new ground while gaining fresh insights into work already done.[11]

The intriguing question here is, why was Ōgai, the advanced medical student, devoting so much of his time to European *literature* at this time? Without pursuing all aspects of this question, let me note here that Ōgai's full genius seems to have been carefully nurtured from his earliest formative years. He had received an exceptional education, which enabled him to pursue the honorable profession of his samurai forebears, who were chief doctors to the daimyo of the Tsuwano domain. Just how exceptional, according to Tokugawa standards, this education was can be surmised from Hasegawa's description:

> At a very young age, Ōgai began studying Confucianism with a private tutor and later continued his training at the Yorokan, the fief school, where he studied Confucianism, Classical Japanese Literature, and Dutch, the language of medicine. Offering courses in the Japanese Classics and studies in Dutch made the Yorokan unique for a fief school because the tendency at the time was to emphasize Confucian studies to the exclusion of everything else. The man responsible for instituting this sort of progressive curriculum in anticipa-

tion of the needs of a new Era was Kamei Koremi, the daimyo of Tsuwano fief. Kamei, who believed in special education for the intellectually gifted, sent a few outstanding students from the fief school to Tokyo each year so that they could be educated as leaders of the new age.[12]

Ōgai was sent to Tokyo and first lived in the Kamei residence, moving later to the home of a relative, Nishi Amane, one of the leading figures of the early Meiji "civilization and enlightenment" movement. Nishi had a similar background in Confucian and Dutch studies. But even during this time, when the young Ōgai was preparing in earnest for the entrance examinations at Tokyo University, he began translating into modern Japanese poems from the *Genji monogatari* and other Japanese classics. He also read extensively in Tokugawa literature. Thus, given his linguistic abilities, which in due course included German in addition to Japanese, Chinese, and Dutch, it comes as no surprise that Ōgai continued to develop his literary tastes during his sojourn in Germany as a medical student.

The oblique autobiographical dimension in most of Ōgai's writings provides the reader with a fascinating set of clues, as it were, into Ōgai's psychological development. For example, we can read *Vita Sexualis* (1909), an ostensible sexual history of Ōgai's adolescence and young manhood, in this way. This work gives us many fleeting glimpses into Ōgai's school days, his exceptional study habits, his early linguistic talents (especially in Chinese). It also documents his voracious reading of such Tokugawa writers as Bakin, Kyōden, and Shunsui during his formative years.

If these clues were not enough, eight years later (in 1917) Ōgai began his biography "Saiki Kōi" with this explicit recollection of the impact of late Tokugawa fiction upon his psychological and literary development.

When I was young I devoured the books of a lending library man who used to walk around with books stacked on his back in something like a monk's backpack. These books were mainly of three kinds: historical romances (*yomihon*), copy books (*kakihon*), and popular love stories (*ninjōbon*). The *yomihon* consisted mainly of the works of Shunsui and Kinsui; the *kakihon* were what we now call scenarios for professional storytellers. After going through all of these I asked the booklender if he had any others I hadn't read, and he recommended I try reading *zuihitsu*, or miscellaneous essays. If one can get through these too, even through the likes of the antiquarian writings of Ise Teijō, he deserves a degree in lending library literature. I got this degree.

I was first addicted to Bakin, then came to like Kyōden more; but I always preferred Shunsui to Kinsui. I developed a similar partiality later on when I read German literature, always having a greater taste for Hauptmann than Sudermann.

In this passage, I submit, we have a pregnant reminiscence by Ōgai, then fifty-five, on the development of his own literary sensibility, and perhaps on his own place in modern Japanese literature. Ōgai's literary sensibility evolved as a process of integration of his youthful absorption in Japanese classical literature and the popular romance-type literature of the late Toku-gawa period, on the one hand, and his pioneer role in introducing the values of German Romanticism through translation, literary criticism, aesthetic theory, and his own creative writing, on the other. (Particularly noteworthy in this latter regard was the influence of Ōgai's long-standing project of translating Goethe's *Faust*.)[13]

This fusion of Japanese and European literary forms is an example of the multi-level character of Japanese culture discussed above. It may be thought to be an essential dimension in "Maihime," "Utakata no ki," *Gan*, and other Ōgai romances, and it formed the basis for Ōgai's further idealistic recollection of "history in itself" in his final phase of writing. The material of some of the late historical stories and biographies can even be traced to Ōgai's later researches into Bakin, Kyōden, Shunsui, and other late Tokugawa writers.[14] But Ōgai conducted these researches and wrote his historical stories while he continued to translate such modern European authors as Ibsen, Strindberg, Dostoevski, and Gorki.

When Ōgai returned to Japan in 1888, his double career as both army medical doctor and man of letters blossomed almost simultaneously. In 1889, the twenty-seven-year-old Ōgai published *Omokage*, an anthology of seventeen poems in translation from such authors as Shakespeare, Byron, Goethe, and Heine. In the same year he organized a literary group called the Shinseisha (New Voice Society), which commenced publication of a magazine, the *Shigarami-zōshi*.[15] This magazine was dominated by Ōgai's monthly translations and literary criticism, and became one of the most important literary publications in its day.

With this start, Ōgai became the medium of wholesale importation of Western, particularly German, literature into Meiji Japan. His eventual translations included works of Goethe, Lessing, Hauptmann, Rilke, Suder-mann, Wedekind, Schnitzler, Bahr, von Hofmannsthal, Weid, von Kleist, Hacklaender, Stern, Holz, Dehmel, Wasserman, Strobl, Schiller, Eduard von Hartmann, Lermontov, Heyse, Karamazin, Pushkin, Gorki, Tolstoi, Turgenev, Zola, Rousseau, Racine, Corneille, Daudet, Aristotle, Shake-speare, Wilde, Shaw, Dunsany, Calderon, Ibsen, Bjornson, Hans Christian Andersen, Strindberg, Varhaeren, Maeterlinck, and d'Annunzio. It is significant that Ōgai continued to translate even after he had become

surgeon general of the Japanese army and had established his own reputation as a creative writer.[16]

Ōgai also became a powerful influence on the formation of the Meiji
literary consciousness through his polemics in the field of literary criticism
and in the philosophy of aesthetics.[17]

Yet all this time his army medical career developed apace. He earned
promotions as director of the Military Medical College and as chief of the
medical staff to the Imperial Guard Division. After a three-year "demo-
tion" to Kokura in Kyushu between 1899 and 1902, he returned to Tokyo,
then achieved a brilliant record for his medical contributions in innoculation
and other services at the front during the Russo-Japanese War of 1904–1905.
(At this time and afterward Ōgai was a personal and professional friend of
General Nogi, one of the heroes of the Russo-Japanese War.) He was elevat-
ed to the rank of surgeon general of the Japanese army in 1907 and became
one of Yamagata Aritomo's personal advisors at the top of the Japanese
governmental bureaucracy. Ōgai retired from the Japanese army in 1916,
and became head of the Imperial Museum and chief librarian in 1917.

Ōgai's contributions to the Japanese medical profession paralleled his impact upon the development of Meiji literature. He frequently attacked the
leaders of the Japanese medical world for their lack of scholarship and competence. He secured legislation against antiquarian medical practices, and
fought a protracted battle to organize the Japanese Medical Association on a
modern charter. Entrenched conservatives in the medical establishment at
one point forced Ōgai's resignation as editor-in-chief of the *Japanese
Medical Journal*; he countered by founding his own medical journal to continue his more progressive views.[18]

In all of these facets of his career, Ōgai gives the impression of prodigal
talents and energy. Even after his bureaucratic "exile" to the military garrison in Kokura between 1899 and 1902—during which time he is said to
have begun to formulate his philosophy of "resignation" (*teinen*)—Ōgai
studied French and Sanskrit, practiced Zen meditation, lectured on Clause-
witz's *Philosophy of War* to the officers of the Kokura army division, finished his *Sokkyō shijin* (a celebrated translation of Hans Christian
Andersen's *Improvisatoren*), and remarried (in January 1902). From Kokura
he also wrote a critique of the Tokyo-centered literary world in a work entitled "Ōgai gyōshi to wa tare zo" (in 1900).[19]

As for Ōgai's own literary works, totaling over one hundred twenty titles
(mostly short stories and novellas), three general areas of development are
discernible. The first was comprised of three romantic novellas written after
his return from Germany, namely "Maihime" (1890), "Utakata no ki"

(1890), and "Fumizukai" (1891). It has been said that Ōgai virtually established the Japanese tradition of the "I novel" (*Ich Roman*) in his own way through "Maihime," although he was ultimately to reject the naturalistic assumptions on the basis of which the same genre was later exploited by Japanese writers.[20]

The second period, which runs from the end of the Russo-Japanese War to the death of the Meiji emperor in 1912, more directly reflects Ōgai's antinaturalistic standpoint, his social criticism and philosophical musings. He composed a prodigious number of works at this time. In 1909, he published a novel, *Vita Sexualis*, and two short stories about his life in Kyushu, "Niwatori" [The chicken], and "Kinka" [The gold coin], as well as three short fictional pieces based on incidents in the difficult early days of his second marriage, "Hannichi" [Half a day], "Masui" [Anesthesia], and "Kompira," (a story, named for a famous shrine, based on the death of one of his children). In the same year he composed two of his most important stage works, "Kamen" [The mask], a contemporary drama, and "Shizuka," a historical play dealing with Yoshitsune and the Gempei wars of the late twelfth century, named for the great general's mistress.

In 1910, Ōgai finished one of his most important accomplishments, the novel *Seinen* [Youth], an account of contemporary intellectual life in Japan, and began another, *Kaijin* [Ashes], which, after a promising beginning, was left unfinished and later published only in fragments. He continued to write stories that mirrored the spiritual confusions of Meiji life. Some of these took the form of stories with a strong autobiographical element, such as "Asobi" [Play], "Dokushin" [Bachelorhood], or "Fushinchū" [Under reconstruction]; others were experiments with allegory, such as "Kodama" [The echo] or "Densha no mado" [From the streetcar window]. He wrote essays on contemporary politics, "Shokudō" [The dining room], "Chinmoku no to" [The tower of silence], and on art, "Rue Parnassus Ambulant." His famous story on Rodin's Japanese model, "Hanako," also dates from 1910.

In the following year, 1911, Ōgai continued to explore the emotional relationships between men and women in such works as "Hebi" [The snake] and "Shinjū" [Lovers' suicide], as well as in the most popular of his novels in a modern setting, *Gan* [The wild geese]. His partially autobiographical works of that year continued to explore spiritual loneliness in "Mōsō" [Delusion] and "Hyaku monogatari," which might be rendered as "The Story of a Hundred" and refers to an old-fashioned means of telling ghost stories: the listeners light candles, and when they go out, the ghost appears.

Throughout 1912, Ōgai continued his interests in the conflicts between

Eastern and Western systems of philosophy in the novella (more an intellectual tract) "Ka no yō ni" [As if], and in several short stories that pursue the same themes. He also composed an ironic essay on the Japanese literary world, "Fushigi ga kagami" [The surprising mirror], and wrote a moving, factual account of the life of a young man who, against great odds, wanted to be a doctor but died before completing his medical exams, "Hattori Chihiro."

Finally, after the *junshi* of General Nogi in 1912, Ōgai wrote "Okitsu Yagoemon no isho" and "Abe ichizoku," two stories on the subject of *junshi* set in the Tokugawa period. With this momentum he turned to write, and no less prolifically than before, in the genre of historical literature and biography. In six years he produced twenty-four works, including five novellas, eleven short stories and short biographies before 1916, and three long and five short biographies from 1916 to 1918.[21] This body of literature, to which we shall return below, probably represents one of the outstanding feats of painstaking historical research combined with creative writing, in the twentieth century.

I have said above that Ōgai's early and middle works represent a developing literary sensibility in which conceptual and symbolic elements he discovered in German literature resonated with the stratum of Japanese literature he had internalized as a youth. At the same time, these writings produced an imaginative world that concretely embodied his literary theories and aesthetic ideals. Again, they are a testament to his deepening powers of introspection and self-discipline, on the one hand, and his sensitive reactions to the political and social world, on the other. It has even been noted that Ōgai used the medium of some of his writings to articulate an indirect comment on public policies which, because of his status within the Japanese governmental bureaucracy, he could not set forth in direct terms.[22] The works of Ōgai's middle period, in particular, are a continuing reflection on a wide spectrum of contemporary social issues ranging from the question of the mythology of the Imperial House, the problems of authority in the modern state, of socialism and anarchy, and of the right of free expression, to the tensions of domestic life in Japan's rapidly changing society.

In assessing Ōgai's late phase of "historical literature" as well, we must bear in mind that Ōgai was writing as surgeon general of the Japanese army. He wrote neither for the entertainment of his potential readers, nor for pecuniary gain, nor from the despair of the alienated artist. He wrote from the dictates of his genius, to be sure, and from what I would describe as an abiding "Meiji" sensibility—that is, from a deep humanistic concern for the quality of civilization in his own times. The "historical" material of his late writings, which so remarkably repossessed the values of the pre-Meiji past, became the medium through which Ōgai continued to react to and comment upon the "modernization" process as he experienced it in his own day.[23]

Thus in addition to understanding the fusion of Tokugawa and German literary forms in his works, it is imperative for the reader to gain some insight into the philosophical sense of personal cultivation and social order which Ōgai reflects as a creative Meiji figure. The critic Katō Shūichi has indeed suggested that the greatness of Ōgai and Sōseki is bound up with the fact that they flourished in the "transitional" time of the late Meiji period when the essential philosophical values of the Tokugawa period were still a living, though transformed, part of the spiritual landscape.[24] This opinion seems to accord with Okazaki Yoshie's assessment of Ōgai as having been always an "enlightenment scholar" who strove to interpret the impact of Westernization on the indigenous Japanese modernization process.[25] The sympathetic reaction of many Japanese intellectuals who have revered Ōgai up to the present time seems partly based on the fact that they see his life and attitudes as an objectification of their own problems and concerns for meaning as modern Japanese.

But if this is so, we should ponder the implications of this phenomenon for our own interpretation of Japanese culture. In point of fact, Ōgai's "historical literature" gives the reader a vivid sense of his appreciation of a quality of spiritual life he knew had existed in the premodern, Tokugawa culture. On the whole, these writings bear eloquent witness to the continuity of Japan's premodern civilization in his own case. Simple stories such as "Jiisan baasan," "Suginohara Shina," and "Yasui fujin" bear the imprint of this appreciation. They are able to communicate Ōgai's sense of the beauty of the lives of men and women who personified the values of love, dedication, self-sacrifice, and self-cultivation, which were social ideals in the Tokugawa culture. The significance of his longer historical biography, *Shibue Chūsai*, is usually understood in this light. It probes the public and private life of a medical doctor, scholar, and man of letters of the late Edo period with whom Ōgai came to identify as almost his own earlier incarnation. He brought this project of historical self-recollection to consummation in the sequels to this work, the biographies *Izawa Ranken* and *Hōjō Katei*.[26]

If Ōgai was such a "transitional" figure in the transmission of Tokugawa culture in the late Meiji and early Taishō years, his prowess in classical Chinese was one aspect of his literary genius. This prowess has been noted by many scholars, and constitutes an important dimension of the style of the "historical literature." We can also surmise from the two stories set in T'ang

China, "Kanzan Jittoku" and "Gyogenki," that Ōgai's historical idealism included an abiding affinity with the Chinese cultural tradition. The continuing legacy of Confucian moral and intellectual cultivation, together with the variety of Dutch studies (*Rangaku*) to which he had been exposed in his early education, remained components in Ōgai's psychology as he developed into the scholar, official, and man of letters who so remarkably bridged the traditions of East and West.

But in the final analysis, Ōgai's impact upon his contemporaries consisted in the point that he contributed to their understanding of themselves as modern Japanese. His "historical" works were written, and read, as contemporary literature, expressive of the complex psychological makeup of a prominent public figure who had already communicated his inner life to his readers in the literary works of his early and middle periods.

Basic Themes of Ōgai's Pre-1912 Stories

Let us now briefly work out some of the aspects of Ōgai's inner life as he revealed it in his pre-1912 literary works. In this way we shall be in a better position to understand what he was attempting to do in his post-1912 "historical literature," and what the serious contemporary reader of this literature must have realized was taking place in Ōgai's mature psychology.

We have already noted in passing that *Vita Sexualis* (1909) furnished one clue as to the direction of Ōgai's later writings.[27] The work, a thinly veiled account of his own adolescent sexual life, was at the same time a critique of the self-confessional "I novel" and its underlying credo of Naturalism. Ōgai had engaged in this polemic ever since first returning from Germany in 1889. *Vita Sexualis* rang various changes on the distinction between love and sexual desire. It also recapitulated many of the themes and symbols of his earlier works through vignettes of his experiences and impressions as a youth. At the same time Ōgai weaved allusions to Japanese, Chinese, and German literature into these episodes. At the end he confessed that he did not know whether to call the account fact or fiction.

Vita Sexualis is important in Ōgai's developing literary career for exemplifying his basic concern to include the self-confessional approach in a wider, and more spiritual, value orientation. This unique approach, combining a selected reminiscence of personal and historical detail with an effort at imaginative expression, and both in the service of oblique spiritual autobiography, became the essential programmatic of the historical genre to which he turned only three years later.

Ironically, however, *Vita Sexualis* was grouped with the naturalistic writings of the day and banned by the authorities in the wake of a famous political trial in 1910. The goverment's sweeping suppression of free expression, combined with other political issues of the times, drew forth a complex response on Ōgai's part.[28] Not abandoning his aesthetic intention in the face of these pressures and obstacles, Ōgai began to articulate a complex philosophy of "resignation" (*teinen, akirame*) that gave a deep coloration to his already pensive works. If we bear in mind that Ōgai was himself at this time a prominent figure in the governmental bureaucracy—and commanded a wide audience of intelligent readers—we shall be better able to surmise the nuances contained in the themes and symbols of his stories and essays written between 1909 and 1912.

If we follow Okazaki Yoshie's interpretation, the concept of "resignation" formed one side of Ōgai's earliest literary expression. His first romance, "Maihime" (1898), revolves around the tension between *giri*, that is, loyalty to the performance values of clan and family, and *ninjō*, that is, the dictates of the human heart and aesthetic emotion. In "Maihime," Ōgai wrote a self-confessional account of his student days in Germany that at the same time symbolized the irreconcilable tension between his career as a public figure in the social structure and his desire to be a writer. In this work, *giri* must conquer *ninjō*, but, as Okazaki maintains, the seed had been sown in Ōgai's writings for the eventual transcendence of the former by the latter.[29]

The tension between *giri* and *ninjō*, between *teinen* ("resignation") and romantic love, reoccurs in Ōgai's next works, "Utakata no ki" and "Fumizukai." And we have clear indications of *teinen* and Ōgai's romantic idealism in *Vita Sexualis*. But for schematic purposes we can say that Ōgai's middle-period works, written between 1906 and 1912, rang various changes on the "resignation" theme, while at the end of this period his "Ka no yō ni" (1912) signaled a transition to a "new idealism" in which the "resignation" theme was transcended.

In these terms, the conceptual key to Ōgai's middle-period works can be found in an essay entitled "Yo ga tachiba" [My standpoint], also written in 1909. In this essay, Ōgai stated that he did not care to be classified or compared with such contemporary authors as Tayama Katai, Shimazaki Tōson, Masamune Hakuchō, Nagai Kafū, and Natsume Sōseki. Here "resignation" signified that Ōgai, in his own words, was "giving up all desire" of being appreciated by the Naturalism-oriented critics, and expressed contentment in his intention of "going his own way." He wrote as follows of the "serenity" (*heiki*) which this resolve had produced in him.

. . . the word that sums up my feeling best would be that of *resignation*. My feeling is not confined to the arts; every aspect of society evokes this in me. Others may think I must surely be suffering to hold such an attitude, but I am surprisingly serene. Probably there is some suggestion of faint-heartedness in an attitude of resignation, but I do not intend to make any special defense against this accusation.[30]

Despite the typical Japanese manner of self-deprecation, however, Ōgai's continuing output and unflagging energy had nothing to do with a faint-hearted attitude. It was rather a positive spiritual resolve to follow the dictates of his own self-consciousness. Spinoza's philosophy, itself mediated through Ōgai's long interest in Goethe, played a role in the formation of this "resignation" concept.[31] Like Spinoza, Ōgai was impelled to "neither laugh nor weep," but earnestly to seek to understand the ambivalences and contradictions, and the deeper harmonies, of his own life and times. But, like Goethe, Ōgai conceived of this kind of "resignation" in terms of active pursuit of duty and destiny.

We can assume that Ōgai's contemporary readers were able to understand this fusion of Japanese and German spiritual attitudes in his works. In 1910 Ōgai drew out one implication of his "resignation" concept in a short story entitled "Asobi." "Asobi" literally means "play." The protagonist, Kimura, who is both an official and a man of letters, represents another self-reflection of Ōgai at this stage in his career. Intrinsically related to the "serenity" concept found in "Yo ga tachiba," "Asobi" reexpressed Ōgai's transcendent attitude. But symbolically the *asobi* sensibility functioned as the point of harmony between politics and art, as exemplified in Ōgai's own position in late Meiji society. Other variations on the *asobi* theme appeared in "Fushigi ga kagami" and "Dengaku tōfu," both written in 1912, and can be traced into Ōgai's historical literature and biographies as well. The same sensibility contained the seeds of the contemplative, but culture-oriented, *bōkansha* ("onlooker") theme which came to the fore in Ōgai's "Hyaku monogatari" (1912), as discussed below.

Ōgai took up the question of art in a more direct way in "Hanako" (1910), a short story based upon an account of a meeting in Paris between a Japanese entertainer of questionable artistic reputation and the sculptor Auguste Rodin.[32] Far from being Ōgai's journalistic appropriation of a contemporary French account, however, "Hanako" was a brilliant tour de force in which he expressed certain elements in his own aesthetic subjectivity. This is clear from the concluding scene in which the overseas Japanese student acting as interpreter—one autobiographical reference—browses through a copy of Baudelaire's "Metaphysics of the Toy" while Rodin sketches

Hanako. Here Ōgai enlists his "play" (*asobi*) concept in the service of his theory of the beautiful and the aesthetic imagination. He employs the symbol of Rodin, the creative genius, in another self-reference. Rodin discovers in Hanako's commonplace physique a special "beauty of strength." He observes, in reference to Baudelaire's aesthetic conception:

> The same idea pertains to the human body, that the form is not interesting simply because it is form. It is a mirror of the soul. The inner flame, showing transparently through the form, alone is interesting.

Rodin also becomes a transparent symbol of the "onlooker" endowed with extraordinary spiritual perception. As for Hanako herself, she has been immortalized by Ōgai no less than by Rodin: she is the symbolic link between Ōgai's early aesthetic theory and the theme of spiritual beauty and inner strength which runs through the "historical literature" of his late phase of writing.

It is imperative to be aware of the intricate inner dialogue in Ōgai's writings. If *asobi* was one variation on the *teinen* theme articulated in 1910, Ōgai explored another—and equally autobiographical—dimension of it in "Mōsō," written in 1911. (In this work, Ōgai imagines himself in his old age; there is an intrinsic connection between "Mōsō" and *Hōjō Katei*, a late historical biography which deals with the life in retirement of a spiritual forebear of *Shibue Chūsai*.)[33] A characteristically introspective pronouncement by Ōgai in "Mōsō" has often been cited by Japanese critics as expressive of Ōgai's self-consciousness as an "eternal malcontent" (*eiennaru fuheika*) at this time. He writes of feeling a "hunger of the soul." He continues:

> What have I been doing since I was born? Pursuing always my studies, as if whipped on by something. I keep thinking that this will perfect me, make me able to carry out some task. To some extent this purpose may be fulfilled. But there is a feeling that the things I do are no more than what an actor does, who comes upon the stage and performs a certain role. A feeling that there must exist something else behind this role I play. And there is a feeling that in only being driven on there is not enough time for this something to awaken.

We must recall that Ōgai was surgeon general of the Japanese army at this time. The passage continues:

> Studying child, studying student, studying bureaucrat, studying student abroad—they are all roles. I keep wanting to wash this face painted black and red—to step a while from this stage, calmly regard myself, peek at the face of this something behind—but at my back is the lash of the stage director and I continue to perform role upon role. I cannot believe that these roles are what

life is. I wonder if something behind them might not be real life. But just as I think this something is about to awaken, it drowses and falls asleep again. The feelings like homesickness that I experience so acutely are like a floating weed that moves with the waves and drifts to far places, and yet whose movement somehow penetrates to the root. This is not the feeling of a role acted out upon a stage. But just when such a feeling seems about to raise its head a moment, suddenly it withdraws.[34]

This confession in "Mōsō" can be read in connection with the theme of Ōgai's novel *Seinen* (1910), whose hero, a literary youth named Koizumi Jun'ichi, is not particularly interested in pursuing any vocation, but "cherishes hopes of being creative." (*Seinen* proceeds to unveil a concept of "altruistic individualism," which also formed a component in Ōgai's idealistic historical literature.)

Ōgai's self-consciousness as an "eternal malcontent" in "Mōsō" was linked to his previous concepts of *teinen* and *asobi* through this kind of idealism and romanticism. Ōgai professed he was not satisfied with the actual world, and by implication, with the actual Ōgai. He felt the call to search after and express the richer possibilities of human life, as manifested in his confessed love of learning and art and his sense of the value of culture.[35]

Another intrinsic dimension of this multipolarized sensibility Ōgai elaborated in literary form the following year in "Hyaku monogatari" (1912). In this work, the protagonist Setsuzō is evidently a fusion of the early and middle Ōgai. He confesses to being a "born onlooker" (*umarenagara no bōkansha*) to life. This was related on the one hand to the "eternal malcontent" theme of the previous year, and on the other to Ōgai's "Apollonian" attitude, which already figured prominently in his uniquely "objective" literary style. Now it became an explicit philosophical attitude, tied to his rejection of the natural, instinctive self. The "onlooker" concept thus subsumed the original "resignation," "play," and "eternal malcontent" themes into a new configuration, indicative of Ōgai's spiritual individualism and quest for more adequate self-expression in spite of the internal and external obstacles he felt.

Variations on the *bōkansha* theme appear in his "Kompira" (1909), "Mōsō" (1911), *Kaijin* (1911), *Fausto kō* (1913), and *Goethe den* (1913), *Ōshio Heihachirō* (1914), and "Suginohara Shina" (1916). Of these, I would turn the reader's attention to the last mentioned, as an exemplification of the transformation of Ōgai's symbolism during his final period. In this historical biography, we read of the figure of Date Tsunamune, the young daimyo placed under house arrest in Edo, who had to "look on passively" at the so-called Sendai disturbances which broke out back in his domain. In the following passage, Ōgai weaves together the "resignation," "play," and "onlooker" themes in a historically objective, yet highly personal, self-reflection.

> Tsunamune was no ordinary daimyo. He was a gifted poet, calligrapher, and painter. He succeeded to the head of the Date house at the age of nineteen. He was lord of the 620,000 *koku* fief for barely two years when placed under house arrest for being involved in an intrigue centering around his uncle, Date Hyobu Shoyu Munekatsu. From then until he became a monk at the age of forty-four, Tsunamune was never permitted to see his son Kamechiyo, later named Tsunamura. . . . On the scrolls he did during those lonely years under domiciliary confinement, Tsunamune often used the seal *chika hikkai*, which means when one perceives his faults, he must correct them. Tsunamune's artistic talents were not confined to calligraphy and poetry. He worked in gold-lacquer ware, made pottery, and also forged swords. I find it of particular interest that Tsunamune rechannelled politically inexpressible energies in the direction of art. It is also interesting that Tsunamune's spirits did not dampen under house arrest. In the sliding door of the Shinagawa mansion he inlaid more than four hundred glass tiles, a material still rare at that time. Does this not bear witness to his indomitable spirit? His mistress Shina, who served this magnificent personality Tsunamune into his late years, was surely no ordinary woman either.

In this passage we see a typical illustration of what Japanese critics call the "new idealism" of Ōgai's historical literature. The description of Tsunamune's exceptional qualities—and of Shina, who "was surely no ordinary mistress either"—is one of many recapitulations of the main theme of "Okitsu Yagoemon no isho" written four years earlier. And this latter work, as we shall see presently, carried forward the "spiritual pragmatism" enunciated in "Ka no yō ni" just prior to the *junshi* of General Nogi.

In all of these variations on the general "resignation" concept in Ōgai's middle period, we find the keynote to be a kind of transcendent individualism as Ōgai searched for the proper vehicle to express his sense of the true and the beautiful. The turning point in this quest came in 1912 with "Ka no yō ni," which, together with "Fujidana," "Shakkuri" (both 1912), and "Tsuchi ikka" (1913), constitutes what is known as the Hidemaro series after the name of the protagonist. These works give evidence of Ōgai already beginning to transform the *teinen* sensibility of his middle years in the direction of the explicit idealism of his post-1912 historical literature.

"Ka no yō ni" represented Ōgai's endeavor to ponder the relationship between art, morality, and religion, on the one hand, and scholarship and science, on the other. It took its point of departure from the "As if" (*als ob*) idealistic philosophy of Hans Vaihinger, a German thinker who interested Ōgai at this time. It was at the same time Ōgai's personal introspection on his own career. This literary dialogue in fact formed the last link between his middle works and the hermeneutical discovery of "history as it is" (*rekishi sono mama*) in his late writings. In "Ka no yō ni," Ōgai philosophized on the phenomenon of literary "fiction" as constituting its own horizon of the expression of life and value, apart from the domain of scientific "fact." He went on to suggest that the world of ultimate values, as reflected in philosophy and religion, requires a similar "spiritual pragmatism" in regard to the "absolutes" we must live by, even though they are not verifiable in the domain of scientific fact. In this way, "Ka no yō ni" takes up the theme of philosophical truth and ideals, and religious beliefs, as "fictions" analogous to literary "fiction."[36]

But it remained for Ōgai to explore the time-honored Oriental genre of "historical literature" as a higher form of creative "fiction" in which the dichotomy between the domains of ideal value and of historical fact could be overcome. Ōgai's career-long struggle to probe the core of his own personality took the form of this progressive integration of the tension between science, scholarship, and bureaucracy, on the one hand, and his literary and philosophical sensibilities, on the other. Thus, in "Ka no yō ni," Ōgai began to shift the center of gravity of his general "resignation" sensibility toward a more explicit idealism which recapitulated his earlier concern for the beautiful and aesthetic value and allowed for the fuller flowering of his genius. The external event of the *junshi* of General Nogi seems to have acted as a catalyst which stimulated the "spiritual pragmatism" already coming to the surface in Ōgai's psyche.

We should note in passing that while Ōgai went on to create in the genre of historical literature between 1912 and 1918, he pursued these same concerns in the modern, *gendai mono* form in such works as "Tsuchi ikka" (1913), "Tenchō" (1915), and "Futari no tomo" (1915). In "Tenchō" [Favor of heaven], for example, Ōgai's belief in *ten* (heaven), reminiscent of a similar attitude in the later Natsume Sōseki and Kōda Rohan, becomes apparent. This maturing of Ōgai's spirituality in "Tenchō" sheds important light on the moral and religious coloration of some of the historical stories—for example, in "Gojiingahara no katakiuchi," "Sanshō dayū," and "Takasebune."

Finally let us observe Ōgai at work in another direction around this time. He published his novel *Gan* [The wild geese] in serial form between 1911 and 1913, and thus it was completed only after the *junshi* of General Nogi and the appearance of Ōgai's "Okitsu Yagoemon no isho" in September 1912. *Gan* has usually been acclaimed as an outstanding work in the rich canon of modern Japanese literature.[37] Its sophisticated romanticism does not well accord with some characterizations of Ōgai as an aloof or cold writer. As is true of *Vita Sexualis*, there is something intensely personal in *Gan*, although expressed by Ōgai under the powerful discipline of his "Apollonian" standpoint.

The heroine of *Gan*, Otama, appears to be a projection of Ōgai's own feminine *anima* (in Jung's sense). (This is true of the female personages who appear in Ōgai's historical literature as well—for example, Yü Hsüan-chi in "Gyogenki," Sayo in "Yasui fujin," Anju in "Sanshō dayū," Run in "Jiisan baasan," Shina in "Suginohara Shina," and Ichi in "Saigo no ikku.") Ōgai, noted for his powerful masculine mind and Apollonian vision of life, appears to have been equally possessed of a delicate feminine sensitivity in the depths of his unconscious. His creative imagination strove to integrate the two sides of his psychological makeup through the medium of his literary expression.

Otama is a hauntingly affecting character into whom Ōgai poured his own mind and soul. She becomes in the course of the novel a transparent symbol of the "onlooker" as she waits each day for the student, Okada, to pass by her house. She is made to take on the full weight of Ōgai's attitude of "resignation" as well. She falls in love with Okada but has no way of revealing or consummating her emotion. She "saves" the situation for her aging father, for whose sake she has become the mistress of a moneylender, Suezō. Through her "resignation" she also saves the situation for Suezō himself. (The novel recollects many of the themes and symbols of Ōgai's earlier works, from "Maihime" onward, in the course of events.) *Bōkansha* and *teinen* sensibilities come together in this tragic but beautiful tale of the Meiji value system as internalized by Otama, and of the pull of historical forces that finally take Okada from her through his trip to Germany.

Okada, of course, represents another autobiographical dimension in *Gan*. He is another variation on Ōta, the protagonist of Ōgai's early romantic *Ich Roman*, "Maihime." We are given to feel that just as Okada and Ōta have their lives permanently touched by the tragedy of unfulfilled love, so Ōgai must ever be the "eternal malcontent" because of his pursuit of the beautiful. Read in the light of such works as "Mōsō" and "Ka no yō ni," *Gan* also suggests the inner longing, the still unexpressed genius, of Ōgai's own psyche.

Gan, at any rate, is a highly nuanced, personal expression. It is full of an intense but subdued emotion. It is clear that these sensibilities were carried over into the "historical literature" which Ōgai began to write in 1912. They contributed to the emergence of a school of literary idealism centering around Ōgai and Sōseki at this time.[38]

In retrospect, Okazaki Yoshie seems to be right in contending that the tension between "resignation" and "romantic love" formed the subcurrent of Ōgai's literature from his earliest work, "Maihime," onward. These were the two conflicting aspects of his "double career." But in this light we cannot fail to see that there is an intrinsic link between "Maihime" (1898) and *Gan* (1911–1913). We have now to see that Otama and Okada of *Gan* were, in turn, metamorphized by Ōgai into the various personages of his "historical literature." The essential thrust of his post-1912 writings involved Ōgai in transforming the various polarizations of his public and private, outer and inner, rational and emotional, scholarly and aesthetic, roles into one whole. Far from being merely "historical," his literary writings after 1912 represent Ōgai's final phase of self-expression, and the most adequate realization of his aesthetic conception of the beautiful.

The Spiritual Naturalism of Ōgai's Historical Literature

Let me begin to approach the aesthetic idealism of Ōgai's final writings by way of comparison with a similar sensibility found in the films of Ozu Yasujirō, who has often been cited as the greatest of the Japanese filmmakers. Like the ending of a typical Ōgai story, Ozu's films usually conclude on a quiet, almost hushed note. Through this means the serene beauty of the film story lingers on in the subjectivity of the viewer. The quiet endings of Ozu's "Late Spring," "Tokyo Story," or "An Autumn Afternoon," for example, seem to have a literary precedent in the calm dignity and affecting tone of the closing paragraphs of Ōgai's "Sakai jiken," "Jiisan baasan," "Takasebune," and other stories.

Apropos of this parallel, I refer the reader to the following description of the quality of restraint in an Ozu film.

> This traditional view is the view in repose, commanding a very limited field of vision but commanding it entirely. It is the attitude for watching, for listening; it is the position from which one sees the Noh, from which one partakes of the tea ceremony. It is the aesthetic passive attitude of the haiku master who sits in silence and with painful accuracy observes cause and effect, reaching essence through an extreme simplification.[39]

Allowing for the differences in aesthetic media, it might strike us that this description can be applied intact to Ōgai's "onlooker" attitude, both as a view of life and as an aesthetic technique. And to the reader of "Takasebune," "Gyogenki," or "Saiki Kōi," for example, the following words also seem apposite.

> The end effect of an Ozu film—and one of the reasons he is thought of as a
> spokesman for the Japanese tradition—is a kind of resigned sadness, a calm
> and knowing serenity which persists despite the uncertainty of life and the
> things of this world. It implies that the world will go on and that mutability,
> change, the evanescence of things, also yield their elegiac satisfactions. One
> lives with and not against time, as with environment. The Japanese call this
> quality . . . *mono no aware*, for which the nearest translation might be
> *lachrimae rerum*, Lucretius's reference to those tears caused by things as they
> are.[40]

Indeed, it was precisely such sensibilities which formed the undercurrents of
Ōgai's middle stories, and which resurfaced in his "historical literature." It
is a complex of emotions found in many Japanese aesthetic works, both ancient and modern. Ōgai was able to repossess this tradition in the genre of
"historical literature," which itself constituted the modernization of an ancient literary form.

Ōgai described his own attitude here as "Apollonian." But the more we
probe the nuances of this term, the more we shall discover Ōgai's repossession of fundamentally Shinto, Confucian, and Buddhist sensibilities. The
questions of "love" and "self" in Ōgai's earlier writings become the
themes of self-transcendence and the worth of high ideals in his later stories.
Ōgai's earlier preoccupation with the question of domestic relations and the
broader issues of social order and authority similarly return in the coherent
spiritual humanism of his "historical literature." From "Okitsu Yagoemon
no isho," which was written immediately after the *junshi* of General Nogi
and his wife, Ōgai's historical stories and biographies usually depict characters who, by transcending the instinctive, natural self, establish a deeper,
"ideal" self in relation to lord, or parent, or husband, or wife, or the honor
of their house and ancestors, or of the Japanese nation.

Further to clarify this intrinsic thematic relationship between Ōgai's middle and late phases of creative writing, let me cite two passages from his
novel *Seinen* (1910–1911), another reflection of the "resignation," "play,"
and "eternal malcontent" complex of sensibilities at that time. In the first,
the hero of the novel speaks directly of the impact of Naturalism in Japan.

> Naturalism has real and true materials, has minutely delineated each part with
> an equally rich and sensitive language, and these are really the merits of natur-
> alism. Naturalism, however, should try to put more emphasis upon the spirit-
> ual values of human beings. Miracles should not be explained in terms of sen-
> sualism. Man has two parts, body and soul, which are delicately fused into one,
> are rather huddled together. If possible, the novel should treat Man from these
> two aspects. And writers should address themselves to the reaction, struggle,
> and harmony of the two parts. In short, it is desirable that while the writer
> treads the path along which Zola has been walking, he should also build an-

other path high in the air, parallel to Zola's. . . . He should erect a spiritual
naturalism. Realize it and it will be another glory, another perfection, another
power.[41]

Ōgai was responding to his own challenge as early as *Vita Sexualis* (1909), as
we have seen. As he realized his full literary genius in his late phase of
writing, he concentrated his energies on reflecting that other glory, perfection, and power through the vehicle of his historical literature.

If the above passage is evidence of Ōgai's philosophical propensity, the
second citation from *Seinen* is equally revealing. Through the character
Omura he articulated one dimension of his "spiritual naturalism" in terms
of the standpoint of "altruistic individualism":

> We make a stout self-defense and, without flagging, we also make all life our
> concern. We render loyal service to our lord. This service, however, we render
> in our capacity as citizens, not as the slavish retainers of a former age. We
> endeavor to be filial towards our parents. We do this, however, in our capacity
> as modern children and not as previous ages when it was even possible for
> parents to sell or kill children. In short, loyalty and filial piety give value to the
> entirety of the life which we have made our concern. Thereby, daily life too at-
> tains value. It is on this basis that we can be dedicated, can sacrifice and still re-
> tain our individualism. The highest affirmation of loyalty is, similarly, to die
> in battle. When life in its universal aspect becomes our concern, individualism
> dies or, rather, is transformed into universalism. This is entirely different from
> the ordinary modern individualism which merely seeks death by rejecting
> life.[42]

The typology of ideal human qualities we find in Ōgai's late historical literature was clearly a further elaboration of these tendencies in his thought.

Among the late works, "Sahashi Jingorō" and "Gyogenki" are the hard-
est to classify in the above terms. The cunning Sahashi and the poetess Yü
Hsüan-chi are not so much paradigms of Confucian virtue or Buddhist enlightenment as embodiments of "genius." But as such they were far removed from the "common man" depicted in the naturalistic and realistic
literature which Ōgai was repudiating. Ōgai appears to have cherished a
similar unique quality in the life of Saiki Kōi, a "great man of taste" who
patronized the Tokugawa gay quarters. It is clear from other sources that
Ōgai had little literary interest in the "common man."[43] In "Suginohara
Shina," we recall, Date Tsunamune "was no ordinary daimyo" and Shina,
who dedicated her life to him, "was no ordinary mistress either." In other
variations on the theme, Okitsu Yagoemon did not think to serve his lord in
ordinary terms; the prisoner Kisuke in "Takasebune" first draws his guard's
attention as "unusual, of a type not seen before"; Ichi in "Saigo no ikku"
is no ordinary young girl. Stories emphasizing heroic samurai attitudes such

as "Abe ichizoku" and "Sakai jiken," and even biographies of memorable individuals such as "Tokō Tahei" and "Tsuge Shirōzaemon," similarly draw the reader's attention to Ōgai's perception of extraordinary human qualities.

Ōgai in fact endeavored to create an uncommon kind of literature in his late works, focusing in the main upon the idealized samurai spirit as the vehicle for his personal self-reflection and contemporary perception of society. As Donald Keene has written:

> . . . the suicide in 1912 of General Maresuke Nogi after the death of the emperor Meiji moved Mori so profoundly that he abandoned fiction in favor of painstakingly accurate historical works that depict samurai morality. The heroes of several of his works are warriors who, like General Nogi, commit suicide in order to follow their masters to the grave. Despite his early "confessional" writing, Mori shared with his samurai heroes a reluctance (akin to traditional Japanese impassivity) to dwell on the emotions. His detachment, in part possibly the result of his scientific training, made his later works seem cold, but their strength and integrity were strikingly close to the samurai ideals he so admired.[44]

Ōgai's uncommon vehicle of literary and philosophical expression has required of even his Japanese readers an unusual degree of concentration in order to be able to appreciate the precise degree of strength and integrity of his stories.

In this connection, of course, we should reiterate that the samurai ideals Ōgai admired were as much the creation of his own mind and art as Ōgai's mere return to the Japanese past. The paradox remains that Ōgai did not endeavor to write *realistic* historical fiction. The subject matter of his historical literature, accordingly, was not that of feudal values per se, but rather the universal spiritual qualities Ōgai endeavored to distill from the given historical context he portrayed.

The thematic of his first historical story, "Okitsu Yagoemon no isho," for example, is that of the value of the tea ceremony—itself a symbol of cultural sensibilities in general—in a military age. It was Ōgai's shrewd comment on Japan's modernization process in his day—and on ours, and every modernization process. The "spiritual pragmatism" of this work is directly relatable to the theme of "Ka no yō ni," as we have seen. Even Ōgai's response to General Nogi's *junshi* was expressed in this same universalizing intentionality—he obliquely commemorates General Nogi's deed as an act of *beauty* in the standpoint of universal humanity. (Sōseki, of course, achieved a similar effect in *Kokoro*.[45])

Ōgai's next work, "Abe ichizoku," took a typically more ambivalent attitude toward the subject of *junshi*. But it would again be a mistake to read this masterpiece in realistic terms. The main theme, as Okazaki Yoshie has pointed out, is rather the ideals of loyalty and sincerity, and the tragic consequences of their absence, as universal human values.[46] And "Gojiingahara no katakiuchi," while dealing with the subject of a feudal vendetta sanctioned by the Edo shogunate, has its primary aesthetic intention in the presentation of the sterling qualities of Kurōemon, Bunkichi, and Riyo, in contrast to the "modern" rationalistic doubts and consequent spiritual collapse of the son Uhei. But Kurōemon's manly pride, Bunkichi's unswerving loyalty, and Riyo's single-minded resolve are not so much depicted as customs of the late feudal age as universal forms of man.[47] Ōgai achieved a similar aesthetic effect in the tale of multiple *seppuku* in "Sakai jiken."

Ōgai's "spiritual naturalism," then, involved the predominant intentionality of presenting the beauty of the lives of persons who have lived and died according to a basically *ideal* conception of "self." He succeeds sublimely at times in capturing the self-transcending "will" and "pride" that are essential elements in the Japanese national character. But the final impact of his historical literature is not precisely the ethical quality of his characters, but rather the aesthetic beauty they embody as human beings. In this way Ōgai ultimately repossessed the aesthetic philosophy of his earlier debates on literary criticism.

"Yasui fujin" is one of the short stories that clearly reveals Ōgai's final aesthetic sensibility and technique of literary self-reflection. Its protagonist, the scholar Yasui Sokken, is depicted with a sympathetic identification which anticipates Ōgai's "spiritual autobiography" in *Shibue Chūsai*. But, as the title attests, the real subject of "Yasui fujin" is Sokken's wife Sayo. In an important passage after Sayo's death, Ōgai reflects as follows:

> What kind of woman was Sayo? Wearing rough clothing over her own beautiful skin, she passed her life serving Chūhei [Sokken], with his simple tastes. Another member of the Yasui family named Rimpei lived at Kofuse, about two *ri* from Aza-Hoshikura of Agata-mura in Obi. His wife Oshina, remembering the anniversary of Sayo's death, took to Chūhei's house a gift of lined kimono of striped cotton. Probably Sayo had rarely worn anything made of silk during her life.
>
> Sayo never refrained from the hard labors of serving her husband. Nor did she ever ask for anything in return. Nor was it a question of her being content merely with rough clothing. She never said that she wanted to live in an elaborate house, nor that she wanted all the proper things to use in her home, nor that she liked to eat good things or to see interesting things.
>
> She was surely not so foolish that she did not understand what luxury was, nor could she have been so selfless as to have no needs or desires for anything physical or spiritual. In fact Sayo did seem to have had one uncommon desire, before which all else was only dust and ashes to her. What was her desire? It was that the intelligent persons of society would say that she had hoped for the

distinction of her husband. I who write this cannot deny it. Yet on the other hand, I cannot crudely agree with the view that she merely gave her labors and her patience to her husband as some merchant invested capital for profit, but dying before any recompense could come.

Sayo had a dream, some image of the future. Until her death, did not the look in her beautiful eyes seem fixed on some far, far place; or was it that she had no leisure even to feel that her own death might be unfortunate? Was not the very object of her hope something which she never precisely clarified for herself?

Here Ōgai has departed from the historical narrative to recapitulate the "eternal malcontent" theme of "Mōsō," and has reiterated a similar Romantic effect of "looking off into the distance" that can be found in such works as "Fumizukai," "Shizuka," "Mōsō," *Gan,* "Sanshō dayū," and other stories. Sayo's precise psychology is left unclarified by Ōgai, and yet she seems to be closely related to Shina, the mistress of Date Tsunamune in "Suginohara Shina," and is perhaps even more a reincarnation of Otama in *Gan.* She takes us to the edge of gaining insight into Ōgai's own inner psychology.

Sayo functions as an important access to Ōgai's aesthetic intention in another passage:

Sayo did her housework without any care for her own looks. Still the earlier traces of "Ono no Komachi" remained there to see. About this time a man named Kuroki Magoemon came to call on Chūhei. He had formerly been a fisherman in Sotoura of Obi, but because of his detailed knowledge of natural history he had been summoned to Edo to serve under a shogunate Censor. After Sayo served them tea, Magoemon's eyes followed her back to the kitchen, and then with a crafty and humorous look he inquired of Chūhei:

"Sir, is she your wife?"

"Yes, she is," Chūhei answered noncommittally.

"Indeed. Has your wife been educated?"

"No, not to the degree of a formal education."

"Then your wife has insight over and above your learning."

"Oh, how so?"

"Because even though she is such a beautiful woman, she became your wife."

Ōgai's technique here is that of superb impressionism.

That Sayo was not only physically but spiritually beautiful—she is thus the reincarnation of the "Hanako" theme—and was blessed, or fated, to feel the call of some transcendent purpose which gave meaning to her obscure life, is an exemplification of the kind of Platonic sense of the Beautiful Ōgai seems to have felt in his own life. This kind of intimation of the Idea of the Beautiful, often accompanied by a sense of the sublime, is integral to the mood of several of Ōgai's historical stories.

The character of Anju, the young girl who sacrifices her life for the sake of

her brother's escape from slavery in "Sanshō dayū," is another illustration
of this theme. As Okazaki Yoshie has observed, Anju is the central figure of
this famous, and exquisitely written in Japanese, transformation by Ōgai of
an old Japanese legend.[48] ("Sanshō dayū" is perhaps the work in which
Ōgai has most poignantly elicited the traditional Japanese aesthetic sense of
mono no aware.) In the course of the story Anju takes on a "mystical"
dimension that sheds important light upon a similar expression of Ōgai's
symbolic imagination in other female characters—in Otama of *Gan*, for example, in the old lady Run of "Jiisan baasan," in Sayo of "Yasui fujin," in
Yū Hsüan-chi of "Gyogenki," in Ichi of "Saigo no ikku," in Suginohara
Shina in the biography of the same name, and in Iyo, the wife of Shibue
Chūsai. Anju represents the tragic, unrequited, repressed, obscure sides of
these female characters in the most extreme form. She is also a reincarnation
of Elisa of "Maihime."

   Ōgai wrote of his devotion to "history in itself," in contrast to giving free
play to his fictional imagination, in his essay "Rekishi sono mama to rekishibanare" (1915). This essay was in fact written directly after he published
"Sanshō dayū," and can be read as an exegesis on that work. At the same
time, we must bear in mind that Ōgai used the historical, or in this case
legendary, medium as a vehicle of his hermeneutical discovery of ontological
dimensions of personal and cultural experience—and as a vehicle of his literary typology of ideal human qualities. "Sanshō dayū" was a tour de force in
that Ōgai worked within a predetermined story frame to create an idealization of Anju, the central expression of his creative imagination, in his own
version of the legend. But even Zushiō is a reincarnation of other male
characters—of Ōta of "Maihime," Okada of *Gan*, of many of the samurai
personages of the late stories and biographies.

   Let us take note of only one illustration of this in "Sanshō dayū." At
precisely the point when Anju has led her puzzled brother to the peak of a
small mountain to announce her startling plan for his escape, Ōgai employs
another variation on the central Romantic symbol that appears in such works
as "Mōsō" and *Gan*, and that we cited above in our comments on "Yasui fujin":

> Anju stood there staring intently toward the south. Her eyes followed the up-
> per reaches of the Okumo River as it passed Ishiura and flowed into the harbor
> of Yura; she stopped when she saw a pagoda thrusting from the dense foliage
> on Nakayama, a mountain about two miles from the other side of the river
> bank.

After persuading Zushiō of her fateful plan, Anju "stood by the spring and
watched the figure of her brother grow smaller as he appeared, then disap-

peared behind rows of pine trees." With Zushiō now on his precarious way to safety and to the climax of the original legend, Ōgai swiftly completes the Romantic symbolization in regard to Anju:

> Later the search party sent out by Sanshō Dayū to catch the pair picked up a pair of small straw sandals at the edge of the swamp at the bottom of the hill. They belonged to Anju.

Anju's death, as well as her parting from Zushiō, retell the tragically beautiful endings of "Maihime," "Utakata no ki," *Gan*, and other works.

Against this background it becomes possible to gain insight into "Jiisan baasan," a brief masterpiece which expresses Ōgai's continued idealization of his female characters. Written six months after "Sanshō dayū," the story revolves around the spiritual beauty of the wife Run. It would, of course, be a gross misreading of this jewel of what the Japanese call *shibui* (understated) and *sabishii* (lonely) qualities to dwell on the swashbuckling samurai episode it contains. Run's exiled husband Iori suffers the consequences of his manly pride; but the story as a whole centers around the love and faithfulness of Run, and is essentially expressive of Ōgai's characteristic sense of the fate, and often tragedy, that is associated with beauty and the attainment of worth in human life. Undoubtedly another reflection of Ōgai's inner spirituality, this writer recommends that "Jiisan baasan" also be read as the sequel to *Gan* and "Sanshō dayū."

"Saigo no ikku" portrays another side of Ōgai's own psychology, emphasizing the power of will and pride in an idealized way. His oblique comment on bureaucratic types is apparent in this story and in "Kanzan Jittoku," which builds to its dramatic and ironic conclusion in similar fashion.

But all the above elements came together in "Takasebune," which we recall was written in the same year as "Shibue Chūsai" (1916). "Takasebune" raises ethical and social questions important in Ōgai's own life—such as euthanasia—in a symbolic way, and is evidently a medium for his own latter-day transformation of the *teinen* and *asobi* sensibilities of his middle years. But the work as a whole is enveloped in a mystically serene atmosphere that may best typify the "Apollonian" quality of Ōgai's final perception of life. It is a consummate expression of the fusion of intellect and emotion in Ōgai's mature temperament.

From this brief sampling of the themes of some of the historical stories we can conclude that Ōgai created his "historical literature" in an imaginative horizon which transcended the domain of formal historiography. The concepts of "history in itself" and "history as nature" which Ōgai set forth in "Rekishi sono mama to rekishibanare" were primarily *aesthetic* concepts, and not a retreat by Ōgai into the domain of scientific fact. Accordingly they do not represent a conversion to literary "realism" either, but rather an innovative effort at synthesis of his classicism and romanticism.

Ōgai always wrote autobiographically, and in this, to be sure, he retained the attitude and habits of a scholar and historian (often, self-historian) to a noteworthy extent, rather than giving free rein to his "fictional imagination." This was his own confession in "Rekishi sono mama to rekishibanare." In this way Ōgai strove to remain truer to his own disposition and genius than if he had striven to follow the contemporary standards of novelmaking. One purport of "Yo ga tachiba" (1909) was to assert his independence from the "Western" novel-making criterion which contemporary critics were exercising. In "Tsuina," published in the same year and one month after *Vita Sexualis*, he wrote: "I, with my 'thoughts in the night,' have concluded that what we call literary prose may be written about anything and in any style."[49] Like every authentic artist, Ōgai succeeded in finding his own inimitable material and style, that of historical literature as oblique spiritual autobiography. Even *Gan*, perhaps the most "novelistic" of Ōgai's writings, becomes wholly intelligible only in the light of the continuing inner dialogue which Ōgai's stories as a whole represent.

Because of the concentrated form of that inner dialogue, Ōgai's writings place heavy demands upon the reader. His stories are a complex system of interlocking and interresonating parts, an ever-compounding fund of conceptual and symbolic elements. One is left wondering, for example, at the precise relation between "Hannichi" and "Hebi," two stories that are clearly autobiographical in respect to the tense relationship that existed between Ōgai's second wife, Shigeko, and his own mother. A much more complex synthesis of symbolic elements obtains in the vivid snake symbols employed in "Hebi" (where the sight of a snake at her mother-in-law's funeral altar causes the wife to go mad) and in *Gan* (where the student Okada saves Otama's caged canary from being devoured by a snake). Often Ōgai spreads out his own self-reflection in several characters, both male and female, in the same story, only to reverse the symbolic variables in another, but interresonating story. As I have tried to suggest above, the reader must be aware that Ōgai continued this inner literary dialogue in his late historical stories: "Jiisan baasan" (1915) is the sequel not only to *Gan* (1911–1913) but to "Maihime" (1898). The reader who will take the trouble to explore this labyrinth of symbolic clues will be rewarded by a growing insight into an intense psychology and intricate genius of genuine "East-West" proportions.

According to all commentators, the most important, if not also most difficult, clues to Ōgai's spiritual autobiography came in *Shibue Chūsai*

(1916), a full-length work. He then continued this self-reflection for over a thousand more pages in *Izawa Ranken*(1917) and *Hōjō Katei* (1918). And it is of great interest that in these late historical biographies Ōgai pursued his imaginative identification not only with Chūsai, Ranken, and Katei, three generations of Tokugawa Confucian scholars, but that his essential humanity and intellectual energy is also revealed in his exploration of the historical record of Chūsai's wife Iyo, of their seven sons and seven daughters, and of more than fifteen of his friends and teachers. This extraordinary project of Ōgai's declining years, as Okazaki Yoshie has pointed out, did not originate from any external influence.[50] The same commentator has observed that the aestheticized elements in *Shibue Chūsai* are reminiscent of a similar effect in such historical classics of the Japanese tradition as the *Kojiki, Heike monogatari,* and the *Nihon gaishi.*[51] *Shibue Chūsai* is Ōgai's "classic."

In conclusion, there is a revealing passage in the opening pages of *Vita Sexualis* in which the protagonist, a philosopher named Shizuki Kanai, says he has a habit of reading many contemporary novels, but does not find many of real aesthetic worth. To Kanai, a work achieves real aesthetic value only if it meets a very high standard.[52] This observation was perhaps part of Ōgai's own self-reflective "eternal malcontent" theme and a confession of his own unrealized genius at that time. Ōgai clearly felt a high aesthetic demand. He seems to have come closest to satisfying it in his historical literature between 1912 and 1916.

Ōgai will perhaps always remain an elusive and difficult genius. Like the characters in his historical stories, he has already become an enigmatic reflection of a particular sense of values embedded in his time and circumstance. Of the Ōgai we can understand, however, we can say that he bore witness to a sense of "civilization and enlightenment" that had few parallels among his contemporaries. And his career remains paradigmatic of the strength, dynamism, and integrity of the indigenous process of Japanese modernization in the last century. We might ponder these high distinctions as we read Ōgai's historical literature. More importantly, perhaps, we should take cognizance of the fact that not only is Ōgai a great figure in this Japanese Renaissance, but that he has sought out problems that are also *our* problems, as co-inhabitants of the twentieth century.

DAVID A. DILWORTH

THE STORIES

SAHASHI JINGORŌ

THE STORY, which bears the name of its main character, is set in a period chosen by Ōgai for a number of his major historical works: the generation of consolidation just after the battle of Sekigahara in 1600. In this particular story he brings the reader close to the grandest figure of the whole period, Tokugawa Ieyasu himself, but Ieyasu is shown under rather atypical circumstances, at the end of his career and after he has officially retired from his duties as head of state.

Ōgai has written also of an important, yet often neglected, aspect of the early years of the Tokugawa period, that of foreign relations. While it is true that Ieyasu's successors maintained a policy of isolation, the early seventeenth century saw considerable activity with foreign nations. The Japanese campaigns in Korea under Toyotomi Hideyoshi just before the turn of the century ended badly for the Japanese and devastated Korea; as a result communications between the two countries were not resumed until the arrival of the mission described in Ōgai's story.

Against this tense and exotic background, Ōgai sketches a series of striking vignettes, many of them sensational and violent in nature. His understated yet precise style permits him to avoid the merely colorful, and indeed, the counterplay of cunning between Ieyasu and Sahashi tie the incidents together to provide an evocative image of the realities of the period.

ALTHOUGH TRAVEL between Japan and Korea had been discontinued since Hideyoshi had attacked the peninsula, Yoshitoshi,[1] the lord of Sōtsushima, received orders from the Tokugawa family to use his influence to negotiate a renewal of official visits. Thus toward the end of the ninth year of Keichō [1604], three priests from Korea, named Song Un-son, Nun Ik, and Kim Hyo-sun, arrived on an unofficial preliminary visit. Tokugawa Ieyasu[2] had them put up at the Daitokuji temple in Murasakino of Kyoto. Soon after the New Year ceremonies were finished, he granted them an interview when they came up to Edo in the retinue of Hidetada.[3]

The first official Korean embassy came in the fourth month of 1607. Since Ieyasu had already gone into retirement in Sumpu, the legation, which had reached Kyoto, was directed to proceed first to Edo. The members of the group reached the Honseiji in Edo several weeks later, and were granted an interview with Hidetada on the sixth day of the fifth month. The legation members left Edo on the fourteenth, and arrived at the Seikenji in Okitsu five days later. Ieyasu invited the envoys to appear for an interview at his castle in Sumpu on the twenty-first, at eleven in the morning. The envoys went first to the mansion of the Minister of State Honda Kōzukenosuke Masazumi,[4] where they changed into ceremonial robes before proceeding to the castle.

The three highest envoys on this occasion were the Grand Administrator Ryŏ Sŏk-kil, and the Grand Councillors Kyŏng-sŏm and Chŏng Ho-Kwan. They rode in palanquins decorated with Korean designs. In Ryŏ's palanquin, a doll holding an artificial flower had been placed on the right of the sitting mat. The message from Yi Yŏn, the king of Korea, was to be presented to the shogunate in Edo. The next three highest officials, Kim Ch'ŏm-chi, Pak Ch'ŏm-chi, and Kyo Ch'ŏm-chi, rode in palanquins of unpainted wood made for them in Nagasaki. They were followed by twenty-six high officials, eighty-four middle grade officials, and one hundred and forty lower officials, making a retinue of two hundred and sixty-nine persons. The whole procession consisted of one hundred and fifty saddled horses in a line, followed by more than two hundred pack horses, and over three hundred men on foot.

Before the interview at the castle took place, the official gifts from the envoys were spread out on the great veranda. There were four types of articles: sixty catties of ginseng root, thirty rolls of white hemp cloth, one hundred

TRANSLATED BY J. THOMAS RIMER

catties of honey, and a hundred catties of beeswax. Compared with the eleven articles presented to the shogun in Edo, the presentation arranged for Ieyasu was a far less formal one. In the beginning there had been no intention on the part of the envoys to divide the gifts between Edo and Sumpu, and therefore the latter arrangements were no doubt made in light of these sudden difficulties. In Edo, the list which accompanied the king's message mentioned eleven articles, but it was said that the document showed that it had undergone some revision.

On this occasion Ieyasu was dressed in green. He sat on a cushion covered with a striped brocade placed on top of two tatami mats. The three envoys advanced to the base of the dais, bowed deeply twice, and then ranged themselves from right to left. The three highest officials, Kim Ch'ŏm-chi, Pak Ch'ŏm-chi, and Kyo Ch'ŏm-chi, all stood together on the veranda and bowed. At this time there was no presentation of papers or documents. Nor were tea and sake presented by the hosts. After a while, the highest envoys again bowed deeply, and the three envoys on the veranda did the same. They then withdrew in order of rank.

Ieyasu, as he watched the six Koreans depart, unexpectedly inquired of his attendants, "the third man who was on the veranda—haven't I seen him before?"

Nearby Ieyasu stood Honda Masazumi and over ten other personal attendants; Yoshitoshi, who had escorted the envoys to Ieyasu, was also there. Sensing their lord's words to have some meaning concealed in them, no one replied for a certain time, until finally Yoshitoshi spoke out with a degree of caution.

"The third man is named Kyo Ch'ŏm-chi."

Ieyasu cut off Yoshitoshi with a cold glance, and he turned his eyes on the whole company.

"Does no one remember him? I am now sixty-six years old, but rarely do my eyes fail me. He was twenty-three when he fled from Hamamatsu in the eleventh year of Tenshō, and so he is forty-seven now. The brazen fellow! He's now posing as a Korean. That man is Sahashi Jingorō."

All those present exchanged glances, but this time no one ventured to speak for an even greater length of time. Honda's gaze probed Ieyasu's mood, waiting to ask him something.

Ieyasu looked at Honda. "That will do. I leave their entertainment in your charge."

Since the orders relaying Ieyasu's decision to retire to the castle at Sumpu had only been received on the twenty-fifth day of the first month of the year, the building was still under construction. Ieyasu had thus requested that the banquet be held in Honda's mansion.

As if to test his lord's mood, Honda said, "Shall we investigate that matter?"

"No. Everyone will say they know nothing about it. In fact, perhaps the senior officials do not know anything about it. In any case, it would be wise to send these envoys away as soon as you can. Make sure that the local people here have as little contact with them as possible."

Having received his lord's instructions, Honda withdrew hurriedly. Preparations for the banquet had already been made. The Korean envoys were to be entertained after returning to Honda's mansion and changing back into their ordinary clothes. When Honda came back from the castle, he found Ryŏ Sŏk-kil resting after his change of clothing. Through Yoshitoshi, Honda inquired in a round-about-manner whether, among those who had presented themselves that day, there might have been someone whom Ieyasu had known previously. The answer came back through the interpreter that Ryŏ knew nothing whatsoever about such a situation. Indeed, since he seemed truly surprised by the question, he gave no sign at all of holding back any information.

There was no commingling with the Koreans as they were entertained. When the trays of food were removed, Ōsawa Jijū, Nagai Ukonnoshin, and Jō Oribe came as messengers from Ieyasu. They presented gifts to the three highest officials: three sets of armor, three long swords, and three hundred pieces of silver. To the next three, Kyo Ch'ŏm-chi and others, they presented three ordinary swords and one hundred fifty pieces of silver. The next twenty-six in rank received two hundred pieces of silver, and those remaining were given five hundred *kwan* in coin.

By Honda's order, the entourage left before sundown and went as far as Fujieda. They had first arrived in Murasakino in Kyoto on the twenty-ninth day of the fifth month; they were now, on the eighth day of the sixth month, on their way back to Osaka, where they boarded their ship three days later.

On orders from Edo, one thousand three hundred forty men and women, taken prisoner in the attacks on Korea, were released and sailed home with the legation.

When the castle at Hamamatsu was finished in 1570,[5] Ieyasu, who then was the lord of Mikawa, went to live there and sent his son Nobuyasu[6] to live in the castle of Okazaki, where he, Ieyasu, had previously resided. It was then that Nobuyasu received the name of Okazaki Jirōsaburō Nobuyasu. When Lord Okazaki was about eighteen, he was served by a page two years younger named Sahashi Jingorō. Sahashi was a youth so quick-witted that he would begin to carry out a command even before the order was finished, and among his comrades of the same age he had no peer in the martial arts. In addition, he was known for his aesthetic sensibilities, and was especially accomplished in playing the flute.

Once, when Nobuyasu and his party returned from visiting a temple, they passed near the edge of the castle grounds. It was early in the spring, when the water was just beginning to grow warm. Suddenly they saw a heron standing on the other side of a wide pond, a pinch of cotton above the black earth at the edge of the water that shimmered in rows of sparkling silver. One of the pages asked if the bird were in range. Most in the group seemed finally to agree the bird was too far off. Jingorō said nothing at first; but after all the others concluded that the bird was impossible to shoot, he spoke, as if talking to himself, ''I wouldn't say that it was entirely impossible . . .''

At this a page named Hachiya spoke sharply to him, ''If that's what you think, let's see you do it.''

''I wouldn't mind trying, but what will you give as a wager?'' Jingorō replied.

''I'll bet you anything I've got with me,'' Hachiya countered.

''Fine! Then I'll give it a try,'' Jingorō agreed, and went over to Nobuyasu to ask his permission. Nobuyasu, now quite interested in the whole affair, asked for his own rifle from a foot soldier and handed it over to Jingorō.

''This is a question of pure chance. So don't laugh if I miss,'' Jingorō exclaimed; and then without the least hesitation, he fired. Everyone watched with bated breath; the heron seemed to start to lift its wings to fly away, but the pinch of white cotton against the black earth never moved. A spontaneous cry of praise rang out. Some foot soldiers were left behind to pick up the heron in a borrowed boat, while the rest of the party returned to the castle.

The next morning the residents of the castle were jolted by the unexpected report that the page Hachiya was dead. No sign of any wound could be found on his body. Jingorō had disappeared completely. After the heron had been shot and the company entered the castle, one of the pages overheard Jingorō say to Hachiya, ''We will talk about your promise later.'' Those who investigated Hachiya's corpse noticed that in place of his long and short swords, which had silver inscriptions, there were swords which seemed to belong to Jingorō. Otherwise, there was no evidence whatsoever to help explain this strange event. According to some of the pages, Hachiya had claimed that his swords belonged to his ancestors and that he always took very good care of them. Others remembered that Jingorō had often admired them.

Jingorō's whereabouts went unknown for a considerable time. Eventually the first anniversary of Hachiya's death passed. Then one day a cousin of

Jingorō named Sahashi Gendayū appeared at Ieyasu's castle at Hamamatsu with a request. The cousin had learned that Jingorō was hiding not far away in the countryside, and came to ask that Jingorō's life be spared. He contended that Hachiya had made a wager to Jingorō that if he hit the heron he would be willing to forfeit anything he had with him. As Jingorō had been lucky enough to hit the heron, he claimed the swords which he had been admiring for a long time. Moreover, Jingorō did not merely propose to take them, but to trade Hachiya for his own in return. But Hachiya refused, saying that these engraved swords were important in the history of the Hachiya family. Jingorō would not accept this. "After a warrior makes an oath, he will give up his life if necessary. Even if these swords are something special to you, they are the only things on your person I claim. You must give them to me." "No, I cannot. If it were my life, I would surely give it up. But even my life is not enough to give in exchange for the treasure of our house," Hachiya replied. Jingorō rejoined with the curse, "You are a dog to go back on your own promise." Hachiya, now enraged, began to draw his sword, and Jingorō gave him a good and strong blow. Hachiya never revived. Thus, the cousin said, Jingorō, who normally accomplished what he set out to do, finally took the swords from Hachiya's body, left his own behind, and fled. Gendayū related this to Ieyasu, stressing that whatever else might be said, Jingorō was a very young man, and expressing the hope that his lord might spare him, or, if that were not possible, that Jingorō might at least be permitted to commit suicide and not be reduced to dying by the hand of another.

Ieyasu heard him out and then, after some thought, gave his reply. "Your account seems to make Jingorō's motives and actions seem reasonable, although such is really not the case. However, as you say, he is a very young man, and therefore if he will perform some outstanding service for me, I will spare his life."

Gendayū acknowledged Ieyasu's words, holding his head bent almost to the floor for several moments. Finally he lifted his tear-filled eyes and looked at Ieyasu, and asked: "This service which Jingorō should perform . . . ?"

"Jingorō is said to be a very clever young man who is skilled in the martial arts. If he can, I want him to kill Amari," Ieyasu said as he rose from his mat.

There was a full moon over the castle of Koyama in the district of Haibara in the province of Totomi, where Lord Takeda Katsuyori of Kai[7] had placed his liege vassal Amari Shirōsaburō in charge of the fortification. Preparations for a moon-viewing party had been made. Amari, a very tall and heavy-bodied man, drained one large cup of sake after the other as he commanded the young warriors to display their various artistic accomplishments.

> Mikawa no mizu no
> Ikioi mo
> Koyama ga sekeba
> Tsui oreru
> Susamaji no wa
> Oto bakari

> The rush
> Of the waters of Mikawa
> Will be stopped
> By the mountains of Koyama
> Only their sound
> Is awesome!

The whole group began to sing in a boisterous fashion. After many hours had slipped by, Amari bade his guests good-night, with the exception of a newcomer among the young men there.

"Ah, what a noisy bunch they were. The moon is loveliest from this time on. Why don't you play your flute for me?" Amari asked, as he invited the young man to kneel on the pillow opposite him.

The young man played. As he was frequently called on to play at unexpected times, he always carried his flute with him. The night deepened. The wick of the candle, which now stood thin and tall where the wax had melted away, turned white on the top and cinnabar on the bottom, while the wax hung like icicles and piled up below. Its dim and muddy light was now overwhelmed by the brilliance of the moon, which bathed the whole room in its glow. The chirping of crickets nearby blended with the deep mood of the flute. Amari's eyelids grew heavy.

Suddenly the sound of the flute was cut.

"Should you be cold, my lord?"

Putting down his flute, the young man pressed softly on the left side of Amari's upturned chest, just where the family crest had been dyed into his pale blue kimono.

Amari, half dreaming, was happy to feel the young man making sure that his collar was not open. At the same instant, something as cold as ice sunk deeply into his chest from the spot where he felt the youth's warming hand. A new warmth now spread from his chest to his throat. Amari's life blood ebbed away.

Having so easily despatched Amari, a man of tremendous power and influence in Mikawa, and then having cut off his topknot as proof of the deed,

Jingorō slipped away like a weasel from the castle at Koyama. Before long, his cousin Gendayū returned to Ieyasu's mansion in Hamamatsu. Ieyasu, as he had promised, summoned Jingorō, but during the interview there was not a single word exchanged concerning Amari. Hachiya's family was by no means pleased to see Jingorō return, but they could scarcely protest against Ieyasu's wishes.

Even after Amari's death, however, the forces in the castle at Koyama did not surrender to Ieyasu. Meanwhile, a number of events took place. Uesugi Kenshin died several years after Takeda Shingen.[8] After Ieyasu was appointed commander of the Right Imperial Guards at the age of thirty-six, his family began to flourish, but in this year, when his first son Nobuyasu was twenty-one, and Ieyasu's second son Ogimaru (later Hideyasu)[9] was five, Nobuyasu was mercilessly forced to commit suicide because of a suspicion of Oda Nobunaga in regard to what became known as the "Tsukiyama Incident."[10] This very year Ieyasu's third son Nenosamaru, who later as Hidetada became the second Tokugawa shogun, was born; his younger brother Fukumatsumaru (later known as Tadayoshi)[11] was born the following year. Two years later, the forces at the castle at Koyama, an obstacle for Ieyasu for so many years, finally capitulated; indeed this event served as prelude to the tragedy which brought Takeda Katsuyori to ruin.

About the time of the destruction of the Takeda clan in 1582, the fate of the Tokugawa house hung in the balance. Akechi Mitsuhide[12] suddenly rebelled and killed Nobunaga. Hideyoshi made peace with the Mōri family in Kyushu and returned to meet Mitsuhide's challenge. Ieyasu, away from his own home base at this time as well, barely managed to escape and return to Okazaki through the combined help of Chaya Shirōjirō's money and Honda Heihachirō Tadakatsu's soldiers.[13] Ieyasu was mustering troops as far away as Narumi when a messenger from Hideyoshi arrived, announcing the death of Mitsuhide.

Just as Ieyasu was in the process of persuading the former retainers of Takeda to join with him, Hōjō Shinkurō Ujinao of Odawara fomented an uprising in Kai and mounted an attack.[14] Ieyasu, whose troops were deployed as far as Kofu, faced Hōjō's army of fifty thousand with a force of less than eight thousand men. At this time, Sahashi Jingorō, along with another young warrior, Mizuno Tōjurō Katsunari,[15] was active at Wakamiko and wounded. At the end of the year, a number of soldiers were rewarded for their valor; Jingorō was among their number, but neither Jingorō nor Tōjurō was given any special commendation.

In the eleventh year of Tenshō [1583], busy preparations were made in the Tokugawa mansion at Hamamatsu for the impending marriage of Ieyasu's second daughter, Tokuhime, into the Hōjō family in Odawara. An announcement of the marriage was sent to the family of Hideyoshi, who had now moved to Osaka.

Jingorō, who was serving in the Hamamatsu castle, was present in the adjacent room and listening when Ishikawa Yoshichirō Kazumasa came before Ieyasu and received his command to carry the news of the wedding to Osaka.

"Take some shrewd young man with you," said Ieyasu.

"In that case, perhaps Sahashi might do . . . ," Ishikawa suggested.

For a long time Ieyasu said nothing. Just as Jingorō was beginning to wonder what might have happened, Ieyasu finally replied.

"I don't want to use him out of my sight. I learned recently from the people of Kōshū who have come over to my side how Amari had loved him like his own son. And yet the cruel fellow killed Amari in his sleep."

Hearing these words, Jingorō gave an involuntary snort and nodded his head slightly. He rose from his seat and left the room; without even returning to the house where he was living with Gendayū, he vanished into thin air. When Gendayū questioned the others in the house, he learned that Jingorō always carried with him a money belt with about a hundred *ryō* in small coins.

After vanishing from Hamamatsu in 1583, was it really Jingorō who came from Korea as Kyo Ch'ŏm-chi twenty-four years later? Or was it only a mistake on Ieyasu's part? Nobody could tell for sure. When questioned, the Sahashi family all expressed complete ignorance of the matter. However, when it later became known that the family had come into possession of a very large quantity of fine quality ginseng root grown in the shape of a doll, there were persons who voiced suspicions as to where it might have come from.

This account is based on the *Zokubuge Kanwa*.[16] According to the genealogies of the Sahashi family, Jingorō had already joined an Ikkō group[17] and died in battle in 1563. In the *Koshōshi yawa*,[18] an old retainer of the Tokugawa family who participated in the Korean embassy of 1607 is identified as a certain Kakehi Matazō.[19] In works such as Hayashi Shunsai's *Kanshirai heiki*,[20] only two officials, referred to merely as Kim and Pak, are recorded as having had interviews with Ieyasu. If there is any one who knows another version of the incidents surrounding the career of Sahashi Jingorō, I would be most grateful if he would send me an outline of whatever evidence he can produce, indicating his sources.

April 1913

YASUI FUJIN

Ah, how mighty was Lord Tokugawa, his name one to make the earth tremble!
That was as it should be. And Master Bashō was a humble man, with but one
garment to his name, and his fame has come down to us, even as that of Lord
Tokugawa. Men are known not by what they are born to, but by what they do.

Thus, says the eminent modern Japanese novelist Nagai Kafū, the Tokugawa Japanese defined a virtuous man.* Mori Ōgai's story is an attempt to
give a considered portrait of one such person. The record is drawn from life:
Ōgai's model, Yasui Chūhei, or, as he was formally known, Yasui Sokken
(1799–1876), was one of the last great scholars of Chinese learning in the
late Tokugawa period. The portrait is a friendly but by no means idealized
one: Ōgai's account is based on meticulous historical research and at least
some of Sokken's blemishes, physical and spiritual, are recorded. Yet the
man who emerges is an exceptional one.

If Ōgai has managed to portray a good man, he has also succeeded in
making him sympathetic and believable as well, thanks to the cumulative
effect of the considerable detail given about Yasui's life and career, details
that are carefully selected to help construct a reality in which Ōgai's concep-
tions are carefully imbedded; the story, rather than a didactic statement, is a
carefully poised construction.

The title "Yasui Fujin," which might be translated as "The Wife of
Yasui," indicates Ōgai's deepest concerns in composing the story, for the
loving relationship between Yasui and his lovely bride Sayo is the central incident of the narrative; in fact, all that Ōgai has written serves as an explanation in depth of the remark made by Kuroki Magoemon to Yasui that
". . . even though she is such a beautiful woman, she became your wife."

 ALONG WITH THE OPINION that "Chūhei will be a great man," whispered comments that "Chūhei is ugly" spread all over the village of Kiyotake.

Chūhei's father, Yasui Sōshū, had two *tan* and eight *se* worth of land in the village of Kiyotake in Miyazaki in the province of Hyūga, where he had built a large house for himself and now lived. For income he held some nearby rice fields, and although for some years he taught Chinese learning to students in his home, he never ceased cultivating his fields. However, when he was thirty-eight Sōshū went to study in Edo, returning home two years later; because from then on he was increasingly employed by the Obi *han*, he arranged for most of his fields to be tilled by tenant farmers.

Chūhei was Yasui Sōshū's second son. When their father had left them behind to go to Edo in 1805, Chūhei was six and his brother Bunji was nine. After their father's return, the boys, now grown tall, would tuck a book inside their clothes and go off to the fields to work each morning. While the others took a rest, Bunji and Chūhei would bury themselves in their studies.

Several years later, shortly after Sōshū had been made teacher of the Obi *han*, several unpleasant incidents occurred. When Bunji, then seventeen or eighteen, and Chūhei, who must have been fourteen or fifteen, walked along to the fields as usual, passersby on the road, as if by common consent, would stare at the differences between them; if in a group, they would whisper to each other. Indeed the two did seem in every way an ill-matched pair. Bunji was tall, with white skin and splendid features, while Chūhei was short, dark, and had only one good eye. Both brothers had caught smallpox at the same time. Bunji fell only slightly ill but Chūhei was seriously stricken. He remained pockmarked by the disease and suffered the loss of his right eye. As his father had also lost an eye from smallpox as a child, the fact that Chūhei was maimed in the same way seemed proof indeed that mere Chance itself was cruel.

Chūhei began to be self-conscious about walking with his brother. Therefore in the morning he tried to finish up his breakfast before Bunji and set out earlier, and in the evening he began staying behind to finish up something or other so as to return home later. Yet passersby on the road still did not stop whispering to their companions when they saw him. And that was not all. For now they seemed even bolder than when he had walked with Bunji; they whispered louder than ever, and among the whispers there were even those who let themselves be heard.

TRANSLATED BY DAVID DILWORTH AND J. THOMAS RIMER

"Hey! Today there's the monkey walking all by himself."

"Strange to see the monkey reading a book."

"They say the monkey can read better than his trainer!"

"Mr. Monkey. What happened to your trainer today?"

In such a little-traveled place as this, Chūhei knew most of the faces he met on the road. Walking by himself, Chūhei made two discoveries. One was the fact that, although up until now he had been going along under the protection of Bunji, he had not been aware of it. The other was real cause for surprise: both of them had been given nicknames. Not only was he called "monkey" because of his ugliness, but Bunji was the "monkey trainer." Chūhei stored these discoveries away in the back of his mind and said nothing to anyone, but he no longer tried going to and from the rice fields on a separate schedule from Bunji.

Bunji, who had a frail constitution, died in his twenties, while Chūhei was attending the school of the Confucian scholar Shinozaki Shōchiku[1] in Osaka. In the spring of his twenty-first year, in 1820, Chūhei had received the sum of ten *ryō* from his father and had left Kiyotake. He arrived in Osaka at the daimyo's treasury at Tosabōri san-chome, and rented one room in a warehouse. He did all his own cooking. For the sake of economy he used to eat a meal of rice, to which he added soy beans previously cooked with salt and soy sauce. This mixture earned the name "Chūhei Beans" at the warehouse. The others who lived there, fearing that Chūhei's body could not be sustained in such a fashion, urged him to drink sake. Chūhei humbly followed their advice and bought one tiny bottle of sake each day. When evening came, he would tie up the bottle with a paper string and hang it to warm over the candle heat of the night lantern. Then facing the light, he would read through the books he had borrowed from Shinozaki's school. Later, about midnight, when everyone had quieted down, steam would come bursting forth from the mouth of the bottle, warmed at the bottom by the lantern. Chūhei would put aside his book, drink the sake with evident relish, and go to sleep. Two years later, when Chūhei was twenty-three, word reached him of Bunji's death back in Kiyotake. Inferior to Chūhei in learning, Bunji was nevertheless a young man of keen intelligence; but frail as he was, he did not last past twenty-six. When Chūhei received the news, he immediately left Osaka for home.

Later, in 1825, when Chūhei was twenty-six, he went to Edo, where he entered the Shōheikō,[2] enrolling as a pupil of Koga Tōan.[3] Chūhei, who wished to fathom the meaning of the Confucian classics directly without depending on the commentaries made in later ages, would have preferred to study with Matsuzaki Kōdō[4] rather than with Koga, but to enter the Confucian college, it was necessary for him to study first under either Hayashi[5] or Koga. Even here this country-boy scholar with his pockmarks, his one eye, and his short body, had to bear the jibes of his fellow students. Chūhei nonetheless remained silent, paid no attention to the unkind comments, and lost himself in his reading. When his friends came to tease him, they found the following verse written on a narrow strip of ornamental paper pasted on the pillar near his seat:

> Ima wa ne o
> Shinobu ga oka no
> Hototogisu
> Itsuka kumoi no
> Yoso ni nanoran
>
> Now concealing his song
> In the depths of the forest
> The nightingale
> Will one day in the sky
> Sing out clearly!

When his friends saw this they would say, "That's a pretty high-flying ambition!" and go off laughing, but actually they felt a bit uneasy inside. This verse was a momento of the time when, at nineteen, Chūhei had thrown himself into his Chinese studies and yet managed in addition to study something of Japanese literature; imitating the various styles of poetry, he had written the verse in retribution for the teasing of his friends.

While Chūhei was still in Edo, he was made tutor to the lord of the *han* at twenty-eight. When his lord returned to the Obi *han* in the following year of 1828, Chūhei accompanied him. At the beginning of that year, construction was started on a small school for the *han* at Aza Nakano in the village of Kiyotake, and the building was now partly finished. When completed, the new *han* school was to be the lecture hall to be used by both Chūhei's father Sōshū, now sixty-one, and Chūhei, now twenty-nine. It was at this point that Sōshū thought to find a wife for his son.

But this was by no means easily accomplished, for even the villagers who declared that "Chūhei will be a great man some day," upon hearing of his return from Edo and his training at the Confucian college, could not help whispering as well, "Chūhei is ugly," because of his pockmarks, his one eye, and his squat appearance.

Sōshū was now a man of experience who, when he was in his late thirties, had managed to go as far as Edo for his own training. Now that Chūhei's education was already completed and he was going on thirty, Sōshū felt that he must find a proper wife for his son. But he was well aware of how difficult the selection would be.

Sōshū was not as short as his son, but as he suffered also from pockmarks and the loss of an eye, he had lived through his own painful experiences with women because of such deformities. He knew that in his own case it had been impossible to arrange a formal meeting with an unknown girl in order to settle an engagement, and he knew that the same would be true for Chūhei, who, in addition to having his father's defects, was of much shorter stature. There was no solution other than to choose as soon as possible from among the girls who already knew Chūhei. Sōshū thought about another aspect of the situation in the light of his own past experience. Since even a woman considered beautiful cannot hide a lack of intelligence over a short period of contact, at some point her beautiful face will be forgotten. As she loses her youth in her thirties and forties, this lack of intelligence will appear on her face, and her former beauty will later seem to have been impossible. And on the contrary, even if a woman's face is flawed, if she is a person with any mental qualities, then as one comes to know her, her ugliness will come to be forgotten. Indeed as she grows older, these qualities of mind will make even her features beautiful. As for Chūhei, when one looked at him, his one black eye sparkling when he spoke, he was certainly a splendid man. These thoughts were not merely the favoritism of a parent. Indeed, Sōshū wanted to find Chūhei a wife who appreciated human character. This is more or less the way he looked at it.

At the gatherings of the relatives at yearly festivals and family memorial services, Sōshū would look over the marriageable girls. The most lovely girl, and the one who attracted the most attention, was named Yaeko. She was nineteen. Her father had worked for the daimyo's representative in Edo and had taken a bride from the capital, where Yaeko had been born. Yaeko wore her makeup in the Edo style, she spoke the Edo dialect, and her mother was teaching her to dance. Sōshū thought she was not yet at the proper age to marry, and that in any case, the choice would not be a good one. He thought that there must be some girl who was modest in appearance and yet refined, and who perhaps might even read books a little. Unfortunately there did not seem to be any such girl. They all were of the most ordinary sort indeed.

After wavering in his choice from one girl to another, Sōshū's selection finally fell on the daughter of the nearby Kawazoe family living in the Koaza-Oka section of the same Ōazaimaizumi section of Kiyotake. They were relatives of Sōshū's wife. There were two girl cousins of Chūhei in the Kawazoe family. The younger sister Sayo was sixteen and too young to be

the bride of Chūhei, who was thirty. Besides, she was considered a very attractive girl: the young men there called her "Oka no Komachi"[6] among themselves. She seemed quite unsuitable for Chūhei. As for the older sister Toyo, she was already twenty, old for an unmarried girl, although in this case, the differences of age did not present an insurmountable gap. She had very ordinary features. Her character was surely not extraordinary, but for a woman she was extremely cheerful and she said precisely what she felt. Her way of speaking her mind was very direct, and never involuted. Her mother used to say, "I am embarrassed at her lack of shyness," but it was precisely this quality which attracted Sōshū to her.

Setting his mind on Toyo, Sōshū carefully considered what means to take to broach his intentions. Whenever he spoke to the two girls, they always listened very respectfully. Thus he felt he could not speak directly to Toyo. After Sōshū's wife lost her father and mother, all the remaining family members were in an inferior position to Sōshū himself; if he announced his intentions to them, they would probably be put in an embarrassing position. He knew of other cases where after such a subject had been broached and found unsatisfactory, the two families had become estranged, at least for a time. In the case of relatives it was all the more necessary to be prudent.

Chūhei had an older sister whom people called "the wife of Nagakura." Sōshū decided to reveal his intentions to her.

"If the girl were to become the wife of Bunji, before he died, there would be no question or hesitation at all . . ." she first replied, in a diffident way. She had never looked at Toyo from the point of view her father Sōshū suggested. However, now that he asked her directly, she realized that while it indeed never occurred to her that Toyo would make a suitable wife for Chūhei, she did not know that Toyo would automatically refuse. Thus she eventually took on the role of envoy for Sōshū.

In the Kawazoe house, preparations were being made for the Doll Festival. Boxes with various labels indicating their contents were strewn out on the straw mats in the back room and from them Toyo was taking out the dolls representing the emperor and empress and the five court musicians. As she removed the cotton and Yoshino paper wrappings, her younger sister Sayo put her hands out eagerly to touch them. "It is fine the way it is. Just leave things to me," Toyo scolded her, "I'll take care of them myself."

Just then the wife of Nagakura opened the sliding door and looked in. She was carrying some branches of dark pink peach blossom which she had cut as a present. "Oh, I see you two are very busy," she said. Toyo was taking out the Jōuba dolls.[7] Putting the rake and hoe in their hands, she

stopped to look up at the peach blossoms. "Are your p
full bloom like that?" she asked. "Ours still have ver

"Since I was in a hurry to come, I just had a few
a flower arrangement, please send someone over to
like," Nagakura's wife said as she handed Toyo the branch.

Toyo took the peach branches and started for the kitchen wi
ing to her younger sister, "Just leave everything here as it is."

Nagakura's wife followed her.

Toyo took a wooden pail from a kitchen shelf, carried it out to the well,
drew a bucket of water and put the peach branches to soak. Every motion
she made was very efficient. Thinking of her reason for coming, Nagakura's
wife could not help smiling as she speculated to herself how this efficient
Toyo would quickly be a benefit to the Yasui house if she became Chūhei's
bride. Toyo, who had slipped out of her wooden clogs and entered the kitchen, was drying her hands on a towel hanging on the wall. Nagakura's wife
came over to her side.

"In the Yasui family it has been decided to arrange a wedding for Chūhei," she announced directly to Toyo.

"Oh, from where?" Toyo said.

"The bride?"

"Yes, who?"

"The bride chosen," she said as she looked straight into Toyo's eyes, "is
yourself."

Toyo's face registered annoyed astonishment, but she said nothing. After
a while she began to smile and said: "It must be a lie."

"It's true. I've been sent to tell you. Then I'm going to speak with your
mother."

Toyo let the towel slip from her hands which now hung limply by her
sides as she studied her guest's face. The smile faded from her lips. "I am
sure that Chūhei is an excellent person, but I would not want to be his
wife," she said calmly.

Toyo's refusal was so frankly expressed that Nagakura's wife could not
find any grounds to continue the conversation. However, remembering that
she had come on such an important mission and could not return without
speaking about it with the two girls' mother, she related the details of her
unsuccessful attempt to speak directly with Toyo to the wife of Kawazoe.
Then, after drinking some white wine poured out in a ceremonial cup, she
took her leave.

Since Kawazoe's wife was herself fond of Chūhei, she was quite unhappy

---

quest directly to him. Still, our introspective
you, didn't she?

"Yes she did. I am still astonished. We m
thing going on in our children's minds, but
speak with your father about her, then let me ca
to her yourself," she said, and then called Sayo i

Sayo opened the sliding panel and entered the
Her mother said to her, "About what you
would take you for his bride, you would accept, wo

Blushing right up to her ears, Sayo answere
lowered her already bowed head even farther.

Sōshū was just as surprised as Nagakura's wife. The
all was the prospective bridegroom, Chūhei! The
enced a mixture of surprise and joy, while the you
hood felt a mixture of surprise and envy. They circul
Komachi is going to the house of the Monkey." As
Kiyotake, there was no one who was not surprised at
a surprise without either joy or envy.

The marriage was sponsored by the Nagakura
held even before the peach blossoms had falle
hitherto merely attractive and doll-like Sayo
her cocoon, left behind her retiring and
a house busy with the coming and go
The new school building, call
tenth month, and as old frie
join in the celebration, the
this young wife who w
ferent from the u
gossips.

In t
thei

the bride of Chūhei, who was thirty. Besides, she was considered a very attractive girl: the young men there called her "Oka no Komachi"[6] among themselves. She seemed quite unsuitable for Chūhei. As for the older sister Toyo, she was already twenty, old for an unmarried girl, although in this case, the differences of age did not present an insurmountable gap. She had very ordinary features. Her character was surely not extraordinary, but for a woman she was extremely cheerful and she said precisely what she felt. Her way of speaking her mind was very direct, and never involuted. Her mother used to say, "I am embarrassed at her lack of shyness," but it was precisely this quality which attracted Sōshū to her.

Setting his mind on Toyo, Sōshū carefully considered what means to take to broach his intentions. Whenever he spoke to the two girls, they always listened very respectfully. Thus he felt he could not speak directly to Toyo. After Sōshū's wife lost her father and mother, all the remaining family members were in an inferior position to Sōshū himself; if he announced his intentions to them, they would probably be put in an embarrassing position. He knew of other cases where after such a subject had been broached and found unsatisfactory, the two families had become estranged, at least for a time. In the case of relatives it was all the more necessary to be prudent.

Chūhei had an older sister whom people called "the wife of Nagakura." Sōshū decided to reveal his intentions to her.

"If the girl were to become the wife of Bunji, before he died, there would be no question or hesitation at all . . ." she first replied, in a diffident way. She had never looked at Toyo from the point of view her father Sōshū suggested. However, now that he asked her directly, she realized that while it indeed never occurred to her that Toyo would make a suitable wife for Chūhei, she did not know that Toyo would automatically refuse. Thus she eventually took on the role of envoy for Sōshū.

In the Kawazoe house, preparations were being made for the Doll Festival. Boxes with various labels indicating their contents were strewn out on the straw mats in the back room and from them Toyo was taking out the dolls representing the emperor and empress and the five court musicians. As she removed the cotton and Yoshino paper wrappings, her younger sister Sayo put her hands out eagerly to touch them. "It is fine the way it is. Just leave things to me," Toyo scolded her, "I'll take care of them myself."

Just then the wife of Nagakura opened the sliding door and looked in. She was carrying some branches of dark pink peach blossom which she had cut as a present. "Oh, I see you two are very busy," she said. Toyo was taking out the Jōuba dolls.[7] Putting the rake and hoe in their hands, she stopped to look up at the peach blossoms. "Are your peach trees already in full bloom like that?" she asked. "Ours still have very tiny buds."

"Since I was in a hurry to come, I just had a few cut. If you want to make a flower arrangement, please send someone over to take as many as you like," Nagakura's wife said as she handed Toyo the branches.

Toyo took the peach branches and started for the kitchen with them, saying to her younger sister, "Just leave everything here as it is."

Nagakura's wife followed her.

Toyo took a wooden pail from a kitchen shelf, carried it out to the well, drew a bucket of water and put the peach branches to soak. Every motion she made was very efficient. Thinking of her reason for coming, Nagakura's wife could not help smiling as she speculated to herself how this efficient Toyo would quickly be a benefit to the Yasui house if she became Chūhei's bride. Toyo, who had slipped out of her wooden clogs and entered the kitchen, was drying her hands on a towel hanging on the wall. Nagakura's wife came over to her side.

"In the Yasui family it has been decided to arrange a wedding for Chūhei," she announced directly to Toyo.

"Oh, from where?" Toyo said.

"The bride?"

"Yes, who?"

"The bride chosen," she said as she looked straight into Toyo's eyes, "is yourself."

Toyo's face registered annoyed astonishment, but she said nothing. After a while she began to smile and said: "It must be a lie."

"It's true. I've been sent to tell you. Then I'm going to speak with your mother."

Toyo let the towel slip from her hands which now hung limply by her sides as she studied her guest's face. The smile faded from her lips. "I am sure that Chūhei is an excellent person, but I would not want to be his wife," she said calmly.

Toyo's refusal was so frankly expressed that Nagakura's wife could not find any grounds to continue the conversation. However, remembering that she had come on such an important mission and could not return without speaking about it with the two girls' mother, she related the details of her unsuccessful attempt to speak directly with Toyo to the wife of Kawazoe. Then, after drinking some white wine poured out in a ceremonial cup, she took her leave.

Since Kawazoe's wife was herself fond of Chūhei, she was quite unhappy about Toyo's refusal. She requested that her daughter's frivolous answer not be revealed to the house of Yasui since she wanted to try to persuade Toyo herself. Nagakura's wife therefore promised to refrain temporarily from reporting Toyo's answer. Not believing that Toyo was about to change her mind, she said, as she took her leave, "Please don't attempt to force her."

Nagakura's wife had gone about two or three cho from the Kawazoe residence when Otokichi, their man servant, came running after her. He brought the message that something important had come up, and would she please be kind enough to come back to the house?

Nagakura's wife thought this strange. She could not believe that Toyo had suddenly changed her mind. "Talk about what?" she thought, as she came back to the Kawazoe house with Otokichi. Kawazoe's wife, who was waiting for her, began to speak even before she fully entered the guest room: "Please excuse me for calling you back after you were on your way home, but something unexpected has occurred."

"Yes?" Nagakura's wife said as she studied Toyo's mother's face. "It's about Chūhei's wedding, you see. I personally feel that we would be unexpectedly fortunate to have him as a son-in-law and so I spoke to Toyo myself. However, she still refuses. Toyo told her younger sister Sayo, who then came to me as if she had something on her mind. When I asked her about it, Sayo inquired if she could be Chūhei's bride in Toyo's place. I thought that she must be saying this without clearly understanding what becoming a bride really meant, but when I questioned her further, she positively said that she wants to be Chūhei's bride, if his family will accept her. It is extremely impertinent of me, of course. Not knowing how the Yasui family will react, I'd like to ask your advice." The mother chose her words very carefully.

Nagakura's wife thought this new development even more strange. When Sōshū had brought up the matter he had said "Sayo is too young," and added "She's too pretty anyway, isn't she?" However, it was plain from her daily observations that he was not unfond of Sayo. Probably he had chosen Toyo, the older and less-exceptional sister, because she was a better match with Chūhei. Yet if the younger and more beautiful Sayo came, that was all the better. Indeed Sayo, who was not known as either aggressive or outspoken, had been able to make her feelings quite clear to her mother. After Nagakura's wife speculated in this wise, she decided she would inform her father and Chūhei of this turn of events; then, if possible, Sayo might have her wish.

"Really?" she now said to Sayo's mother. "Father has chosen Toyo, but as I think about it, Sayo might also be acceptable to him. I will take your request directly to him. Still, our introspective little Sayo certainly surprised you, didn't she?

"Yes she did. I am still astonished. We mothers think we know everything going on in our children's minds, but we're so wrong. If you will speak with your father about her, then let me call Sayo now and you can talk to her yourself," she said, and then called Sayo into the room.

Sayo opened the sliding panel and entered the room very timidly.

Her mother said to her, "About what you said before . . . if Chūhei would take you for his bride, you would accept, wouldn't you?"

Blushing right up to her ears, Sayo answered "Yes, I would," and lowered her already bowed head even farther.

Sōshū was just as surprised as Nagakura's wife. But the most surprised of all was the prospective bridegroom, Chūhei! The Yasui household experienced a mixture of surprise and joy, while the young men of the neighborhood felt a mixture of surprise and envy. They circulated jokes like "Oka no Komachi is going to the house of the Monkey." As the jokes spread around Kiyotake, there was no one who was not surprised at the news. But theirs was a surprise without either joy or envy.

The marriage was sponsored by the Nagakuras, and the ceremony was held even before the peach blossoms had fallen to the ground. Now the hitherto merely attractive and doll-like Sayo, like a butterfly coming out of her cocoon, left behind her retiring and introspective manner and took over a house busy with the coming and going of young students.

The new school building, called the Meikyōdō, was completed in the tenth month, and as old friends and relatives came to the Yasui house to join in the celebration, the guests bowed spontaneously and sincerely before this young wife who was so beautiful yet so unaffected. She was entirely different from the usual kind of young bride about whom everyone usually gossips.

In the following year (1829) when Chūhei was thirty and Sayo seventeen, their first daughter Sumako was born. In the seventh month of 1831, the *han* school was moved to Obi. The next year Sōshū, now sixty-five, became head of the Obi school, which was named the Shintokudō. Chūhei, at the age of thirty-three, served under him as assistant instructor. A neighbor, a man named Yuae, moved into their former house in Kiyotake, while the Yasui family received an estate in Kamo of Obi.

At the age of thirty-five, Chūhei accompanied the lord of the *han* to Edo, returning in the following year (1835). Sayo was for the first time left in charge of the house during this somewhat long sojourn of Chūhei.

Sōshū died of paralysis at the age of sixty-nine, the year after Chūhei returned from his second sojourn in Edo.

At the age of thirty-eight, Chūhei went to Edo for the third time, while the twenty-five-year-old Sayo again remained at home in the *han*. The following year (1838) Chūhei became a teacher in the Shōheikō school, the official Confucian college in Edo. Chūhei was then also given the office of Head of the Garrison at the *han*'s Edo mansion in Sotosakurada. He returned home the next year, then went back to Edo after only a brief stay. On this occasion he promised to call Sayo to Edo as soon as their place of residence was settled. He had resolved to resign from his *han* posts in order to open a private school and teach.

About his time Chūhei's learning was gradually gaining public recognition. Among his friends there was an excellent scholar named Shionoya Tōin.[8] As they walked along together, neither of them cut a very fine figure, but still, since the tall Shionoya stood out in contrast, people used to make jokes like "Shionoya's hips are up in the clouds, while Yasui's head is somewhere down in the grass."

Even after he went to Edo, the simple Chūhei lived an extremely frugal life. On his most recent visitation there, before entering the Shōheikō school he lived at the branch mansion of the *han* in Sendagaya. Later he lived at the main mansion in Sotosakurada and also at one time in the Konjiin within the precincts of the Zōjōji temple. In each case he cooked his own meals. More and more resolved to move into his own quarters, he lived for a time in Sendagaya, but only after a fire broke out in the lower mansion did he purchase a house sold on bankrupt terms in Gobanchō for twenty-nine *mai* of silver.

After he again moved his residence from Gobanchō to Kaminibanchō he called Sayo to Edo. They called their home the Sankei Juku.[9] Downstairs there were a few three and four-and-a-half mat rooms, and upstairs there was a study in which he hung some calligraphy in a frame of elegant spotted bamboo. Chūhei had brought the roots of this special variety with him when he left his temporary house at Kariya in the Tanomura section of his native *han* at the time he moved to Edo. Chūhei was now forty-one, Sayo twenty-eight. They had two more daughters after Sumako, Mihoko and Tomeko, but Mihoko died suddenly from unexpected complications during a minor illness. Sayo came to the Sankei Juku accompanied by Sumako, who was eleven, and Tomeko, now five.

Chūhei and Sayo did not employ any servants at the time. Sayo cooked their meals and Sumako did the shopping. Because Sumako's Hyūga accent was unintelligible to the shopkeepers, she often came home in tears without having fulfilled her missions.

Sayo did her housework without any care for her own looks. Still the earlier traces of "Oka no Komachi" remained there to be seen. About this time a man named Kuroki Magoemon came to call on Chūhei. He had formerly been a fisherman in Sotoura of Obi, but because of his detailed knowledge of natural history he had been summoned to Edo to serve under a shogunate Censor. After Sayo served them tea, Magoemon's eyes followed her back to the kitchen, and then with a crafty and humorous look he inquired of Chūhei,

"Sir, is she your wife?"

"Yes, she is," Chūhei answered noncommittally.

"Indeed. Has your wife been educated?"

"No, not to the degree of a formal education."

"Then your wife has insight over and above your learning."

"Oh, how so?"

"Because even though she is such a beautiful woman, she became your wife."

Chūhei couldn't help smiling a little. Amused at this impolite flattery of Magoemon, he played a game of go with him—something Chūhei loved to do although he was not a good player—and then saw him off.

The year that Sayo came from the *han* to Edo, Chūhei moved to Ogawa-machi, and the following year he bought a house near Ushigome-mitsuke. The price was barely two *ryō*. The eight-mat room had a tokonoma and a veranda; in addition there was a four-and-a-half mat room, a two-mat room, and a small wooden corridor. Chūhei placed his desk in the eight-mat room, piling up mountains of books around him. About this time he used to borrow books from the library of Kajimaya Seibē[10] of Reiganjima. Although Chūhei was himself a learned scholar, he never developed the habit of accumulating a library. By nature always frugal, now, although he never was short of daily necessities, it was another matter when it came to buying books. He used to borrow and return the borrowed books after reading them through and copying out the important passages. Even a trip he made to the Shinozaki private school in Osaka was for the purpose, not of studying there, but of borrowing books. He also stayed once in the Konjiin in Shiba in order to hunt out old books.

In this same year, the death by sudden illness of their third born, Tomeko, was followed by the birth of their fourth daughter, Utako.

The next year the lord of the Obi *han* became Master of Ceremonies[11] for the shogunate, and Chūhei was offered the office of Recording Secretary.[12] He declined with the excuse that his vision was bad, and indeed since he did read so much in dim light, his eyesight was not good.

The following year Chūhei moved to Nagasaka-uradori in Azabu. The house was constructed by bringing materials from the old house in Ushigome. Immediately after moving in, Chūhei made a sightseeing trip to Matsushima. He wore a slit outer coat of light-blue woven cotton, a samurai *hakama*, swords of silver design at his waist, a sedge hat on his head, and straw sandals on his feet. After his return home, Sayo now thirty-one, gave birth to their first son Yōzō. He grew into a handsome youth very much resembling his mother "Oka no Komachi," a genius of a boy who would "someday rule the empire," as it says in the twenty-ninth chapter of the *Chin-wên shang-shu*.[13] Unfortunately he died of cholera in the summer of his twenty-second year.

Two years later Chūhei and Sayo took up temporary quarters in the main mansion of the *han*, then later moved into a residence in Sodefurizaka of Banchō. That summer Sayo, aged thirty-three, gave birth to their second son, Kensuke. Unable to nurse him properly, she gave the baby over to the village headman of Zōshigaya to be cared for by a wet nurse. Kensuke grew up to be rather strange-looking, resembling his father. He took the name of Andō Ekizai and practiced medicine in Higashigane and Chiba. He also taught Chinese learning as a secondary occupation. He later committed suicide there during one of his inborn fits of anger, at the age of twenty-eight. His grave is in the Dainichi temple in Chiba.

When the American warships came to Uraga in 1846 and the whole world seemed in an uproar, Chūhei was forty-eight and Sayo was thirty-five. Chūhei had by then earned a considerable reputation and was known as the great Confucian scholar, Master Sokken. He barely managed to escape being caught up in the whirlwind of the times.

In the Obi *han*, Chūhei served as a Councillor. In 1848 he presented a plan for coastal defense. At fifty-four, in 1852, he became the friend of Fujita Tōko;[14] now Chūhei's ideas gained influence with the lord of the Mito clan.[15] The following year, in response to the threat posed by Perry's visit, he developed "A Plan to Repel the Foreigners and Defend the Harbors." Since the *han* authorities did not approve his plan, he resigned his position. Yet although he left his position of Councillor and remained only a Steward, his duties were exactly the same as before. When he was fifty-seven, he prepared "A Treatise on the Development of Hokkaidō." When he was sixty-three, he requested permission from the head of the *han* to retire. This was in the year 1860, when Ii Naosuke[16] was assassinated at the Sakurada Gate and the lord of Mito died.

The family had moved to Hayabusa-chō in 1849. The next year, because of the earthquake, they sold off what remained of their burned storehouse and various house fittings and moved to Banchō; when Chūhei was fifty-nine, he and his family moved to Zenkokujidani in Kojimachi. When they were living in Banchō, Chūhei wrote in calligraphy the phrase "no discussion of frontier matters" and hung it on the wall of his second-floor room.

Sayo had managed to recover from a serious illness when she was forty-five, but in the spring of her fiftieth year she took to her bed and died on the fourth day of the following New Year. Chūhei was then sixty-four.

Among their children were two boys, Yōzō, whose own life was soon to end as well, and Kensuke. Two of their daughters were still alive. Sumako had married the son of a steward of the Akimoto family, Tanaka Tetsunosuke, had been divorced, and then later, through the intermediary of Shionoya Tōin, had married Nakamura Teitarō,[17] a loyalist from Shimabara in Hizen who went by the pseudonym of Kitaarima Tarō. When Sumako's second husband died in prison in 1861, she returned home to her father's family with her two children, the girl Ito and her son Kotarō. Seven months after Sayo died, her daughter Utako followed her to the grave at twenty-three.

What kind of woman was Sayo? Wearing rough clothing over her own beautiful skin, she passed her life serving Chūhei, with his simple tastes. Another member of the Yasui family, named Rimpei, lived at Kofuse, about two ri from Aza-Hoshikura of Agata-mura in Obi. His wife Oshina, remembering the anniversary of Sayo's death, took to Chūhei's house a gift of a lined kimono of striped cotton. Probably Sayo had rarely worn anything made of silk during her life.

Sayo never refrained from the hard labors of serving her husband. Nor did she ever ask for anything in return. Nor was it a question of her being content merely with rough clothing. She never said that she wanted to live in an elaborate house, nor that she wanted all the proper things to use in her home, nor that she liked to eat good things or to see interesting things.

She was surely not so foolish that she did not understand what luxury was, nor could she have been so selfless as to have no needs or desires for anything physical or spiritual. In fact Sayo did seem to have had one uncommon desire, before which all else was only dust and ashes to her. What was her desire? It was that the intelligent persons of society would say that she had hoped for the distinction of her husband. I who write this cannot deny it. Yet on the other hand, I cannot crudely agree with the view that she merely gave her labors and her patience to her husband as some merchant invested capital for profit, but dying before any recompense could come.

Sayo surely had a dream, some image of the future. Until her death, did not the look in her beautiful eyes seem fixed on some far, far place; or was it that she had no leisure even to feel that her own death might be unfortunate? Was not the very object of her hope something which she never precisely clarified for herself?

In 1863, six months after his wife's death, Chūhei was brought to Edo castle, at the age of sixty-four. Two months later he was summoned for an interview with the shogun, Tokugawa Iemochi, and was given the position of Chamberlain. The next year he was awarded the even greater title of Keeper of Documents and was made a Head of the Pages. Chūhei now became a Liege Vassal, while his son Kensuke was given an office in the Obi *han*. Kensuke also later became a teacher at the shogun's Confucian college. As for the family line of succession in the *han*, in 1859 Nakamura chose Takahashi Keizaburō as a son-in-law for his daughter Ito born to Sumako. However, the young couple died soon afterward. Later Sumako's son Kotarō succeeded as head of the Yasui family.

At sixty-six, Chūhei was to be made Intendant of Hanawa in Mutsu, with an income of sixty-three thousand nine hundred *koku* a year. But pleading illness, he declined the honor and took a lesser position.

When he was sixty-five, Chūhei moved his home to Kachimachi in Shitaya. When he was sixty-seven, he lived in the main mansion of the *han* for a time, then bought a house near Hanzomon no Horibata in Kōjimachi 1-chome, and moved there. The Sea Cliff Tower where he viewed the moon with the conspirator Kumoi Tatsuo[18] was actually the second floor of that house.

In 1869, during the period when Edo suffered terrible confusions in the wake of the collapse of the shogunate, Chūhei, now seventy, made public his resignation. Soon afterward his Sea Cliff Tower was destroyed in a fire, and he lived for a time in the upper and the lower mansions of the Obi *han*. While the uproar in the city was at its height, he retired to the home of Masakichi, the younger brother of a farmer, Takahashi Zembē, at Ryōkeimura in Ōji. Since Chūhei's daughter Sumako had returned to Obi three years earlier, he was now joined by Kensuke's wife Yoshiko, who came from the Amano family, along with her child Sengiku, born the summer before. Yoshiko's body had been weakened by the childbirth, and six months after she came to live with Chūhei she died at twenty-nine, without ever seeing her husband who was then away in Shimofusa.

Chūhei remained in his place of retirement until winter and then moved to the mansion of the Hikone clan in Yoyogi. He was invited to do so because he had published for the Hikone clan a commentary on the *Tso Chuan*.[19] When he was seventy-one, Chūhei moved back to the Sakurada

mansion of his old *han*, and at seventy-three, he moved again to Dote sanbanchō.

Chūhei died on the twenty-third day of the ninth month of his seventy-
eighth year. His grandson of ten, Sengiku, born of Kensuke and Yoshiko,
became the heir to the family. After Sengiku's premature death, he was succeeded by Jirō, the second son of Kotarō.

April 1914

TSUGE SHIRŌZAEMON

IN 1869, Tsuge Shirōzaemon assassinated Yokoi Shōnan, a leading thinker and political figure of the time who, in a moderate and enlightened way, hoped to open Japan to foreign influence. Conservatives of the time approved of the violent act, yet within a few years, Tsuge's name was all but buried in oblivion as the public mood shifted dramatically to espouse a philosophy of "civilization and enlightenment" during the first decade of the Meiji period. No more eloquent statement of the effect of historical change on a generation can be imagined. The transmission to the next generation of these confusions of attitude is also an integral part of the meaning of this somber rendering by Mori Ōgai of the life and death of a man now only remembered and admired by his son, a friend of Ōgai's brother. As the son searches for the meaning of his father's life, and by implication for his own, it is easy to understand why Ōgai wrote that ". . . in studying historical records, I came to revere the reality that was evidenced in them. Any wanton change seemed distasteful to me."*

Ōgai's fidelity to history plunges the reader into the midst of the details of early Meiji history, seen not from the elevation of generalization but as it was lived and suffered through, and indeed the richness of the material provides a perfect vehicle for Ōgai's characteristic reflections on the fragility and ambivalence of the values by which men live and die. In this sense, the story is a shrewd comment on the process of "modernization."

Ōgai's final appendix gives additional details, especially those concerning Nihoko, a striking figure involved in the periphery of the account. One only regrets that he had no more materials on which to draw.

TSUGE SHIRŌZAEMON was my father. But the name probably means nothing to people now. That's only natural. Were anyone to suggest that my father died without contributing a thing to society, that he merely withered away like a weed, I would have to agree.

If I were to add by way of explanation that Tsuge Shirōzaemon was the man who beheaded Yokoi Heishirō, people no doubt would exclaim: "Oh, so that's who he was!" While no one knows my father, everyone has heard of Yokoi Heishirō. Everyone has heard of "Shōnan Sensei"[1] from Kumamoto.

To my way of thinking, the Yokoi family was a respected house, favored by fortune, while the Tsuge family was a disgraced, ill-starred one. I can only lament this circumstance. What brought about such differences of good and bad fortune, with the obscurity and fame attending each? I would like to present the whole story and clear my father's name.

At the close of the Tokugawa period, the nation was divided into two views: "Revere the Emperor" and "Support the Shogunate." Those for whom moral integrity meant anything at all clung to the former view. In all the slogan spouting at that time, "Expel the Foreigners" (*jōi*) was paired with "Revere the Emperor" (*sonnō*), and "Open the Country" (*kaikoku*) with "Support the Shogunate" (*sabaku*). In each pair the two phrases were indissolubly linked. It was impossible to conceive of one without the other—that is to say, in the minds of the people.

Viewed in the context of the general trend of history, opening of the country was inevitable, expulsion of the foreigners was impossible. The men of wisdom[2] knew that. Though knowing it, they concealed it. They thought the best way to destroy the declining shogunate lay in urging the impossible policy of expelling the foreigners. Their secret did not filter down to the attention of the masses at all.

Opening of the country was inevitable for the simple reason that Europe and America, though regarded as foreign barbarians at the time, possessed a civilization superior to ours. The men of wisdom knew that. Yokoi Heishirō was one of those who knew that earlier than others. My father was among those who, to the very end of their lives, did not grasp that fact.

In 1847 Yokoi's elder brother fell ill. Yokoi had him taken care of by a doctor of Dutch medicine, a certain Fukuma. Yokoi then was consorting with such men as Motoda Eifū,[3] and he had his own school of Neo-

TRANSLATED BY EDMUND R. SKRZYPCZAK

Confucian studies; yet when it came to treating the illness of his own brother, he turned to the medical skill of Europe. Yokoi was thirty-nine then.

In 1852 Ikebe Keita opened a school of Dutch gunnery in Kumamoto, and Yokoi sent a pupil of his to study there. Ikebe was a disciple of Takashima Shūhan[4] of Nagasaki; when Takashima had fallen under suspicion and been summoned up to Edo, Ikebe had been imprisoned along with him. Yokoi knew that Europe was superior both in military weapons and in the technical use of them. He was then forty-four.

The next year, when Yokoi was forty-five, Perry came to Yokohama. Yokoi very quickly sensed the necessity of opening the country. In 1854, at forty-six, he went to Nagasaki in order to meet the Russian envoy.[5] During his absence Yoshida Shōin visited his home, where he left a letter for Yokoi.[6] The hidden thoughts of one thinker were beginning, ever so slightly, to be communicated to another. The next year, when Yokoi turned forty-seven, the pupil studying at Nagasaki became acquainted with Katsu Yoshikuni,[7] who had gone there to study naval science, and Katsu and Yokoi began to meet. This was another contact between thinkers.

In 1866, when Yokoi was fifty-eight, he sent two nephews, Saheita[8] and Tahei, to America to study naval science. The two students were both sons of Yokoi's elder brother; the older of the two was later called Ise Tarō, and the younger, Numakawa Saburō. Yokoi had earlier succeeded to the house of his elder brother, and he in turn ceded it to Ise Tarō.

There were wise individuals among both imperial loyalists and shogunate partisans. But the former took pains to conceal the light of their wisdom, for concealment was more expedient for controlling the masses. They kept their secret so well that the necessity of opening the country did not filter down to the populace. A record which dispassionately portrays the events of that period in careful detail, like a drama, is the story of Iwakura Tomomi and Tamamatsu Misao in Inoue Kowashi's *Goin zankō*.[9] Since extracts of it appear even in textbooks, there is no need to repeat it here. But if the story is true, how was the secret kept? Why did the "secret back door" of the hermitage in Iwakuramura remain unnoticed?[10] The mass of people are fools, that's why.

I hate to say this, but I must admit my father was one of them. Yes, he was a fool. But in his defense I wish to submit two facts: first, father was a young boy at the time, and secondly, his social position was a low one.

When father was born, the wise man Yokoi was forty years old. The latter had studied in Edo at thirty-one, and at thirty-two he had returned to Kumamoto. The journey from Edo in those days was equivalent to a trip across the ocean today. Yokoi was sixty-one and in the important post of Junior Councillor when father cut him down. Father was a vagrant youth of twenty-two.

Whereas Yokoi was the son of a magistrate of the Hosokawa family (albeit his stipend came to less than two hundred *koku*), father was the son of a village headman in Okayama. When Iki Wakasa[11] became Supreme Commander of Pacification Forces in Bitchū and Echizen, father tried to join the foot soldiers of Iki's Valiant Fighting Force (Yūsentai), but even in this he met many obstacles.

Wisdom develops with age. Even though father was not intelligent by birth, who knows but that he died before he had a chance to develop the little he had? Again, wisdom grows through experience. Though father was a fool, he might have been able to correct his erroneous ideas had he had opportunities for close contact with wise men. He may not have had the makings of a prophet, but wasn't his inability to join the group of *consacrés* and learn the secret of the times due entirely to his low social position? People may say that I am just prejudiced in favor of my own kin, but I find it impossible to arrive at any other conclusion.

Our family served for generations as village heads of Ukida-mura in Jōdō District, Bizen Province. Ukida-mura used to be called Numamura; it contains the ruins of Ukita Naoie's castle.[12] The Tsuge family home was located within what still remained of the castle moat. Three ri east of Okayama, it was backwoods country with not a single feature to attract attention.

My grandfather was called "Village Headman Tsuge Ichirōzaemon." In accordance with a custom widespread in old families, he took a wife from a branch house of the same family. My grandmother's personal name was Chiyo. She was said to have been related to the Marquis Ikeda family of Bizen,[13] and to have been privileged to ride to Okayama palace in a palanquin. I imagine she was probably a wet nurse. These were my father's parents.

Father was born in 1848. His childhood name was Shikata. Again in accordance with a custom in old families, his future was arranged by his parents and he had a wedding ceremony while still a child. He exchanged nuptial cups with a girl named Take, daughter of the Shiomi family. I think this probably took place in 1851, when Shikata was four and Take, a year older, was five.

Little Shikata grew up in a turbulent world, in the midst of rumors about Perry's "black ships." In the conversations of visitors to his father's house he invariably overheard such remarks as "so-and-so is a man of 'righteousness,' " "so-and-so is a man of 'irresolution.' " "Righteousness" meant reverence for the emperor and expulsion of the barbarians, while "irresolution" meant support of the shogunate and of opening the country. Opening of the country should by rights have meant a bold, progressive policy, yet it was termed "irresolution" because it was seen as capitulation to the foreign barbarians from fear of their threats. Behind this was the subconscious influence of Chinese history, which depicts those who discuss amity with foreign barbarians as traitorous subjects. Lurking in the background of people's hatred for anyone who advocated opening the country lay a revulsion against such historical figures as Ch'in Kuai.[14] Shikata longed to grow up as fast as possible—to grow up as soon as possible and become a man of righteousness.

In 1862, at age fifteen, Shikata celebrated his coming of age and shaved his forelocks. When the tall, well-built lad bound his hair in a long queue, he looked a magnificent specimen of manhood. He was given the ordinary name Shirōzaemon, and the formal name Masayoshi. I am told the former was abbreviated in the public register to Shirō, out of deference to the Saemon in the Ikeda family. My grandfather, Ichirōzaemon, also publicly went by the name Ichirō.

Shortly after Shikata came of age, he and Take, whom till then he had treated as a sister, became true man and wife. From about this time Shikata became a resident apprentice of Abe Morie of Okayama[15] and studied swordsmanship. Abe was at that time renowned through all of Kansai for his swordsmanship.

I was born in the second month of 1863,[16] when father was sixteen and mother seventeen. I inherited father's childhood name and was called Shikata.

In the winter of 1867, long-fermenting changes in society finally reached the boiling point; Tokugawa Yoshinobu[17] restored the reins of government to the emperor and resigned his position as shogun. In Okayama, among the Han Elders who served Ikeda Echizen no kami Shigemasa, was an imperial loyalist named Iki Wakasa. This Iki had once given lodging to Kagawa Keizō of Mito, Kawada Sakuma of Inaba, Katsura Kogorō of Nagato,[18] and other such well-known loyalists, and this is why he was made Supreme Commander of the Pacification Forces of Bitchū and Echizen in January the next year, 1868.

Iki had a force of but three hundred foot soldiers. This was inadequate, so acting upon the advice of Matsumoto Minosuke,[19] he first organized what was called the Valiant Fighting Force. This he did by recruiting volunteers from the samurai of Okayama *han*. Shirōzaemon immediately tried to volunteer, but he was rejected because he was the son of a village headman, hence of low social rank.

It did not take long to assemble the Valiant Fighting Force; Noro Katsunoshin[20] was put in command, and they set out for Matsuyama in Bitchū. Shortly after the force left Okayama, Noro happened to look up front and saw, just ahead of the vanguard, a man marching briskly down the middle of the road. He looked as if he might be the force's guide. A tall, well-built fellow, he was all dressed up in court apparel, with a long-sword in his belt. Noro halted the force and had the man summoned. He identified himself as one Tsuge Shirōzaemon, pupil of Abe Morie, and went on to tell Noro his story. He had long embraced the imperial cause; when the Valiant Fighting Force was being formed, he had so desperately wanted to join that he had applied at once; for being a village headman's son he had been turned down; from a distance he had witnessed the force's stirring departure, and the thought of remaining alone in Okayama had been more than he could bear; if fighting broke out he wished to be of some help, however slight, so he was marching along with them. Noro was taken by the man's attitude and manner of speaking; without further delay he appealed to Iki and had Shirōzaemon admitted into the force. Shirōzaemon was twenty-one.

Itakura Iga no kami Katsukiyo[21] of Matsuyama was a former member of the shogun's Council of Elders, yet he had no desire to oppose the trend of the times by offering resistance to the imperial forces, so Iki's army was able to carry out its objective of pacification without shedding any blood. For about half a year, till the sixth month, the army was stationed in Matsuyama, where Iki mustered a second army. This was the so-called Loyal Fighting Force (Gisentai), commanded by Fujishima Masanoshin[22] of Bitchū.

One day a trial of martial arts was scheduled for the training ground outside the castle; divided into Bizen and Bitchū teams, the men pitted their skills against one another. Since the Bitchū team had more able swordsmen, the Bizen side was taking a bad beating. Then Shirōzaemon stepped forth and defeated several of Bitchū's most formidable swordsmen. Iki was so delighted he presented Shirōzaemon with the horse he himself rode. When the contest ended and Shirōzaemon rode back on this horse, people along the route, thinking it was Iki, bowed in obeisance.

In the sixth month Iki united the Valiant and Loyal Fighting forces and withdrew to Okayama. Both forces were billeted at a temple, the Shōrinji on Mt. Misao in Kokufu-mura. In addition to his army duties Shirōzaemon became a personal attendant of Iki Takumi,[23] member of an Iki branch family, and gave instructions in swordsmanship.

While Shirōzaemon was in the Valiant Fighting Force he made friends with Ueda Tatsuo,[24] who was something like an advisor to the commander of the Loyal Fighting Force, Fujishima Masanoshin. Whenever the two men met they spoke about the imperial cause; stirred to indignation, they saw traces of "irresolution" in the Bakufu's "total reform of the nation" (*banki-isshin*)[25] treatment of the court, and they were unhappy about the way foreigners were being accorded undeserved respect. This all stemmed from the secret intention, held all along by the senior and junior councillors, to open the country, a purpose which finally surfaced in their operation of the government.

One day Shirōzaemon and Tatsuo decided to desert the *han* and go to Kyoto. Together they would live near the imperial residence and observe at firsthand what was being done in the government. Already a plan to ferret out the root of the maladministration and promptly eradicate all the traitors on the imperial side began to take shape in the two men's hearts.

They left for Kyoto. There they inquired about, trying to ascertain which councillors were favorably disposed to the foreign devils. The one they judged to be the chief of the traitors had become a *chōshi*[26] and had come up from Kumamoto in the third month, had spent some time as a judge in the Bureau of Institutions,[27] then had been promoted to junior councillor: Yokoi Heishirō.

Yokoi had long enjoyed the confidence of his lord, Matsudaira Echizen no kami Yoshinaga;[28] he had advocated the union of court and Bakufu (*kōbu-gattai*) and had submitted to Yoshinaga a plan for opening the country. Also, through Ōkubo Kaname,[29] steward of the warden of Osaka castle (Tsuchiya Uneme no shō Tomonao),[30] he wrote to Tokugawa Yoshinobu; through the good offices of Fujita Seinoshin[31] he also wrote to Mito Nariaki.[32] Popular hearsay distorted the contents of the proposed plan. "It suggests dethronement of the emperor," people said; "He is planning to make a secret agreement with the foreigners and grant official approval to Christianity," and so on.

That the *kōbugattai* advocate Yokoi should appear somewhat suspect in the eyes of pure and simple *sonnō* loyalists was completely natural; that he appeared to them absolutely guilty stems from a different cause. Yokoi was a wise man in his day, but his way of thinking was comparatively straightforward; when he expressed his views he did not take the necessary precautions to allay men's suspicions. Yokoi recognized, in the light of political history, the value of republican government; he felt that there had existed a republican form of government in China as far back as the times of Yao and Shun, several centuries before the Athenian government: "How can we say the monarch is appointed by Heaven? The monarch is said to rule the people as the representative of Heaven, but Heaven is not a human, a person of great virtue, so how can the monarch claim he is fulfilling the mandate of Heaven? Yao turned over the reins of government to Shun. This is what tru-

ly great virtue is.'' But this did not mean he was advocating republican government in Japan. Again, Yokoi saw how the Christian religion was extremely powerful in the West because of the way it united men's minds, so
he deplored the stagnation of Shinto, Confucianism, and Buddhism. ''The
West says it has the true Teaching. This Teaching is centered around a
Supreme Being. It guides people by means of commandments. It en-
courages good and castigates vice. Both high and low believe this Teaching.
They establish their laws by it. Government and Teaching are as one. In this
way the people are inspired to action.'' This does not imply he wanted to
spread Christianity in Japan. At the close of the above lines he wrote: ''Ah,
ah! In the time of T'ang and Wu the Way was as clear as a morning sky; yet
we have abandoned it, are ignorant of it, and are instead content to become
slaves of the West.'' Yokoi was politically a *sonnō* partisan, ideologically a
Confucian. His resentment at the Japanese people's passively becoming
slaves of the West in no wise differed from the sentiment of any *jōi* partisan.
But the loyalists ended up misunderstanding Yokoi since their thinking at
that time was even simpler than his.

This was not the first time Yokoi had been considered a traitor by the
loyalists. In 1861, six years before, while serving in Edo during his lord's
absence, he was drinking in a restaurant in Gofuku-chō with Tsuzuki Shirō
and Yoshida Heinosuke[33] when assailants rushed in and tried to kill him.
Yoshida stood up to the attackers; he sustained a deep cut on one shoulder
and died as a result. Yokoi managed to slip away and fled the scene with
Tsuzuki. Yoshida's son, Shikuma, set out in revenge and slew one of the
assailants in Tsurusaki in Bungo Province. On the grounds that Yokoi's action in Gofuku-chō was sheer cowardice, he was deprived of his stipend as
soon as he returned to Kumamoto.

Ueda Tatsuo and Shirōzaemon made up their minds to watch for a chance
to slay Yokoi. But Yokoi no longer was the simple *han* warrior he had been
six years earlier. He was now a high official of the court and went about in a
palanquin, surrounded by followers and attendants. If the two attacked
alone they were bound to fail. Thus they quietly hunted among the *rōnin*
then in Kyoto and found four allies. One was Yanagida Tokuzō from Kōri-
yama *han*,[34] another was Kashima Matanojō from Bishū *han*;[35] the other two
were both from Totsugawa: Maeoka Rikio and Nakai Toneo.[36]

Shirōzaemon changed his name to Tsuchiya Nobuo and went into hiding
in the home of Miyake Tenzen[37] in Tsutsumi-chō, to the south of Shirakawa
bridge in Awata, Kyoto. From time to time the seven[38] accomplices met and
discussed plans for ''slaying the traitor.'' However, Yokoi suffered from an
intestinal ailment and for quite some time did not go to work. Reconnais-

sance of his residence revealed only that a messenger from the Cabinet[39] was making frequent trips back and forth bearing a large letter box.

The accomplices were for rushing into the residence and attacking. But Ueda, who had assumed leadership of the secret band, would not hear of it. He argued that Yokoi realized full well that he was hated by the *rōnin* and was taking full precautions at his residence; if they stormed the place, even their contingent of six men would have no guarantee of success.

As the year drew to a close, Yokoi recovered and started going to work every day. The accomplices met and resolved to carry out the job very early the next year. Once arrangements were settled, Shirōzaemon set off for his home to bid farewells.

Even after Shirōzaemon had gone to Kyoto, his father kept sending him money from the family in Ukida-mura by means of a secret messenger. The accomplices' meetings were held in a geisha house in a new section of the Gion area in order to mislead prying eyes and ears; the one who usually paid the bill for their meetings was Shirōzaemon. Fair-complexioned, gentle and calm, good-mannered even when drinking, Shirōzaemon, it is said, was idolized by the geishas and maids. One of the accomplices once said of him: "I remarked that it was a shame to make only Tsuge shell out money the way we did; there were ways to raise funds for our cause; why not imitate other people and try dunning some skinflint? At this Shirōzaemon drew himself up straight, looked around the group, and said: 'Ours is an association of righteousness. Since I am to offer myself in service of the empire, I cannot lend myself to behavior no better than that of a common thief. Even if on my deathbed I cared nothing for my own dishonor, I must not sully my ancestors' name or bequeath shame to my posterity. I, at any rate, cannot agree to the idea.' "

It was a snowy night, the last day of the year. From the house of Sugimoto, a relative of the Tsuge family also living in Ukida-mura, a messenger arrived at the Tsuge home. The matter was urgent, he said, and everyone in the house was requested to come over together, but in a manner that would not draw attention. The old couple felt something was amiss, but nevertheless told Shirōzaemon's wife, Take, to hurry and get ready. Though apprehensive that it must have something to do with her husband, my mother, who was twenty-two at the time, took me (I was six) and followed on the heels of my grandparents.

My father was waiting at the Sugimoto house. Being a mere child at the time, I cannot even recall clearly how he looked. All I faintly remember is that he said, "Hi there, son!" and smiled as he patted me on the head. I heard later he told his parents and my mother that his absence would be quite long, so he had come back for a brief visit. He set out from Ukida-mura before daybreak and hastened back to Kyoto.

The attack occurred on the afternoon of the fifth day of the first month in 1869. Yokoi Heishirō was on his way from the Cabinet office, and his palanquin had just come down the Teramachi to the section south of Goryōsha.[40] Flanking both sides of the palanquin were his followers, Yokoyama Sukeno-jō and Shimotsu Shikanosuke.[41] In addition to two attendants, Ueno Yūjirō and Matsumura Kinzaburō,[42] a sandal-bearer also accompanied the party. Suddenly a pistol shot shattered the leaden air of that cloudy day; from between two tradesmen's houses a half-dozen warriors stepped out, drawing their swords in unison. It was Ueda and his band. Nakai had purposely fired the pistol into the air to frighten the palanquin bearers and retainers.

The palanquin bearers dropped the palanquin and ran. Yokoi's followers, Yokoyama and Shimotsu (he had expected some incident on the way and had picked competent swordsmen), drew their swords and faced their adversaries. Yokoyama crossed swords with Kashima; Shimotsu crossed swords with Yanagida. Maeoka and Nakai held the attendants at bay.

As Ueda and Shirōzaemon stood watching a short distance behind the others, the flap of the palanquin opened, and out stepped Yokoi. The oldest of all the *chōshi*, he wore his slightly thinning white hair in a topknot. That year he had turned sixty-one. Without the slightest sign of panic, he gripped a short-sword in his right hand and cooly surveyed the band of men. Yokoi had once spent time learning fencing. He had refused to face the assailants in Shinagawa seven years before because there had been a chance to escape. Seeing that flight was impossible here, he was determined to fight to the bitter end.

"Now!" said Ueda with a glance at Shirōzaemon. The latter, expecting it to take but a stroke, swung down upon Yokoi. But Yokoi easily parried the blow. Fighting on equal terms with Shirōzaemon, who so prided himself on his swordsmanship, Yokoi deftly caught some fifteen blows. This short-sword remains in the Yokoi family; the blade is so badly nicked it looks more like a saw.

While Yokoi was fending off Shirōzaemon's blows, Yokoyama gashed Kashima on the forehead. With the blood running into his eyes, Kashima retreated a few steps. Ueda saw Yokoyama trying to follow up the advantage and finish off his man, so he fell upon Yokoyama from the flank. The ferocity of Ueda's attack proved too much for Yokoyama and, though he managed to graze Ueda on one arm, he broke off fighting and started to run. Hot in pursuit, Ueda slashed him across the back of the head, then gave up and returned to the scene.

Met by Yokoi's unexpected resistance, Shirōzaemon's anger flared; finally
under the vicious onslaught of Shirōzaemon's blade, the short-sword was
knocked from Yokoi's hand. In a flash Shirōzaemon plunged his sword
home; shoving Yokoi to the ground, he took hold of his topknot and cut off
his head.

"Let's go!" he shouted and started running with Yokoi's head dangling
from his left hand. Townsmen from Teramachi Street and passersby, who
had gathered round the group of combatants and stood watching in great
terror, now, when they saw Shirōzaemon coming toward them with bloody
sword and dripping head, were quick to clear the way.

Meanwhile, Yokoi's follower Shimotsu, undaunted by a gash on his forehead administered earlier by Yanagida, ended a hard-fought struggle by
putting a deep slice in Yanagida's shoulder. Unable to bear the pain, Yanagida crumpled to the ground. Just then Shimotsu saw Shirōzaemon take his
beloved master's head and run from the scene, so he abandoned Yanagida
and set off in pursuit of Shirōzaemon.

At this point Ueno, one of the attendants held at bay by Maeoka and
Nakai, slipped away from the group and joined Shimotsu.

Ueno, fleeter of foot than Shimotsu, had almost caught up with Shirōzaemon when the latter whirled around and flung the head straight at him. It
struck him hard on the right arm. He stumbled, and in that instant Shirōzaemon made good his escape.

After Ueno had raced off in pursuit of Shirōzaemon, the attendants kept
falling back under a rain of blows from Maeoka and Nakai. When the latter
saw that Shirōzaemon had taken Yokoi's head, they changed tactics and
fled. Kashima, cut on the forehead by Yokoyama, and Ueda both saw their
chance and also fled. The only one of the band left at the scene was the badly wounded Yanagida.

Ueno, in his hands the head hurled at him by Shirōzaemon, and Shimotsu were returning to the place of their master's corpse when Yokoyama also
came back. Out of the crowd of bystanders, other attendants stepped forth
and truncated corpse inside the palanquin. It was about then that a large
number of police on duty in the city arrived on the scene, arrested Yanagida, and led him away.

After racing through the city and coming out onto a path through some
paddyfields, Shirōzaemon washed the blood from his sword in a creek that
ran beside the path, replaced it in its sheath, and then turned off the path
and headed for the home of Miyake Sakon,[43] in Saga. Sakon was a swordsman whom Shirōzaemon had met at the home of Miyake Tenzen. Behind

the Sakon place was a small sake shop. Shirōzaemon bought a three-pint jug of sake there and with the jug in one hand went through a back gate hidden in a bamboo thicket. After Shirōzaemon's capture and death, I am told, that jug was wrapped in a purple silk-crepe wrapper and carefully stored away in Sakon's house.

The prisoner Yanagida would not utter a word, and the judges and other officers ordered to conduct an investigation did not try to force any information out of him, so the names of the accomplices remained unknown for some time. But those who had had any dealings with Yanagida were summoned one by one, and some were clapped into prison.

Shirōzaemon went into the city every day; he made inquiries wherever he went, hoping to find out whether Yanagida was alive and who had been arrested. That Yanagida was badly wounded but still alive, that he would not reveal the names of his accomplices, and so on—these were common gossip in the city. Those who had been summoned and detained in the government office, or captured and put in prison, were for the most part people publicly known as proponents of *sonnō-jōi*. Best known among them was Naka Zuiunsai[44] of Izumi; he was imprisoned with his eldest son Katsuki, his second son Kanae, and third son Takeshi. Kanamoto Kenzō from Izumo, Masuda Jirō from Totsugawa, Koyasu Riheiji from Shimōsa, Ōkuma Kumaji from Echigo,[45] and others, were also imprisoned. Of Shirōzaemon's fellow countrymen, Kaima Jūrōzaemon[46] was summoned, but after some questioning he was immediately set free. Kaima was owner of the Yoshidaya, an inn for travelers in Kamiya-chō in Okayama and was rumored to be rendering assistance to the group.

Opinion in Kyoto was in general sympathetic to the band; indeed, it tended to censure the crimes of the slain Yokoi. Yanagida's silence was lauded. The way the little band kept their secret so well and covered up their tracks was admired. Having a lot to do with this general attitude was a document posted at all crossroads a few days after Yokoi was slain. Who the author of this document was, the band did not know; to judge from its contents, it was not written in the same jesting mood as the lampoons,[47] but seemed to be an outright attempt to defend the band. The police officials lost no time going round and ripping down the posters, but several copies of it circulated in the city. The text read as follows:

On the fifth preceding, the *chōshi* Yokoi Heishirō was slain by the sword in broad daylight in Teramachi. One of the assailants was captured; it is said that the remainder, who fled, are diligently being sought out. I do not as yet know what manner of men cut Yokoi down, but their actions would seem to be motivated by an intense concern for the welfare of their country. The wickedness of this Heishirō was something known to all in the land. In the beginning he played up to the Bakufu; then he advocated—I hesitate even to say it—dethronement of the emperor, and placed in jeopardy the line of emperors unbroken for ages eternal. In addition, he made criminals out of true patriots by use of slander, and had them killed. Recently he secretly contacted the barbarians and agreed to propagation of the Christian religion in our empire. Also, he tried to shunt aside the court's most urgent need, military arms. His other evil crimes are too numerous to mention. At a time when the country is being reformed into a land of imperial rule and has become the center of attention of the whole world, this traitor in key position was obstructing progress, introducing irregularity in court practices, breaking down imperial authority, creating chaos in the empire, and attempting to turn this majestic divine land of ours into a dependency of barbarians no better than brute animals. His assailants, finding such things intolerable, were forced to slay him by sword. The heroic daring of their deed is comparable to that of the Mito warriors at Sakurada gate.[48] For these reasons, there is no one with an iota of righteousness who does not rejoice over their deed. In general, such incidents as this occur because the opinions of ordinary citizens do not reach the ears of the statesmen. From the beginning the Five Articles of the Imperial Oath called for free exchange of views between high and low, but this has remained empty, insubstantial verbiage. A man of loyal heart, one upright and true, is cast aside as a bigot, and a traitorous subject like Heishirō, who betrays the court, is appointed instead; around him gather men of the very same breed; they corrupt the government of our land, and the barbarians grow more and more powerful. Loyal men, concerned about the situation, could tolerate it no longer and at an opportune time made known their true views, but these were dismissed as insubstantial and not adopted. Hence it was that they took strong action, slew the chief of the traitors, and have caused us to reflect on past political errors in regard to the court. The above is because views between high and low are not being exchanged. I make a heartfelt plea that the court harken to the truth in what is said above, proclaim an imperial edict requesting the whole nation to speak up freely, banish all traitors, appoint to office faithful and upright men, abandon erroneous views, and let the law of justice shine bright. Also, as for the assailants who slew this Yokoi fellow with the sword, be pleased to commend their sentiments, overlook their crime, and release them at once. If this is done, not only can the national polity most surely be secured and the barbarians' insolence be requited, but also warriors throughout the land will admire the court's speed in admitting and rectifying its own mistakes, and such acts as the slaying of traitorous subjects will cease entirely. But if the court hesitates to carry out the above matters, it will be filled with traitors, the emperor's grip on the reins of administration will slacken, and one calamity will follow upon another. There will be no difference between this government and the Bakufu government that collapsed. When things come to such a pass, loyal patriots will rise up in anger and sweep away all treacherous subjects without exception. The above is not the right way to keep intact the prestige of the imperial court. Yet the Sun Goddess, founder of the imperial family, watches from Heaven. Whether what I say is correct or not requires no proof. Let all who agree with my view when they read this written appeal assemble at Mt. Hiei; let us together discuss how to achieve the great task of reforming our country.

spring, first month, 1869

A son of Great Japan who laments
the present state of affairs

To this poster was appended an additional piece of paper, on which was written: "This notice should be posted for three days. Anyone removing it without cause will be cut down." This was copied from an official document by Shirōzaemon's instructor in swordsmanship, Abe Morie, who afterward worked in the Justice Department.[49]

On the fourteenth day of the first month, nine days after killing Yokoi, Shirōzaemon went to the home of a friend from Shinshū, Kondō Jūbē,[50] who at the time was an official in the Cabinet. While he was inquiring about rumors in government circles, police officials stepped in and led away both host and guest. This resulted from Ueda's capture together with Kashima at the base of Mt. Kōya, at which time the police decided that Shirōzaemon, Ueda's close friend, should also be arrested. When Kashima was first called in, the judge had questioned him about Bizen loyalists, but Kashima was evasive in his replies and kept suspicion from falling upon Ueda and his men. But when Ueda was arrested because of the sword wound on his arm, Kashima's efforts came to naught.

Yanagida died from his injury on the sixteenth, two days after Shirōzaemon was captured. Since customs from the old Bakufu times were still being observed in prisons, the corpse was packed in salt. After Ueda and Shirōzaemon were captured, the organizer of the Valiant Fighting Force in Bizen, Matsumoto Minosuke, was put into prison, and a retainer of the Han Elder Tokura Sazen, Saitō Naohiko,[51] who assisted in organizing it, also underwent questioning.

In the absence of any reliable records, and because those involved in the affair are all dead, I do not know the details of what happened in the tribunal at that time; but if the story is true that even some of the judges were sympathetic to the accomplices, this would explain why they did not take severe measures. I also heard that there was a certain woman named Nihoko,[52] who petitioned to have Shirōzaemon released. I was a mere child at the time, and when told she tried to save father, imprisoned for acting for the sake of His Majesty, I envisioned a court lady with long hair hanging down her back and dressed in a scarlet garment. In reality, though, I do not know what her social position was. I heard that later, around 1878 or 1879, Nihoko came to Okayama, gathered some followers and spoke to them of respecting the gods and revering the emperor; she also composed poems which she sent to various people, but I was no longer in Okayama by then.

I was told that father was executed on the tenth day of the tenth month of 1870. He was buried in an unmarked grave, so as not to offend government circles. I have no parental grave where I can place incense and flowers. I do not recall clearly now, but people tell me that, when I heard the news of father's death, I asked how he died. Mother's answer was that he died by the sword. I replied that if so he must have had some enemy, and this is how I would cut that enemy down—at this I leapt out into the garden and with a wooden sword snapped a branch off a jasmine tree. Mother was so alarmed that she stopped speaking about father in my hearing from that time on.

After father died, grandfather's spirits fell; he even stopped supervision of the tenant farmers working our fields. The harvests gradually diminished, our finances declined, and afterward mother and I were left almost propertyless. We were not just an ordinary widow and orphan child. We were the wife and child of a man who had been executed as a criminal. We were people with a dark past.

To bring me up and, as I gradually grew older, to send me to school, mother worked herself to the bone. Thanks to her I eventually gained admission into Tokyo University, but on account of various problems I withdrew before finishing. I do not wish to enumerate all those problems here, to make feeble excuses over them. One thing I do want to state, however, is that, driven from childhood by a fierce desire to clear my executed father's name, I was unable to set my mind to acquiring an education.

People may say that acquiring an education, making a name for myself, and restoring the fortunes of my house would have been the way to clear father's name. But that is abstract theory. My heart ached day and night for my deceased father; I could not apply my mind to study. The power of cool reason was too feeble to calm my burning emotions.

Father killed a man. To do so was bad. But if the slain man were a bad man, if he were always regarded as bad, killing him would have been taken for granted. Unfortunately, the slain man was not a bad man. No one looking back from our present perspective would say he was bad. Did father, then, kill someone good? No, he killed someone who was, in his eyes, bad. This is not to say that father was the only one who made this judgment. At that time people in general judged Yokoi to be bad. Criteria for good and bad change with times and places. Father, living in a certain age, killed a man who, in that age, was bad. Why did father have to be executed? Why must his wife and child become social outcasts? Rambling, repetitive, vicious circles of thought such as these wrapped themselves round my mind like spider webs; they forced me to shut books and cast aside writing brushes poised in hand.

After abandoning my studies, I joined the ranks of lower-echelon public servants and received enough pay to feed mother and myself. Since the jobs I took up afterward were limited to mechanical, mentally tedious tasks, I tried to use all my strength to clear father's name. But it was an indescribably arduous undertaking.

First of all I tried to learn in as minute detail as possible the things father did. Convinced he was a good man, I felt that the more people knew about what he did, the greater his glory would be. Every time I had a vacation I went on a trip and finally I traversed every district father had. When I learned of someone who knew father, or who had heard about him, I visited the person and listened to his story, regardless of the distance. However, fifty years had passed since father's death. Though the mountains and rivers were the same as before, old roads had disappeared, new roads had been cleared, paddies and fields had been converted into residences and city streets. The same with the people. There were very few around who had even heard of father, let alone who knew him personally, and even they were so old they complained of failing memories or poor hearing.

The things I recounted earlier are what I have pieced together as I could from scraps of data collected in the manner just mentioned. There may have been errors in the telling; there may have been errors in the hearing. Again, it is not impossible that in some places my imagination unconsciously asserted itself and put in things that were not there. For the most part, however, I believe I can say the following. My expectations did not play me false. They were not biased. Father was a good man. He was a man who esteemed moral integrity. He was a loyalist. A patriot. A man who possessed something more precious than life or property. He was an idealist.

While I believe this, I also can console myself. On the other side of the picture, however, I also have to admit that father was a simpleton and a fool, unable to see the signs of the times. I have to deplore his lack of natural endowments, and lament that no one was kind enough to enlighten him.

This is my concluding judgment—the eulogy I append to father's biography. I here express my thanks to those who told me about father. One of the principal of these is the widow, Lady Kaima. Possessing a woman's natural delicate sensitivity to the slightest stimuli, she recalled things which others could not; as a result, I was given numerous details of father's personal history. Another is the son of Miyake (Sakon), Takehiko; sympathizing with father in his destitute wandering, he harbored him in his home for a long time. Next I mention the names of two men who spoke in defense of father: Niwa Hiroo and Suzuki Muin.[53] Niwa was a senior statesman in Bizen with a stipend of three thousand *koku*. He had this to say: "To criticize Shirōzaemon as a simpleton is too harsh. Japan was an isolated country at the time, and Bizen was an isolated fief within an isolated nation. People in Okayama could not set foot outside the fief boundaries. When young lads had a hankering for women, they went to Miyauchi, about one ri west of Okayama. If they were treated insultingly by anyone they could not take the fellow to task because it would betray the fact that they had gone into Bitchū territory. To blame these lads for being out of touch with trends in the world is unreasonable. When I was in Kyoto I too once tried to stab a certain individual. But circumstances prevented me from doing so and I returned to Okayama without realizing my purpose. Before long, due to my comparatively high social position, I was appointed a minor government official. After that I associated with higher authorities and gradually heard about conditions in foreign lands. I am not pretending to be wise, but between Shirōzaemon and me there was no difference whatsoever." Suzuki was a scholar versed in domestic and international law who had worked on national affairs with Arao Sei and others. He sent me the following message: "I knew Shirōzaemon. He was no fool. There were fitting reasons for his slaying Yokoi." But Suzuki died before I could meet him. I do not know what story he had to tell me, but I feel cheated.

I was not satisfied with just digging up father's past. My desire since childhood was to do something positive to clear father's name, as if I were to wash away mud smeared on his face. As a child I thought to myself: "Father acted for the sake of His Imperial Majesty. Yet somebody killed him. I must kill the man who killed him." When I grew a little older I realized it was not a man who killed father, but the law. I felt I had lost my purpose in life. I felt life had become meaningless. I remember that this discovery tortured me for days and months on end.

After I passed through this internal struggle I lived in a daze for some time; as equilibrium of mind gradually returned, the positive means of clearing father's name that I had adopted in the past rose into consciousness again in completely new guise. I resolved to have my deceased father some way or other granted a special imperial favor. Father had been among the first to rise up at the time of restoration of imperial rule and serve the court's cause. He had slain Yokoi because their political views were incompatible. Yokoi was a victim of political conflict. Now that the times had changed and both fanaticism and hate had subsided, what was there to prevent his dry bones from being bathed in imperial favor? With this idea in mind, I first consulted a senior official from my part of the country and then appealed to the proper high authorities. This was after I had abandoned my studies.

From 1886 to 1887 the pros and cons of conferring posthumous rank on Tsuge Shirōzaemon were discussed by the authorities, I was told. But in the end it was decided that conferral of posthumous rank on someone not given amnesty and executed as a criminal could not be sought from the emperor. I was dismayed; once again I felt life had become meaningless. Still, compared with the previous time I had lost my object of revenge, my suffering this time was rather slight and short-lived. Perhaps it was because I had matured; then again, it could very well be that I had grown callous.

I have given up my cause. What with one compromise after another, my ambition has gradually shrunk to the point where now my only desire is to have someone put this story in writing for future generations.

The narrative ends here. The "I" of the tale is the son of Tsuge Shirōzaemon Masayoshi, the person named Shikata. This much is already clear from the story. This is not all, though. The reader no doubt has also been able to size up to some extent Shikata's character, circumstances, and past history.

As the editor of this narrative, I feel no need to make numerous additions. I only wish to explain the events which led to its being made public at my hands. It all started when I was already out of college but still at home, and my younger brother, Tokujirō, was still going to college. I asked Tokujirō, "Tell me, are there any outstanding fellows among your schoolmates?" My brother immediately mentioned the names of two of his classmates. One was K., a big-hearted person, the other was Tsuge Masataka, an uncompromising fellow, he said. My brother later came to consider a man of talent as ideal, but his ideal then was still the outgoing type. He introduced K. and Tsuge to me. K. was as huge as a wrestler and liked judo. Unfortunately, under the influence of alcohol he did something that was interpreted as robbery and was expelled from school. Tsuge, or Shikata, is the author of this narrative.

Tsuge was a light-complexioned youth with an oval face, his brows knitted in a perpetual frown. It seems to me his family's misfortunes were, like the sign of Cain, written on his countenance. He was a reticent person, and, since I also was not much of a talker then, our first meeting almost ended up with us staring at each other. But from then till the present day, a span of thirty years, Tsuge has not been remiss in writing to me. My own negligence in replying has not bothered him. Shortly after we met he left college and started drifting from place to place. His letters have come from Hokkaido. They have even come from Korea. Still he has never completely disappeared from sight.

On 13 October 1913, Tsuge suddenly visited my house and told me the story of his father, Shirōzaemon. The narrative is almost exactly as he told it. He wanted me to revise it, but because the words have so much forcefulness, flowing as they did from the heart, I am publishing them almost verbatim. All I did was verify points regarding the times and places mentioned in his story with Sugi Magoshichirō, Aoki Umesaburō, Nakaoka Moku, Tokutomi Iichirō, Shimizu Koichirō, and Yamabe Takeo;[54] then I made two or three corrections. During the long period since we last met, Tsuge became a robust, cheerful-looking fellow; not a shadow remained of his old melancholic gloom. As I bring this postcript to a close, I sincerely wish him good health.

The story above, originally published in *Chūō kōron*, was the means of my coming to know a good many people. Among them were even some who had been friends of Shirōzaemon. Through these people's conversations, letters, documents in their possession, and so on, I made a few editorial changes in regard to the names appearing in the story. I adopted what I judged to be comparatively accurate. I was also able to learn the following several facts:

That, in appearance, Tsuge Shirōzaemon resembled the Masataka mentioned above can be surmised from the text. However, Shirōzaemon is said to have had a slightly larger physique and a somewhat rounder face.

The storehouse of the Miyake Tenzen family in Kyoto, where Shirōzaemon stayed in hiding, is said still to retain its old exterior even though the main building was later rebuilt; one can see it from the road. The woman who carried food to the storehouse and otherwise looked after Shirōzaemon is still alive and living in Hakusan Goten-machi, but she does not want her name made public.

In the text I wrote that when Ueda Tatsuo and Shirōzaemon left their fiefs and went to Kyoto they soon determined on a plot to assassinate the traitor. But this might not necessarily have been the case. After the two of them arrived in Kyoto, they took an active part for a while in the "Imperial Bodyguards Affair."[55] One of the court nobles left his family, recruited some lordless samurai, and laid plans for protecting the imperial family. He wanted the roster filled by lordless samurai because he feared *han* samurai would scheme for their own masters. I leave the name of that court noble unwritten here. But if some day materials on the Restoration are made public, this matter might not be able to remain a secret.

Among the *rōnin* were many samurai from Totsugawa. The rest were from various other provinces. Foremost among those samurai of note who were enrolled in the imperial bodyguards was Naka Zuiunsai.

The Naka family used to be called Urikami, and was an illustrious Kawachi family. In 1653 they moved to Gomon in Kumatori-mura, Izumi Province, and for generations were known as rural samurai. Included among the branch houses of the Naka family was the Negoro family[56] living in Hon-jō in Edo—direct vassals of the shogun, with an income of three thousand six hundred *koku*. Born third son of the Negoro family, Zuiunsai succeeded to the main family and himself had three sons. The eldest was Katsuki, the second Kanae, and the third Takeshi. In addition he had an adopted son, Kaoru.

Zuiunsai early passed the house on to Katsuki; he then went to Kyoto and joined the loyalists. When Shirōzaemon and the others were imprisoned, Zuiunsai was arrested along with his three sons. He was sent under guard to Aomori Prefecture, but died en route; Katsuki and Takeshi died in a Kyoto prison; Kanae was released after ten years' imprisonment. Meantime their three sisters were living in their home town of Kumatori-mura. A certain guardian looked after them; he made arrangements with Tatsunosuke, the second son of Hara Bumpei of Kotani-mura, and married him to the eldest daughter, Sumi. After his release Kanae was not kindly received by Tatsuno-suke and his family, so, changing his name to Ken'ichirō, he moved to Sakai and set up in business; when he ran out of capital, he became the priest of Homuda shrine in Furuichi-mura, Minamikawachi District, Osaka. Ken'i-chirō's children were Kanae, Takeo, and Yukio; Kanae is a lower-echelon official in the tax office, Takeo an assistant engineer under the Governor-General of Formosa, and Yukio a student of history in college. The eldest daughter married the grandson of Miyake Tenzen, Tetsuo. I owe this family history to Yukio.

Among the accomplices of Zuiunsai was Miya Taichū of Totsugawa.[57] At that time he was known as Ōki Mondo. Taichū was well known for his proficiency in Japanese, Chinese, and Western studies. He was put into the same prison as Shirōzaemon and the others, then banished to Miyake Island; after being pardoned he was able to return to his home. Taichū's son Taimo lives at 19 Kita Iga-chō, Yotsuya-ku.

Another Totsugawa samurai imprisoned in the same way was Kamihira Chikara (if one is careless in writing the horizontal stroke in his name, the result will be Shimohira); exiled to Nii Island, he also was able to return home.

Ichinose Tonomo[58] was another Totsugawa samurai imprisoned; exiled to Hachijō Island, he was later pardoned and returned home.

Naka and company wanted to form a band of imperial bodyguards but were unable to do so because they were thwarted by such people as Kanda Kōhei,[59] Nakai Hiroshi,[60] and Yokoi Heishirō.

At this time a document titled "On Reform of the Way of Heaven" circulated among the loyalists. According to contemporary reports, the text was composed by Yokoi Heishirō, the document was issued by the priest of Aso shrine, and it was passed around by Koga Jūrō.[61] The text runs as follows:

> Just as the human body has four limbs and a hundred bones, so there are mountains, rivers, trees, grasses, human beings, birds, and beasts. Hence, he who does not know the essence of the universe is no different from one who does not know that his body is equipped with arms and legs. Now, all countries in the world are like one body, and there is no distinction between "others" and "self." It is necessary to understand the principle of proximity and distance and grasp that interior and exterior [Japan and other lands] are one and the same. From ancient times, it has been customary for an illustrious sovereign to spread his dignity and virtue all over the world, and all countries that submit to him, without exception, find, because of the sovereign's magnanimity, entrance into his expansive heart; nothing proves impossible to grant; his heart, evolving in accord with his beneficence, is in harmony with this constantly changing world. Thus this sovereign can be lord of the world and monarch of all people. However, if through shallowness of mind he does not know the principle of the whole world being one body, one being, it would be as if the whole body were insensate and felt neither pain nor itch. A hundred generations would not suffice for such a one to gain understanding. Is this not something to be pitied? . . . Today there is a movement—indeed, since the beginning of time there has never been a greater one—toward renovation of political rule, and thus many foreign countries are striving to understand, to discover, and to attain a high level of culture on the basis of natural principles. However, Japan alone huddles to its isolated small islands . . . and so cannot achieve this. Its fall is inevitable. We must at once sweep away the great evils of narrow-mindedness and deep-rooted abuses, must, guided by the idea that we are "eternal as heaven and earth," see through distorted opinions and must be intent on our land becoming the greatest in the universe. If in this way we search for principles, shall we not in the end attain a clear insight into the principles of all things?

> Teibō, third month, at the southern window, on the spur of the moment.

> Shōnan

I have omitted some two to three hundred irrelevant words and transcribed here the remainder. However, both the style and diction can, for the most part, be gathered from this much. "Teibō" is 1867. The general idea is an elaboration of the five-character poem "Human Rulers How Divinely Appointed?" For something supposed to have been written by Yokoi, it is quite inferior.

It is said that when Shirōzaemon and the others read it they were absolutely sure it was Yokoi's writing. Convinced the situation had become critical, they abandoned the imperial bodyguards idea and laid plans to cut down Yokoi.

The spot where Shirōzaemon and the others killed Yokoi is reported to be south of the crossroads of Maruta-machi and Teramachi, beyond Goryōsha, but before one reaches the Hikaru-dō. This information is based on Minami Jun'ichi's *Fūbunroku*.[62] Jun'ichi later changed his name to Hisatoki.

The incident took place on 5 January 1869. On the sixth, a government proclamation was issued.

> The killing of the *chōshi* Yokoi Heishirō was an outrageous act in complete disregard for the imperial constitution. Matters such as assassination cannot be undertaken by anyone who belongs to a *han* or who holds prefectural office. Perhaps assassination was resorted to on grounds that speech and writing are shackled, but after the Restoration of 1868 discussion has become free and there ought to be no *han* or prefecture where communication is impossible. If anybody can desert his *han* and in effect decide what is right and wrong in society, thus undermining the court's laws, how will public discipline be maintained and the empire sustained? This is the question asked by His Majesty, who is extremely distressed by what has happened. He has given orders that, especially in Kyoto but in other prefectures also, deserters from their *han* are to be tracked down relentlessly, and that at all times strict control is to be kept without relaxing of vigilance.

This text is recorded by Osatake Takeshi.[63] The Osatake family now lives in Kasumigaoka-chō, Yotsuya-ku.

Both Miyake Tenzen, at whose house Shirōzaemon stayed in hiding before the incident, and Miyake Sakon, whose house he visited afterward, were from Tsurajima in Bitchū Province. Takehiko, the heir of Tenzen, whose pen name was Gazen, speaks about Sakon in writing as follows:

> In an article about my deceased father reference is made to a wine shop and a sake jug. Come to think of it, at that time, there was an old man named Miyake Sakon, also from Tsurajima, who was a retainer at Saga palace [Daikaku-ji]. A swashbuckling type of old man, with neither wife nor children, he lived in Saga in Kyoto. There was, as a matter of fact, a thicket behind the house, and a sake shop. This Miyake Sakon used to meet with my deceased father in our house, and, because he boasted of his swordsmanship, he and my father finally held a contest; he was soundly defeated. From that time on he felt a respectful admiration for my father and became something of a pupil of his. I imagine that my father did take some sake to the Sakon house. Sakon's real name is Sahei.

I have mentioned before that the Naka family were in-laws of Takehiko. Takehiko lives in Dote Sanbanchō, Kōjimachi-ku.

The woman whom I described in the text as defending Shirōzaemon, Nihoko, was reported to be the daughter of Fushimi-no-miya Shodaibu, Wakae Shuridaibu. The letter Nihoko presented to the Bishū *han chōshi* Arakawa Jinsaku[64] ran as follows:

On what grounds was the decision made in regard to the disposition of the man who killed Yokoi Heishirō? Since it was decided by the authorities, we ought by no means question it; still, in a written document presented by the man who killed Yokoi, it is stated that: "Yokoi's close associates were scheming to spread the Roman Church throughout all of Japan." On the basis of only this one document, one might suspect the man was using a widespread rumor as a pretext to vent a personal grudge; however, since the whole country knew about Yokoi's scheme, it cannot be said the man was taking advantage of a public rumor for his own ends. To have killed a Councillor of the imperial court is a serious matter, and of course it ought to be punished severely. But in view of the fact that this man put to death someone who, as I said above, everyone knew was guilty of a crime, he is, really, a man moved by a spirit of patriotism; although he committed the serious crime of killing a man, still, by special dispensation, please commute the death penalty one degree. This is inconsistent with what I said the other day about it being a well-deserved punishment and it may strike you as suspicious; but if in these present circumstances you were to punish such men with severity, it would immediately alienate men's hearts from the government, and other incidents will, it seems quite clear, flare up everywhere. On top of this, rumor has it that there have been many with no direct part in the matter who have denounced themselves to the authorities as being of the same mind as the slayers. These people who have surrendered themselves are all known to be faultless, righteous men. I think it fitting to use special clemency and pardon them. Indeed, righteous subjects are a nation's strength and vigor; to put even one of them to death as a criminal is naturally to damage the strength and vigor of the nation. If its strength and vigor are damaged, the very life of all those entrusted to it by Heaven will perish. I beg you to give full consideration to these reasons, by special dispensation to commute the death penalty of the leader one degree, and to grant complete pardon to all those who surrendered themselves as being of like mind. Though they may be great criminals, I think they have committed no more than a minor offense when compared with that of the enemies of the emperor. By reason of my speaking thus, I suppose suspicion will fall on me: "She has something to do with this matter; that is why she is asking this . . ." If suspicion does fall upon me, I shall say nothing in my own defense, so be pleased to arrest me at once and punish me—but only me—with death; then I trust you will pardon all the rest. If you punish with severity both the young leader and his comrades as well, without distinction, I think that righteous men throughout the land will at once harbor feelings of indignation and bitterness against the court; you will unwisely arouse public opinion and the situation will get out of control. I understand that at the close of last year you ordered a religious service performed for those punished by death in the time of the tyrannical

Bakufu government; it seems to me that to enroll among the gods those already dead and then punish with death the still living is no policy for stability in government. I know Your Excellency is indisposed at present, but I trust that this matter will be handled with fitting discernment. With earnest entreaty for your kindest consideration.

First month, 21st day, Nihoko.

The recipient of this letter, Arakawa Jinsaku, resigned because of illness from his post as Junior Councillor in the third month of 1868, changed his name to Ozaki Yoshitomo, and is reported to have lived in Nagoya.

Nihoko's letter passed from Tanaka Fujimaro[65] or Niwa Juntarō (later named Masaru)[66] to the Owari *han* warrior Matsuyama Yoshine[67] of the Mighty Fighting Force (Hōhakutai); he was older brother of former Minister of the Navy Yashirō.[68] From him it passed into the possession of Kurachi Iemon of the Komaki Post Office in Owari; Kurachi then presented it, through me, to Tsuge. Kurachi believes that it is the autograph copy of Nihoko herself. Another version has it that the original manuscript of Nihoko's letter is in the possession of one Nishida Jirō, priest of Funae shrine in Funae, Shinjō-mura, Funae District, Tamba Province. This is based on Miyaki Takehiko's account of the facts.

Nihoko's letter has already been published. It appeared in the newspaper *Enkin Shimbun*, number five, published 10 April 1868 and copyrighted by Tsuji Shinji[69] and Gotō Kenkichi, who reside on the campus of Kaisei Gakkō.[70] Osatake has the paper in his possession. What I have transcribed above is the result of using the Kurachi copy as the basic text and then comparing it with the *Enkin Shimbun* copy. There were a few differences between the two texts. That the Kurachi is the autograph copy is somewhat doubtful.

According to what I heard from Mimaki Motoyoshi,[71] Nihoko was not a good-looking woman, but she was a talented one. When the Empress Shōken[72] was still residing in her Ichijō home, Nihoko gave her lectures on Chinese works. Mimaki himself had attended Nihoko's lectures. Because she spoke out about matters of state, she was told to quit her position and was placed with a Tanaka employed by the Fushimi-no-miya family. Later, because of an indiscretion, she was shunned by self-respecting folk; she then dwelt in isolated retirement in the vicinity of Akashi, in Suma, where it seems she died.

Nihoko's poems have made their way here and there into the world. Miyake Takehiko possesses a small book of them. In June of 1915, a Meiji Commemorative Exhibition was held in Manshōji temple in Nagoya. Among the items on display was a scroll with a poem by Nihoko.

The days of seclusion pass drearily. Sitting idle all the day long, I brood in sorrow and lament the times, till day reaches its close. When cool breezes fan the room where I lie dozing, I know the heat of day has passed. Seen from my window at dawn, traces of the night's rain remind me how wearily the night dragged on. The acclaims and strictures of human society are things of the distant past, the vicissitudes of life have vanished like a dream. No matter how many the reverses I have suffered, I remain as rash and senseless as ever.

Early fall; living in confinement. Nihoko.

It had one seal, and on the design was printed "Suga-shi." Wakae seems to have been a Sugawara. This was copied out by Kurachi and brought to me. Also, others have said they saw these words written by Nihoko: "There are so many thousands of men in our divine land, but is there one who grieves as I?"

I have already given supplementary material about Nihoko, the daughter of Wakae Shuridaibu, but since then I have heard from Honda Tatsujirō[73] that the Shuridaibu's personal name was Kazunaga, and that he had once been chief of the Bureau of Imperial Mausolea.[74] As a result of this bit of news I made inquiry of Shiba Katsushige,[75] from whom I received in writing the following information.

The girl Nihoko's father was the head of the household staff of Fushimi-no-miya and a man of court rank. The Wakae family originally was a Sugawara, from the stock of Arikimi, son of the Shikibu Gon-no-taifu, Sugawara no Kimisuke. The name was first Mibu Bōjō, then Nakamikado, then once again changed to Wakae. The Wakae first began serving Fushimi-no-miya in the time of Nagachika, who was the tenth generation away from Arikimi. Nagachika was born on the twenty-ninth day of the third month in 1664, and he passed away on the ninth day of the seventh month in 1720, at the age of fifty-seven. Kazunaga was the son of Kimiyoshi, who was the fifth generation from Nagachika; born on the thirteenth day of the twelfth month in 1812, he came of age on the twenty-eighth day of the third month in 1825 (at the age of fourteen), was appointed Echigo Gon-no-suke, and granted the privilege of attending the imperial court within the hall—all on the same day. Later he became vice-minister in the Imperial Police Department, and then went on to become Shuridaibu; Junior Grade Fourth Court Rank was conferred on him on the twenty-second day, twelfth month, 1842. This much can be known from the *Jige-Kaden*.[76] Besides this, according to the diary of Nonomiya Sadayoshi, on the twenty-fourth day, second month, 1864, restoration of the Bureau of Imperial Mausolea was announced, and the man appointed at the time to become its chief was this Kazunaga. However, it seems Kazunaga had no special knowledge of mountainous regions. Anything to do with mountains, apparently, he entrusted almost entirely to two subordinates, Yamato no Suke Tanimori Tanematsu[77] and Chikuzen no kami Suzuki Katsunori.[78] To come to the point, there is something of interest with regard to his daughter Nihoko. From the account given by Mimaki Motoyoshi it has already been seen that Nihoko was a talented woman and that, because she was well-versed in Japanese and Chinese studies, especially the latter, she went to give lectures on Chinese literature when Empress Shōken was still in her Ichijō home. Now a section in the annals of Toda Tadayoshi[79] contains the following account:

> From 1867 on, their lordships Nijō and Nakayama were extremely concerned about the marriage of H.M. the Empress. Both of them requested me to give the matter some thought. Just as I was at my wits' end, it was brought to my attention that Nihoko, the daughter of Wakae Shuridaibu—he had for some time been working closely with me in connection with the Imperial Mausolea—was teaching *waka* to the daughters of Lord Ichijō; I therefore visited her to seek her advice concerning a suitable prospect, but she told me that His Lordship's second daughter was already specially designated; when I reported this to their lordships Nijō and Nakayama, I was instructed to visit the Ichijō palace at once and very discreetly observe the second daughter firsthand; I accordingly discussed the matter with Nihoko and together with her did visit the palace and meet the daughters, after which I made my report on the second daughter. At this juncture, however, His Lordship Nijō was relieved of his post because of certain suspicions harbored against him; later, however, he was appointed commissioner for the wedding, everything went off well, and the wedding took place. . . .

According to this, then, Nihoko's advice seemed to play a considerable part in the selection of the Crown Princess who was destined to become Empress Shōken. In the sixth month of 1867, announcement was made of Empress Shōken's entrance into court, and shortly afterward women were chosen to serve as her upper and middle ladies-in-waiting; at this time Nihoko was again requested to come to the palace and give lessons. The entry for the ninth day of the eighth month of that year in the court record of Hashimoto Saneyoshi[80] gives the following:

> Also, since the younger sister of Wakae Shuridaibu has for many years been devoted to learning, and since she is well known for her admirable depth of wisdom, would it not be advisable to allow her to visit the palace to give lessons to the Crown Princess? I have been told that the chief of the Imperial Guards has indicated the matter should be left to my discretion; as far as I am concerned, it seems advisable to permit her attendance, and I have submitted a report to this effect.

However, the papers of the Ichijō family have, in the entry for the third day of the ninth month:

> I met with Norikata, the messenger of Fushimi-no-miya, and our discussions lasted for several days. I received answer to the effect that he had no objection to acceding to the Crown Princess' request that Wakae Shuridaibu's daughter, Ofumi, give lessons in recitation of the Chinese classics.

On the tenth day of the same month we find: "The Crown Princess said that, for the instructor on the *Book of Filial Piety* in the Palace, she wished Ofumi to be invited," while for the fifteenth day we find mention of Nihoko's going to the Palace for the lessons, entering by way of the door to the ladies-in-waiting quarters, and giving instructions on the *Book of Filial Piety*. The above-mentioned invitation was probably a formal notification renewed on the occasion of the Crown Princess' formal entrance into court; it surely was not the first time she ever gave lessons there. One thing, though: how does one explain the fact that the Saneyoshi court record gives her as the younger sister of the Shuridaibu? Also, was "Ofumi" an earlier name of Nihoko? I have not been able to find any absolute proof for Nihoko's visiting the palace after Empress Shōken's entrance into court. It could very well be that, because of her participation in political matters and the like, an invitation from the Crown Princess was never forthcoming. It is a shame, finally, that her indiscretions brought her to such an unfortunate end. Ueda Keiji's *History of Empress Shōken*[81] states that, "Even after the empress' entrance into court, Nihoko received special preferential treatment; she died peacefully in 1872 in Marugame in Sanuki, where her remains lie even today." But I have not succeeded in discovering any proof for this statement.

Since Kazunaga used to be chief of the Bureau of Imperial Mausolea, I [Shiba] tried asking Tateo, second son of the late Tanimori Tanematsu (he later changed his name to Yoshiomi), whether he had ever seen or heard anything about him. (Yoshiomi was my maternal grandfather, and Tateo my uncle.) Tateo told me this:

> There was a small shrine in Demizu in Kyoto called "Wakae Tenjin," and the Wakae family lived next to it. I think it was when I was about ten years old; one day my father took me to visit the Wakae residence. I there met two girls who were introduced to me as Wakae's daughters. The younger one was an ordinary girl and looked every bit a court nobleman's daughter, with her hair tied behind and flowing down in back; but the older one was an unusual woman: dark-complexioned, with no makeup whatever, her hair bound artlessly. I recall how, more than a match for any man, she heatedly engaged my father in argument. Even he said he could not stand up to such a woman. This

was Nihoko, probably. I also heard that later her whereabouts became unknown, but as for her having yielded to temptation because of her family's not
being well off, well, maybe what happened deserves our sympathy more than
anything else. It may also be true that she died in Sanuki, but I do not think it
was an ordinary death. I also do not think she was the younger sister of Kazunaga. I remember her being introduced as his daughter.

April 1915

KURIYAMA DAIZEN

"KURIYAMA DAIZEN" makes use of an incident in history to define the nature and quality of loyalty. In particular Ōgai seeks to illustrate the conflict involved between allegiance to institutions and traditions (in this particular case, the great family of Kuroda) as opposed to the men who merely represent them.

The events of the story (all historically quite accurate) take place on the periphery of some of the most important moments in Japanese history: the rise of Oda Nobunaga and Toyotomi Hideyoshi, followed by the establishment of a hegemony over all of Japan by Tokugawa Ieyasu and his descendants. Yet in concentrating on the situation in the country two decades after the battle of Sekigahara, Ōgai has managed in a penetrating way to suggest the legacy of difficulties remaining to the rulers. The story provides a real sense of the quality of life (at least of moral and spiritual life) as perceived by those men of public importance who were determined to see peace and order prevail.

Ultimately the most intriguing aspect of the story remains Ōgai's mastery of the technique of understatement in order to reveal an intricate moral dilemma. There are opportunities for melodramatic and violent scenes throughout, but Ōgai never succumbs to the temptation to provide them. In particular, he refrains from any speculation on the precise nature of the attraction felt by Tadayuki for Jūdaiyū. All the formidable complications of the narrative are marshalled around the central conflict, never resolved until the moment of Toshiaki's quiet testimony to the shogun's retainers in Edo, just before the end of the story.

Toshiaki, Ōgai felt, was the kind of man to inspire the deepest admiration, and in his telling of "Kuriyama Daizen" he makes his reasons for believing so abundantly clear.

ON THE FIFTEENTH DAY of the sixth month of Kan'ei nine [1632], an agent of Kuroda Uemonnosuke Tadayuki,[1] lord of the castle at Fukuoka in the province of Chikuzen, arrested a suspicious-looking man in Dōmachi at the Hakata crossroads. When the matter was investigated, he was found carrying with him a sealed document from Kuriyama Daizen Toshiaki[2] addressed to Takenaka Unemenoshō,[3] the Public Censor of the Tokugawa shogun living at Hida in the province of Bungo. When those at the castle read the document, they found that Toshiaki had accused his lord Tadayuki of fomenting a rebellion.

At this time the relationship between Lord Tadayuki and his retainer Toshiaki had become very strained. Early that year, when Tadayuki returned home from the capital after the funeral services for the former shogun Tokugawa Hidetada, all of his principal retainers came as far as Hakozaki to meet him. Only Toshiaki, on the pretext of illness, shut himself up in his rooms in his quarters in the castle town and did not appear. When Lord Tadayuki's entourage passed by the house, he sent Yamashita Hyōbē as a messenger to inquire after Toshiaki's health, wishing him a complete recovery and requesting his attendance as soon as he was well. Afterward Lord Tadayuki often sent messengers to inquire about Toshiaki's well-being, and he also made inquiries about Toshiaki's condition from the doctor who was treating him, Takatori Chōshōan. Yet from what the doctor and the messenger reported, it seemed clear that Toshiaki was not suffering from any serious disease. Thus, on the thirteenth day of the sixth month, Lord Tadayuki sent Kuroda Ichibē and Okada Zen'emon as envoys to Toshiaki, to inform him that since he was not so ill that he could not be moved, he should appear in attendance, even if he needed help in walking. Toshiaki answered that he could not be moved and that he would come as soon as he was well. Lord Tadayuki sent both envoys back immediately to say that he ordered Toshiaki to come to the gate of the castle, riding, if necessary, in a vehicle, even though the trip might risk making him weak or dizzy. And should that prove impossible, Lord Tadayuki added, then he would come to call on Toshiaki himself. Toshiaki sent back the answer that he could by no means be seen until he was completely well. Lord Tadayuki then asked his envoys how many retainers Toshiaki had with him, and if they had noticed any weapons. They answered that there were about twenty men with Toshiaki, who had kept himself surrounded, and that some weapons were visible. Lord Tadayuki received this report in one of the large open rooms of the castle; now,

TRANSLATED BY J. THOMAS RIMER

seemingly having made up his mind, he suddenly announced that he would go and force his way into Toshiaki's residence himself. Commanding everyone to make proper preparations, he quickly withdrew. Those in attendance all sent servants home to get their arms.

Rumors soon spread throughout the castle town, and guardsmen and young samurai began to throng in front of Toshiaki's residence. At this moment, two of Lord Tadayuki's senior retainers arrived, Inoue Sohō Yukifusa (who went by the name of Dōhaku)[4] and Ogō Kuranojō. Pulling Lord Tadayuki back, they urged him to remember that such behavior on the part of Toshiaki was, after all, only a trifling thing, and that it would be embarrassing to everyone concerned if Edo learned of the matter. They offered to pledge their own honor for Toshiaki, they continued, and surely the matter could be cleared up in some fashion or other; if not, then let Toshiaki commit *seppuku* if that were Lord Tadayuki's order. Lord Tadayuki finally grew calmer. Inoue and Ogō then left to announce that no one at all would be permitted to go to Toshiaki's residence. Anyone who had already gone to the front of Toshiaki's residence was sent over to the mansion of Kuroda Mimasaku (who at that time went by the name of Suiō),[5] the husband of Toshiaki's older sister, and to the office of the *han* Councillors situated across the way from there. On the next day, the fourteenth, Inoue and Ogō conveyed to Toshiaki these decisions made at the castle. Toshiaki immediately cut off his hair and sent his wife and second son Kichijirō as hostages to the castle. There they were placed in the care of Kuroda Hyōgo, Toshiaki's father-in-law. All of these events took place the day before Lord Tadayuki obtained the letter sent by Toshiaki to the Public Censor.

Lord Tadayuki and his retainers who were on duty at the castle found it scarcely credible that Toshiaki had written such a document. Certainly Lord Tadayuki himself had no intention whatsoever of raising a rebellion against the Tokugawa shogun. At this time, however, all the feudal lords had to be on their guard against something or other being seized as a pretext to suggest their disloyalty. It was for such reasons that in the fourteenth year of Keichō [1609], Tōdō Sado no kami Takatora first took the initiative and sent his wife and children to Edo as proof of his loyalty. After the fall of Osaka castle in the first year of Genna [1615], Lord Tadayuki's father Nagamasa[6] also sent his wife Hoshina,[7] their eldest daughter Toku,[8] their second son Inuman,[9] and their third son Mankichi[10] to Edo as hostages. Hoshina was now in Edo, together with Hisamatsu, the wife of Lord Tadayuki. Such were the steps taken to convince the Tokugawa family that no secret intentions were being harbored against them.

Lord Tadayuki and his retainers were shocked to find that, although Lord

Tadayuki harbored no disloyalty against the shogunate, Toshiaki of all people had accused him of doing so. It is true that the relations between the two had become extremely strained. The quarrel between them had grown to the point where Lord Tadayuki would no doubt have ordered Toshiaki to commit *seppuku* if he had made another move of any kind. Tadayuki felt that no matter how faithful a retainer Toshiaki might be, to act in such a way toward his lord was altogether scandalous; for his part, Toshiaki was convinced that, no matter how wise his lord might be, Tadayuki was insulting an older man who had rendered faithful service to two generations of the Kuroda family. Although Tadayuki was furious, he maintained a somewhat diffident attitude, while none of his retainers could comprehend why Toshiaki, whom they respected even while they feared him, should try to ensnare Lord Tadayuki in a false crime.

Not only did the secret letter of Toshiaki surprise and shock everyone concerned, but the whole incident made them visibly full of apprehension. Not only did the letter allege that Lord Tadayuki was planning a rebellion; there was an appendix attached to the letter stating that in order to make sure that it reached proper hands two copies had been made and given to two different persons, sent off by separate routes. It might well be that even if the Kuroda family had been fortunate enough to intercept one copy, the other had probably been received without difficulty in Hida, to be sent on by Takenaka to the Tokugawa house in Edo. Even the impetuous Lord Tadayuki realized, however dimly, that if he put to death such a meritorious retainer of the Kuroda house as Toshiaki, he would surely be accused of violating the laws set down by the Tokugawa family. If the letter reached Edo, as it may well have, then Toshiaki now was the man who could not be put to death under any circumstances: for if Lord Tadayuki was interrogated by the Tokugawa family concerning the question of a possible rebellion, there would be no means to clear himself other than by a direct confrontation with the man who had dared to accuse him of the crime.

Toshiaki's father Kurimoto Toshiyasu[11] was descended from a branch of the Akamatsu family in Harima. His childhood name was Zensuke; later he took the name of Shirōemon and finally the name Bingo. He was born in the castle of Agō in Harima in the twentieth year of Tembun [1551]; when he was fifteen, he entered the service of Kuroda Kambē Yoshitaka[12] at Himeyama in the same province. After the birth of Yoshitaka's son Shōju in the eleventh year of Eiroku [1568], Toshiyasu was appointed as his young lord's personal attendant. Yoshitaka was the grandfather of Tadayuki. His father was Shōju, who later took the name of Nagamasa.

In the sixth year of Tenshō [1578], Araki Settsu no kami Murashige[13] closed himself up in the castle of Arioka at Itami in Settsu and began his rebellion against Oda Nobunaga. Yoshitaka went to the castle to remonstrate with Murashige, who promptly took him prisoner. Toshiyasu, together with Mori Tahyōe Tomonobu (who was later called Tajima) and Inoue Kurōjirō Korefusa (who was later called Suhō), took turns disguising themselves as tradesmen, and managed to loiter around the quarters where Yoshitaka was confined, in order to watch over their lord. At one point Toshiyasu disguised himself as a moneylender of Itami, and under cover of darkness, deceived the sentinels, swam across the irrigation pond behind the prison building, broke in, and managed to speak personally with Yoshitaka. On the eleventh month of the following year, when Takikawa Sakon Kazumasu[14] captured the castle of Arioka, Toshiyasu arrived just as the guards fled, broke open the locks and led Yoshitaka out of his prison. Toshiyasu took him to Arima and had him take healing baths, so that Yoshitaka finally regained the use of his arms and legs.

In the tenth year of Tenshō [1581], Oda Nobunaga was assassinated by Akechi Hyūga no kami Mitsuhide.[15] From that time on, Yoshitaka and his son served Toyotomi Hideyoshi. In Tenshō fifteen [1587], Yoshitaka was made lord over six counties in the province of Buzen. At this time Toshiyasu received a portion of the land. Two years later Yoshitaka retired, taking the name of Jōsuiken Ensei, and Nagamasa became the head of the Kuroda family. Two years after that, on the twenty-second day of the first month, Toshiyasu's wife Murao gave birth to his son Daikichi, who later took the name Daizen Toshiaki. In the first year of Bunroku [1592], Nagamasa took Toshiyasu and Tomonobu with him among the troops crossing to Korea. Yoshitaka later entered the Korean capital as an envoy for Toyotomi Hideyoshi.

In the fourth year of Keichō [1599], when Tokugawa Ieyasu went to the Kantō Plain to attack Uesugi Kagekatsu[16] of Aizu, Nagamasa accompanied him. Before he set out from his home at Temma in Osaka, Nagamasa called together Toshiyasu, Tomonobu, and Miyazaki Sukedayu Shigemasa (later known as Oribe), and left them with precise instructions. While he was gone, should the forces of Toyotomi Hideyoshi advance, they were to take his wife and mother and escape with them to the Nakatsu River before they could be taken as hostages. Since there was a chance that insurrection might not break out, however, they should not act in too great a haste. In any case they should not misjudge the situation and thereby permit the two women to be taken prisoner. He asked that Toshiyasu and Tomonobu concern themselves with any attacking enemy and that Shigemasa remain with the women; if it seemed clear that escape was impossible, Shigemasa was to kill the two women and commit suicide himself.

A short time after this, as expected, Ishida Jibushōyu Mitsunari[17] left his castle at Sameyama and assembled a group of allied daimyo in Osaka. Toshiyasu and the others immediately took the two women, Kushibashi,[18] the wife of Yoshitaka (then a lady of forty-eight), and Hoshina (who was sixteen), the wife of Nagamasa, wrapped them in straw sacks, put them in baskets, and carried them in this fashion through a hole they dug in the base of the wall of the bathing room. The baskets were passed over to Tomonobu who, disguised as a merchant, carried them away on his shoulders. Tomonobu took the baskets along the path, thick with reeds, that followed the river flowing by Nagamasa's mansion. The women were eventually concealed with Naya Kozaemon, a credit merchant in Temma. All of these efforts were made to prevent the discovery of the women by the advance scouts of the forces of Hideyoshi. Both women were hidden in the inner storehouse of Naya's shed. In addition, as a precaution against a possible house search, Naya dug a hole under the wooden floor in the bedroom and placed a mat in it, so that the space would be ready if the women should suddenly have to be moved from the storehouse. Naya's wife took food to them in such a way that even the servants were not aware of their presence. Shigemasa lived there and acted as a guard, while Tomonobu watched over the house from another building close by.

After two or three days had passed, Toshiyasu went to the home of Tōjō Kii no kami Nagayori[19] to learn the latest developments. Talking with him, Tōjō learned that soldiers were gathering to attack the Kuroda mansion. Saying he knew nothing at all about this, Toshiyasu asked Tōjō the circumstances as a means of sounding out his allegiance. Toshiyasu thought that, depending on the answer, he might take Tōjō prisoner and then return to the Kuroda mansion. Tōjō, however, said he knew nothing about it. Toshiyasu leaped on his horse and sped back to Temma. The Kuroda mansion was still quiet. Shortly a secret envoy from Kōri, Shume Muneyasu,[20] arrived with word that the attacking party was approaching. Shortly afterward, fifty samurai mounted on horses and about six hundred foot soldiers, armed with two-hundred-odd guns, surrounded the house. The leader of the party asked if the two ladies were inside. Toshiyasu affirmed the fact that they were. The soldiers withdrew leaving a guard behind. Next came an envoy from the castle asking if the two ladies could be seen, saying that acquaintances of the women were being sent who could identify them. Toshiyasu refused, saying that wives of warriors could not be subjected to such public scrutiny. The messenger said that he was sent to see the wives of other daimyo as well and urged again that the women show themselves, even if screened off from direct view. Toshiyasu, telling them that he could not foresee the reprimand that would be coming when his master returned, agreed there was nothing to be done but let them be seen in this way. The women came who were to identify the two. One had known Kushibashi as a young woman, and the other had known Hoshina when she was twelve.

In Toshiyasu's household was a lady attendant, born in Shinano, the daughter of Ogasawara Kuranosuke, who was about the same age and with roughly the same physical proportions as Kushibashi. Toshiyasu had this woman recline behind gauze mosquito netting and had her daughter, who was also an attendant, sit outside it and converse with her, while the two observers watched from an adjoining room. Fortunately the trick worked and the party withdrew.

Toshiyasu and his men now deliberated as to how to find a way for the ladies to escape. There was a man named Kajiwara Tarōzaemon from Iejima in Harima, a ship's captain who transported goods for the Kuroda family. Plans were made with him for the use of his boat. However, the forces of Hideyoshi had set up a check point to prevent the escape of the wives of the various daimyo. The guard, located below Fukushima in Osaka at the confluence of the Tenryū and Kizu rivers, consisted of a hundred armed soldiers on one large boat, and two smaller ones as well. Toshiyasu and the others waited for a proper occasion, but somehow they were never able to slip through.

It was now the seventeenth day of the seventh month. Wives of various daimyo who sided with the Tokugawa forces had been forced to stay in the citadel of the Osaka castle as hostages. The forces of Hideyoshi first despatched a number of men to the home of Hosokawa Etchū no kami Tadaoki.[21] Without even listening to the protests of the retainers of the Hosokawa family, the soldiers pushed their way right in. Akechi Gracia,[22] the wife of Hosokawa, saying that she refused to expose herself in Osaka castle and did not wish to stand in her husband's way in serving the Tokugawa cause, took her own life. The household retainers, Ogasawara Bizen, Kawakita, Iwanami, and the others, shut the gates for a final defense for the family, then set fire to the buildings and committed suicide. Chastened by this experience, the forces of Hideyoshi abandoned the attempt to hold the wives of daimyo as hostages.

Toshiyasu's men had been keeping their small boat out on the upper reaches of the Fukushima River to study the situation at the guard post. In this way they learned that when the Hosokawa mansion went up in flames, the guards had gone in small boats to the site of the fire. When he received this report, Toshiyasu immediately put the two women into a large box, which he took from the rear door of the shed, and loaded it on a boat. Tomonobu was given a long spear with an immense handle; it was inlaid with pearl, more than seven feet long, and in an elaborate case. He was charged with protecting the boat, along with a group of fifteen strong attendants. When the boat reached the check point, Tomonobu grasped the spear in his hand and demanded to see the guard, an acquaintance of his, named Suga Uemon no Hachi. Tomonobu told the guard that he had business to do in his home village and demanded that the boat be searched so that he might pass. Suga Uemon no Hachi knew very well that Tomonobu was a warrior of great physical stature and tremendous strength; he cravenly replied that the boat need not be searched. So they went down the Dempō River and transferred the two women to Tarōzaemon's boat, which was waiting. One of the serving maids of Hoshina, named Kiku, had escaped from the mansion and followed them. She too was put on the boat. Under Tomonobu's escort the boat arrived without difficulty at the Nakatsu River four days later. Shigemasa went by boat past the borders of Izumi Province, where he boarded still another vessel; Toshiyasu went by land as far as Muro in Harima, then boarded a boat and returned to the Nakatsu River. Kuroda Yoshitaka (who had now taken the name of the lay priest Josui), having surmised the situation in Osaka, tried to send a boat with Mori Yosabē for the two women, but could not manage to do so in time. Shinomiya Ichibē remained behind in the Temma mansion in Osaka where he made desperate excuses to the high officials of the Toyotomi forces. After this, the wife of Katō Kazoe no kami Kiyomasa,[23] led by Kajiwara Sukebē, also escaped from Osaka. The pair made their way to the Nakatsu River, where they stayed in the home of Kajiwara Hachirō Dayū, the older brother of Katō's wife. Josui presented Katō's wife with clothing and had Kiku, who had come to the Nakatsu River accompanying Hoshina, attend her to Kumamoto.

The year following, Keichō five [1600], Nagamasa was awarded the province of Chikuzen for his service to the Tokugawa house at the battle of Sekigahara. At the end of that year, he entered the castle at Najima in Kasuyagōri for the first time. A year later, after discussing the situation with Josui, who had returned from Kyoto for a brief visit, Nagamasa built a castle at Fukuzaki which at that time was in the village of Keiko in Nakagōri. The area is now Fukuoka in Chikushi-gun. Within the six outlying fortifications which were built at the time, Tokiyasu was put in charge of the castle at Matera in Kamizagōri, Tomonobu of the castle at Takatori in Kurategōri, and Yukifusa of Kurozaki in Ongagōri.

In November of Keichō seven [1602], Nagamasa's first son Tadayuki was born in the east citadel of the castle at Fukuoka. His childhood name was Mantoku. The main citadel had been built on the site of a Shinto shrine; in order to avoid defiling this shrine, the eastern citadel, also under the charge of Toshiyasu, was chosen as the place for the delivery of the child. Two years later, Josui died at fifty-nine on the outer fortification of the castle. In 1606, Nagamasa's first daughter Toku was born; his second son Inuman was born four years later, and his third son Mankichi two years after. Inuman was later known as Nagaoki, and Mankichi as Takamasa.

From Keichō nineteen [1614], through the first year of Genna [1615], there were a series of disturbances by the Toyotomi forces in Osaka. In the winter battle of 1614, Nagamasa was in charge of Edo, and the forces of Tadayuki, now thirteen, began to push north from Fukuoka, despite the fact that he had not recovered from a severe fever. Toshiaki served under Nagamasa, while Toshiyasu came down from Edo and took Nagamasa's place in Fukuoka. At the time of the summer battle of 1615, Nagamasa left from Edo and Tadayuki from Fukuoka to join forces in Osaka. Toshiyasu remained behind in Chikuzen, while Toshiaki joined Tadayuki's forces. It was immediately after the fall of Osaka castle[24] that Hoshina took Toku, Inuman, and Mankichi to Edo.

In 1616, the year when Tokugawa Ieyasu died at Sumpu, Nagamasa's third daughter Kame[25] was born. In 1622, when the daughter of Hisamatsu Kai no kami Tadayoshi was seventeen, the shogun Tokugawa Hidetada adopted her as his daughter and sent her as a bride for Tadayuki. A year later, Hidetada turned over the office of shogun to Iemitsu. When Hidetada and Iemitsu went up to Kyoto, they sent Nagamasa on ahead from Edo. Nagamasa, then fifty-three, brought Tadayuki with him and while they were staying at Nijō castle in Kyoto, Nagamasa suddenly died of a stomach cancer. His final testament was heard by Toshiaki and Ogō Kuranojō. Nagamasa's remains were taken back to his home province, and he was cremated at Matsubara in Hakozaki. Toshiaki, now thirty-one, accompanied the coffin in front while Tadayuki, now twenty-two, followed at the foot. When Nagamasa died, Toshiyasu was seventy-three and had taken holy orders. He took the name Ichiyōsai Bokuan.

With such a relationship between them, why were Lord Tadayuki and Toshiaki now embroiled in such a struggle between themselves? It was not that Toshiaki had changed; rather, it was Tadayuki who had.

In the full vigor of his youth, Tadayuki suddenly became a daimyo of more than 500,000 *koku*. As he was naturally intelligent, he thought to manage his territories by his own efforts and with his own wisdom, without the restrictions that might be placed on him by his senior retainers. For this purpose he needed a subordinate of whom he could make use in a free manner. It so happened that there was a clever young man named Jūdayū, the son of the chief of the foot soldiers, Kurahashi Choshirō, who had been employed the year before at the Nakatsu River. Tadayuki made this boy his personal attendant and used him for a variety of purposes; in a very short space of time he had added to the boy's stipend a number of times. Those who wished Tadayuki well grieved for their lord and their province; those who were timid stood in awe of Jūdayū; and those who were vulgar or depraved sought merely to use him to advance themselves.

However, according to the final wishes of Nagamasa, to which Toshiaki and Ogō were witness, three Han Elders—Toshiaki, Kazunari, and Ogō—were to consult together in any affairs of importance concerning the province, while under any exceptional circumstances, Toshiyasu (retired as Bokuan) and Yukifusa (retired as Tōhaku) were to be consulted as well before any final decision was made. Thus the year after the death of Nagamasa, the three Elders prepared a written document of allegiance and presented it to Lord Tadayuki. The document was composed of five sections. First, the three affirmed that they were concealing no treasonous thoughts of any kind against Lord Tadayuki. Second, they affirmed that if they learned that someone, no matter who it might be, was plotting against Lord Tadayuki or attempting to bring harm to their province, they would inform Lord Tadayuki and ask that such a person be properly disposed of. Third, if any party attempted to estrange one of the three from the other two, each would confide in the others so that the truth of the matter would be revealed. Fourth, the three wished to affirm a brotherly feeling between themselves. Fifth, should any of the three Elders encounter any slander concerning themselves, the three would with one heart and mind inform Lord Tadayuki of the allegations. As for Jūdayū, who had received such exceptional favors, they did not feel they understood his real feelings. They watched him night and day, wondering if the second part of their document of allegiance might apply to him.

However, there were no suspicious flaws in the conduct of Jūdayū. The first thing that Toshiaki and the others noticed was merely that decisions about which they had always been consulted were now being made without their consent. At first Lord Tadayuki and his subordinates had only taken independent action in affairs of a trifling nature that could, indeed, be handled in such a fashion; but soon relatively important matters were being handled in the same way. Later, when Toshiaki and the others would ask the subordinates involved, they would reply that no offense of any kind was intended and that it simply had not occurred to them to consult the three. These latter incidents became more frequent. Toshiaki and the others always seemed to be pursuing matters that had already been decided.

The three Elders became increasingly distressed. From time to time they complained directly to Lord Tadayuki concerning the fact that certain official procedures were not being followed with sufficient care. He too replied that he had meant no offense but simply had not thought to consult them. They could get no satisfactory answers from anyone they spoke to, either above or below their rank.

At one point Toshiaki and the others determined to try to put an end to this untenable situation. Needless to say there was a close connection between these abuses they had witnessed and the conduct of Jūdayū, who attended constantly upon Lord Tadayuki. Yet Jūdayū's conduct was impeccable and he had made no obvious blunders in his own administrative activities. It was only that Toshiaki and the others felt instinctively that, somehow or other, the whole atmosphere around them was changing.

They began to observe more sharply. Soon they began to distinguish in precisely what way the changes were becoming apparent.

They first became aware of a certain slackness in the administration of everyday affairs. There was a tendency for Lord Tadayuki to delay arriving for his hours in public attendance, while his retirement to private quarters seemed to begin earlier and earlier. Consequently officials seemed late to appear and quick to withdraw. In his visit to the shogun in Edo, Lord Tadayuki's behavior was precisely the same: he was late in attendance at the castle and he withdrew more quickly than had been his custom. Envoys from the province to Edo, and to the representatives of the Tokugawa in Bungo were always being despatched later than the scheduled date.

Next they noticed that various arrangements were being carelessly made and then changed in a hasty and confused manner. The most flagrant example of this concerned the choice of an envoy to Edo. The person first chosen was Mori Shōzaemon, then a change was made to Tsukigase Umenojō, next Mori was chosen again, finally Tsuboda Shōzaemon. There were also instances when a man who had been treated kindly and who had served Lord Tadayuki well would suddenly seem to incur great disfavor.

It also seemed that trifling things, matters for mere amusement, were given precedence over matters of serious importance, and often serious injunctions over minor matters were set up. Mere *sarugaku* actors were often called upon as special couriers, yet travelers were not permitted to cross through the hawking fields. Returning from Edo, Lord Tadayuki had sent for women entertainers while staying in an inn at Hyōgō, without regard for his own reputation.

Then again, tendencies toward luxurious living became apparent. Clothing and utensils became more splendid, and provisions and menus became more elaborate.

Next they noticed that such important events as funeral ceremonies, certain festivals, condolence calls and similiar observances began to be neglected. On the fifteenth day of the ninth month of the third year of Kan'ei [1626], when the mother of the former shogun Hidetada, Oda Tachiko, also known as Ōmi Daidokoro, died, Lord Tadayuki not only failed to observe ritual abstinence but even was seen on his hawking grounds. Nor did he observe the abstinences on the memorial days for the deaths of Tokugawa Ieyasu or his grandfather Yoshitaka. When he returned from Edo, he did not make the proper visits to the shrines of Yoshitaka and Nagamasa.

It was true that nothing more serious than this had been observed. Yet under the circumstances, there seemed at least a possibility that something serious might well develop. Toshiaki and the others thought that when the proper occasion presented itself, they would speak quite firmly to Lord Tadayuki.

Finally a man was punished for a crime he did not commit, while another was pardoned for an equally serious crime. Jūdayū was involved in both these incidents. In the first instance, a merchant from Hakata refused to give a folding screen painted by an artist named Ukiyo Matabē[26] to Jūdayū, who was anxious to have it. Jūdayū sent his retainers to take the screen by force; when the merchant tried to get it back, Jūdayū had him thrown in prison. In the second instance, a man was apprehended stealing from a farmer in Shimagōri; but when it was discovered that the thief was an elder brother of the mistress of Jūdayū, he was released.

Toshiaki at last gathered his courage, discussed the situation with Kazunari and Ogō, and then wrote out a letter of admonition to Lord Tadayuki. He divided it into various sections, and quoted appropriate examples from the Classics and Histories to buttress his criticisms. In all, he listed twenty-five items. The document was composed in a circumspect fashion: the matter of the false judgments that had prompted Toshiaki to act was placed in a section listing events concerning which neither praise nor blame could clearly be given. Nor did he give too much importance to any censuring of Jūdayū, but rather called on Lord Tadayuki to reflect sincerely on his own conduct. Toshiaki made a clean copy of the document and then asked Bokuan and Tōhaku to read it. This was the twelfth day of the eleventh month of the third year of Kan'ei [1626]. Bokuan and Tōhaku both wrote an endorse-

ment of what Toshiaki had composed. Kobayashi Takumi, Kinugasa Boku-
sai, and Oka Zenzaemon were entrusted with presenting the document to
Lord Tadayuki.

When Lord Tadayuki read it, he was furious. He felt sure that it was composed as the result of jealousy against Jūdayū and prompted by a desire to
find fault. When he saw the many learned quotations he realized at once
that Toshiaki had written it, and all Lord Tadayuki's rage centered on him.
Lord Tadayuki first thought to call Toshiaki and scold him severely. Then he
realized that Toshiaki was not the kind of man to sit and take a scolding
silently. Lord Tadayuki decided that rather than facing disagreeable opinions in a wearisome interview, he would simply dismiss the matter completely without making any comment whatsoever.

Toshiaki and the others waited for Lord Tadayuki to take some kind of action, but there seemed to be no reaction at all. The whole mechanism of administration went on as before. Jūdayū continued to behave in his super-
ficial, clever way. The only difference was that Lord Tadayuki would turn his
face aside every time he met Toshiaki. The letter of admonition had no
other result whatsoever.

Lord Tadayuki carried on this treatment of Toshiaki in a stubborn fashion, and Toshiaki repaid him in kind. It was at this point that the period of
mourning was ended for the death of Kushibashi, the wife of Yoshitaka,
who died in Kan'ei four [1627].

The year following, Lord Tadayuki announced that for his annual visitations to Edo he was having a large boat constructed which he named "Precious Jewel," so that he could sail the distance between his domain and
Osaka. He also announced that Jūdayū should have his own contingent of
soldiers, and without reporting the fact to Edo, he collected together three
hundred foot soldiers for the purpose. The extravagances mentioned in the
letter of admonition were no longer confined to food and clothing: the boat
was constructed in a luxurious fashion and Jūdayū now received his extraor-
dinarily large contingent. Toshiaki no longer felt that he could remain a
bystander in such a situation, and despite the efforts of Ogō and Kazunari to
stop him, he resigned his position as Lord Tadayuki's retainer on grounds of
ill-health. Lord Tadayuki accepted the resignation immediately. Toshiaki
vacated his residence near the castle in silence and secluded himself in his
quarters at Matera.

Lord Tadayuki felt he had removed this annoying source of criticism, but
the year following, he suddenly received an official statement of advice from
the shogun, sent to him by Doi Ōi no kami Toshikatsu.[27] The statement was
a reminder that the Kuriyama family, as retainers to the Kuroda family,

were supposed to lead and guide their young lord. Toshiyasu might be excused from this duty, as he was close to eighty years old, but the fact that Daizen Toshiaki was confined to his home was most improper. A means should be found to persuade Toshiaki to resume his duties. Now, of necessity, Lord Tadayuki was forced to request Toshiaki to return to service.

Toshiaki did eventually take over his duties again, but Lord Tadayuki still continued to turn away from him. There was absolutely no change in the situation since Toshiaki had resigned. As Toshiaki's services were requested by the shogun, Lord Tadayuki could do nothing, which in turn made the secret feelings of ill-will he felt for Toshiaki grow even stronger.

While this tense situation continued, unpleasant as it was to both parties, Toshiaki's father Bokuan suddenly died in his sleep, on the fourteenth day of the eighth month of the eighth year of Kan'ei [1631]. He was eighty-one. By this time Jūdayū had finally managed to gain the rank of Han Elder and received lands valued at nine thousand *koku*. Actually the income they produced was around thirty thousand *koku*. Toshiaki, Kazunari, and Ogō all informed Lord Tadayuki that, although of course Jūdayū was a person who could render good service, it was quite inappropriate to give the status of Han Elder to a man without lineage. Lord Tadayuki did not listen to them.

At a certain point, Lord Tadayuki, declaring that there should be some valuable possessions in the home of his new Han Elder, sent Jūdayū a suit of armor given to his father Nagamasa by Tokugawa Ieyasu at the battle of Sekigahara. When Toshiaki heard this, he went out to the residence of Jūdayū and confiscated the armor himself. Yet even after Toshiaki had taken a step of these proportions, he did not notify Lord Tadayuki. Furious as he was, Lord Tadayuki allowed the incident to pass without a comment of any kind.

The retired shogun Hidetada died in 1632. Lord Tadayuki participated in the funeral procession in Edo and then returned to his domain. It was at this point that the dispute arose concerning Toshiaki's failure to attend upon Lord Tadayuki and Tadayuki's threat to go personally to Toshiaki's residence. Toshiaki was essentially a man of tremendous patience, but so was Tadayuki. On this one occasion, however, there was a particular reason why Lord Tadayuki had become so irritated that he lost his good judgment. Hidetada died on the twenty-fourth day of the first month. The funeral was held on the night of the twenty-sixth at the temple of Zōjōji in Edo. On the twenty-second day of the second month, the imperial messengers were despatched, and on the eleventh day of the third month, Lord Tadayuki took leave of the shogun and left Edo. When he arrived home in the fourth month, a serious incident had just arisen in the adjacent domain of Higo.

On the tenth day of the fourth month, an anonymous letter was brought to the home of Muroga Gen'ichirō Masatoshi[28] in Nagata-chō in Edo. The letter revealed the supposed treachery of the lord of Kumamoto castle in Higo, Katō Tadahiro.[29] Inoue Shinzaemon, the father-in-law of Masatoshi, was intimate with Lord Doi Toshikatsu and so told him about the letter. Toshikatsu ordered the man who brought the letter apprehended. When he was found four days later, at Dobashi in Kōji-machi, he was identified as Maeda Gorōhachi, a retainer of Katō Mitsumasa, the son of Katō Tadahiro. As the shogun Tokugawa Iemitsu was on a visit to Nikkō and was stopping at Utsunomiya in the province of Shimotsuge, Toshikatsu sent Masatoshi there and had him present the charges against Katō. Inaba Tango no kami Masakatsu was chosen to serve as envoy from the shogun to Kumamoto and order Katō to come to Edo. Since Masakatsu passed through Yamaga in Onga of Chikuzen Province on the way to Kumamoto, Lord Tadayuki, just returned from Edo himself, sent a party from Fukuoka to greet him. Jūdayū was chosen as Lord Tadayuki's chief envoy, and Kuroda Ichibē was to serve as his assistant. Jūdayū's party contained, in addition to two hundred of his new retainers, other foot soldiers and some troops armed with muskets, all together about three hundred and fifty men, while those accompanying Kuroda were no more than thirty-eight all together. Arriving at Yamaga, the welcoming party waited on Masakatsu at his inn. Masakatsu announced that he had never heard of the name Kurahachi Jūdayū, but he had heard that Kuroda Ichibē was of good lineage, and so he would confer with Kuroda. Even though Jūdayū was chief of the delegation, he was not granted an interview and had to retire. The townspeople of Fukuoka and Hakata despised the tyrannical ways of Jūdayū, and the whole incident made excellent gossip for everyone.

When Lord Tadayuki heard what happened, he was even more angry than when he had received the letter of admonition from Toshiaki. He ordered that those who spread rumors about the affair should be identified and arrested. Shortly afterward several townspeople were killed. Of two persons who were talking on the street of Amibachō, Sugihara Heisuke was cut down while the other escaped. At Gofuku-chō in Fukuoka, where three people were chatting together, Sakada Kazaemon was killed and the two others escaped. In Tojinchō, Hamada Tazaemon was killed and one escaped. The townspeople were terribly intimidated. The incident about the Katō family came to be interpreted as an attempt by Katō Mitsumasa to slander his father Tadahiro. Tadahiro was eventually accused of taking his two-year-old son, born of a concubine, back to his native province without informing the shogun's authorities; on the first day of the sixth month, he was stripped of his rank and all the emoluments accompanying it.

The anger that almost drove Lord Tadayuki to force his way into Toshi-aki's quarters was manifested in the same nervous excitement that caused the death of several townsmen in repayment for the insults received by his favorite retainer, Jūdayū.

On the twenty-fifth day of the eighth month of 1632 a messenger arrived from the shogun, with an order for Lord Tadayuki's attendance in Edo. For the first time Lord Tadayuki seemed to become aware of the dimensions of the situation, as if awakened from a dream. He left Fukuoka shortly after-ward, taking with him Kazunari and Ogō Kaganojō. When they were close to Edo they learned that a party of Tokugawa liege vassals, captains of ar-tillery, and some twenty or more men of lower rank were waiting for Lord Tadayuki at Shinagawaguchi, with orders to put him in quarters at the Tō-kaiji temple in Shinagawa. Lord Tadayuki felt that even if he could not escape his own ruin, he was determined to end his days in his own mansion in Edo. Ogō devised a plan, and a few retainers, armed with spears, set out about midnight from Kanagawa with Lord Tadayuki in his palanquin. The small group was able to pass quickly through Shinagawa and enter Lord Tadayuki's principal residence at Sakurada in Azabu. When dawn arrived, just as Kazunari and Ogō were preparing to arrange the Kuroda party in a proper procession and go to Shinagawaguchi, a messenger came from the guard house with instructions from Abe Tsushima no kami Shigetsugu,[30] who indicated that Lord Tadayuki was being requested to stop for a short time at the Tōkaiji. Ogō answered that Lord Tadayuki had suddenly been summoned for an emergency and had already entered the capital with a few retainers during the night.

Shortly afterward, a messenger from the shogun's highest councillors ar-rived at Lord Tadayuki's mansion at Sakurada. He came to announce that Lord Tadayuki was to be quartered in the Hase temple in Shibuya. Lord Tadayuki answered that he was unaware of how he had incurred his lord's displeasure, but should prefer to receive his punishment at his own resi-dence. At this, the messenger withdrew. Next, Lord Naruse Hayatonoshō Masatora[31] of the Owari branch of the Tokugawa family, and the lords Andō Tatewaki Naotsugu[32] and Takiguchi Bingo no kami[33] of the Kii branch of the Tokugawa family, came to request an interview. The three, who were usually on excellent terms with Lord Tadayuki, persuaded him to allow him-self to be moved to the Haseji.

Now a special message was despatched by mounted courier to Fukuoka from the mansion at Sakurada. When the messenger arrived in Chikuzen, the retainers in charge of the c..le, the captains of the soldiers, and the other samurai gathered to discuss the situation. When their deliberations were finished, the results were reported to their subordinates in the following terms. Those samurai who wished to hand over the castle and evacuate it were to leave immediately. Those who were determined to take a final stand were urged to make appropriate preparations. No one spoke for evacuation. It was decided to take the women and children into the castle and that all would give up their lives in a final battle. Finally, plans were made to defend the castle.[34]

In Edo, meanwhile, Lord Tadayuki was summoned by the shogun's councillors and went to the West Enceinte of Edo castle on the seventeenth day of the eleventh month. There he was informed that the authorities regarded as transgressions his employment of subordinates in general, and the incident of Jūdayū's serving as chief envoy to Inaba Masakatsu in particular. He was told that an official investigation would be carried out. That night, Andō Naotsugu came to call on Lord Tadayuki and informed him that Naruse Masatora had fallen ill. About eight that evening, Lord Tadayuki went to visit Naruse. On the nineteenth day, Tadayuki was permitted to return to his own quarters, but as he felt some apprehension about occupying the principal mansion, he moved instead to a secondary residence where his younger brother Takamasa had been living. Takamasa moved to the outbuildings.

Early in the second month of 1633, Lord Tadayuki was called three times in the course of several days to the West Enceinte and was questioned by the shogun's councillors. He was also asked about Toshiaki's accusation that he was fomenting a rebellion, but Lord Tadayuki defended himself in a clear and logical manner. After this interrogation Lord Tadayuki deliberately showed great restraint and remained within the Hase temple.

At this time, Takenaka Unemenoshō arrived in Edo, escorting Toshiaki. On the twenty-fourth day of the second month, there was a confrontation between Toshiaki, Jūdayū, and the others, at the mansion of Lord Doi Toshikatsu. Attending were thirteen high officials,[35] ranged around Toshikatsu to witness the discussion. Takenaka, with Toshiaki beside him, sat on one side about three feet from the seat of the Censor General. On the other side sat Kazunari, then Jūdayū.

A brief inquiry was begun. Toshiaki began by asserting that the affair was of no great import and that he would like to request that the investigation be confined to the circumstances surrounding his letter of admonition to Lord Tadayuki the year before and the events that followed, since it was this incident that generated the present situation. He said nothing further. Kazunari and Jūdayū replied that there was no evidence that their Lord Ta-

dayuki had rebellious attitudes against the Tokugawa and could not understand how Toshiaki could make the accusation he did. Following this exchange, both men were questioned by the shogun's councillors concerning
the facts of the alleged misdemeanors of Tadayuki.

During the investigation, Kuroda Kenmotsu was called upon and questioned concerning the unauthorized increase in foot soldiers.

Next Ogō Kaganojō was called in. Since he appeared without having been
officially summoned, his testimony was not considered admissible by the
shogun's inspectors. After Ogō made his obeisances to the assembled officials, he made his usual salutation to Toshiaki. He began by declaring that
Lord Tadayuki had no treasonous intentions whatsoever. Why Toshiaki had
made such a complaint was a mystery to him. When Toshiaki was born, the
previous lord of Chikuzen, Nagamasa, had presented to Toshiaki's father
Toshiyasu a wet nurse, a short sword, baby clothing, and ceremonial rice
wine and fish. Nagamasa himself had taken the gifts to the Kuroda household, and Toshiaki's father had gone himself to the gate in the most humble
way to thank Nagamasa for his great favors. When Toshiaki grew up, he too
received favors from Nagamasa. Thus wondering how Toshiaki could have
lodged such a complaint, Ogō suddenly broke into tears. Then he continued
by saying that, were there any treasonous activities being plotted by Lord Tadayuki, then surely Tōhaku (Yukifusa) would not fail to be aware of them.
Getting up from his seat, Ogō left the room and returned with Tōhaku
himself, whom he brought before the officials.

After Tōhaku paid his respects to all present, he suddenly moved toward
Toshiaki and crouched down before him. "Please move down a little. I am
sitting here," he spoke out. "Please, put yourself at ease," replied Toshiaki, without moving. "But Lord Tadayuki will be coming soon," continued
Tōhaku. "Would you move down just a bit?" At that, Toshiaki moved
down one space. Now Tōhaku took his seat in a position of greater honor
than Toshiaki.

Actually Tōhaku, like Ogō Kaganojō, had not been summoned. However
since Doi Toshikatsu was acquainted with him, he called on him to speak.
Then Andō Naotsugu asked Tōhaku, "You must be the father of Awaji?"[36]
Naotsugu was acquainted with the son of Tōhaku.

Tōhaku next spoke to Toshiaki. "I was a good friend of your father Bokuan. Bokuan never told a lie in his life. You are less worthy than your
father." Toshiaki replied, "Sir, you have not been apprised of recent events
and you are not aware of the situation."

Next Tōhaku faced the shogun's officials and spoke. The empire, he began, is gained by the military arts and protected through the arts of civil

rule. Had Lord Tadayuki any treacherous intentions, he could do nothing without making his accomplices those samurai who had a great deal of experience themselves. Kazunari was the most experienced of the Kuroda family retainers. Ogō Kaganojō and Kenmotsu had also been involved two or three times in military encounters. He himself, Tōhaku continued, had to some extent the requisite experience. Certainly these two or three would have to be consulted, and as for Toshiaki, he was no man to become involved in any warlike battles. The very fact that Toshiaki seemed to be the only one who knew anything about Lord Tadayuki's supposed intentions was surely a proof that no such plans existed. If Lord Tadayuki because of his youth had been negligent in his administrative duties and was thus to be stripped of his domain, then he, Tōhaku, was resigned to obey the shogun's order. But he only wished to remove the false charge laid against Lord Tadayuki. After all, at the time of the battle of Sekigahara, had not Tokugawa Ieyasu himself taken the hand of Kuroda Nagamasa, who was then the lord of Chikuzen, and told him that the success of the Tokugawa family had been greatly aided through the efforts of the Kuroda family? Had Ieyasu not promised that the house of Kuroda would never in the future be slighted by the house of Tokugawa? Such matters, Tōhaku reminded his listeners, were surely known to some there in attendance: Lord Doi, Lord Ii, and Lord Sakai.[37]

Kazunari and Ogō expressed their agreement with what Tōhaku had said. Then the three took their leave. Toshiaki was also sent away, on orders from Naruse Masatora.

Two or three days later, Lord Tadayuki was called by the shogun's councillors to the West Enceinte, where he was given his sentence. As there were clearly evidences of misconduct, his lands in Chikuzen were to be confiscated. Nevertheless, as the military prowess of his family and his own personal loyalty were well recognized, he would be reappointed as lord over Chikuzen. That night Andō Naotsugu sent a letter to Tadayuki saying "You are now free to act as you wish." During the night Tadayuki entered his mansion in Azabu.

At the beginning of the third month, Toshiaki was called to the mansion of Naotaka. Doi Toshikatsu was in attendance, as well as many of those who had participated in the earlier meeting at Doi's residence. Toshiaki, who was without his swords, took his seat. Takenaka Unemenojō informed him of the decision that had been made. First of all, it had been agreed that the incidents mentioned in Toshiaki's original letter of admonition to Lord Tadayuki were substantially correct. Yet the charge that Lord Tadayuki was guilty of treason was certainly false. He was asked to explain precisely how he had come to make such an accusation. Toshiaki replied that he considered it a great blessing that the letter of admonition had been accepted as correct. He had accused his lord of treason, Toshiaki continued, because he wanted to stop Lord Tadayuki from putting him to death for his own personal reasons. Toshiaki was not concerned for his own life and insignificant death, but he knew that if Lord Tadayuki had continued in the same fashion he would have had his lands taken from him without an investigation and without any recourse. His accusation, he explained, was the strategy he chose to save the situation as best he could. Toshiaki's words brought a flush of emotion to the faces of the officials in attendance.

Two or three days later Toshiaki was again called to the mansion of Naotaka. The same officials were in attendance, with the addition of Nambu Yamashiro no kami Shigenao.[38] The decision rendered was conveyed to Toshiaki by Matsudaira Tadahiro, who told him that Kuroda Tadayuki would have his lands confiscated on a temporary basis, because of various improprieties in his conduct. However, in view of Lord Tadayuki's distinguished family and his personal loyalty to the Tokugawa, his lands would be returned to him. Toshiaki was to be placed under the custody of Nambu Shigenao in Morioka. Toshiaki thanked them and respectfully moved back a considerable distance, tears welling in his eyes. "This is a piece of great good fortune for me," he said. Shigenao came forward at this point and said that Toshiaki would receive a stipend of one hundred fifty *koku* from the shogun's authorities, and, until he set out for Morioka he would now be free to travel as he pleased within a space of two or three ri. Toshiaki again paid his deepest respects to all those assembled.

At about the same time, Masatora and Naotsugu came to the mansion at Azabu, where they met with Tōhaku, Kazunari, Ogō, Kenmotsu, and Jūdayū. Masatora said, "On this occasion, the affair with Lord Tadayuki has been successfully resolved. This is a matter to rejoice over. Yet, if he had been sent into exile, what would have happened to all of you?" Tōhaku, after pondering the question for a moment, spoke up. "If such a decision were made, then all of Lord Tadayuki's retainers would retire from all activities."

"All of them? Without exception?"

"Yes," they told Masatora.

As he rose, Masatora said, "Then indeed the house of Kuroda is fortunate to have retainers of such caliber." The conversation served as a commitment from Lord Tadayuki's retainers that the preparations made for a siege in Fukuoka would never become public knowledge.

Again, two or three days after this, Jūdayū was called to the home of

Andō Naotsugu. Masatora was also present, at Naotsugu's request. They suggested that Jūdayū would be well advised to take the tonsure and retire to the Buddhist temples at Mt. Kōya. Jūdayū, overwhelmed, accepted their proposal.

On the eighth day of the fifth month, Lord Tadayuki was granted an interview by the shogun Iemitsu, and good relations between the Tokugawa and the Kuroda families were restored. Five years later, Lord Tadayuki won considerable renown at the battle of Shimabara,[39] and three years after that was put in charge of coastal defense preparations at Nagasaki. From this time on, Dutch ships that formerly called at Hirado were now directed to Nagasaki.

When the Shimabara Rebellion broke out in Kan'ei fourteen [1637], Jūdayū slipped away from Mt. Kōya and joined a group of Christian converts. When the Shimabara castle fell, he was killed in the general tumult.

Toshiaki arrived in the castle town of Morioka in Iwate in the province of Mutsu at the end of the third month of Kan'ei eleven [1634]. The Nambu family welcomed him with a magnificent house prepared for him on the main thoroughfare.

Only two years before, on the fourteenth of the sixth month, Toshiaki had faced the most difficult day he had during the entire affair. He had sent his wife and his second son Kichijirō to Lord Tadayuki's castle as hostages and prepared the two copies of his accusation addressed to Takenaka Unemenoshō, sending one copy by a skilled and trustworthy man on a special route to Hida; the other he sent quite intentionally with a suspicious-looking farmer. It was this man who had been apprehended in the town. Before taking this final step, Toshiaki had gone both to his quarters near the castle and to his residence at Matera in order to put things in proper order, paying special attention to safeguarding the most valuable items he possessed. Among those was a written document dated the nineteenth day of the ninth month of Keichō five [1600], presented to Kuroda Nagamasa by Tokugawa Ieyasu. It was a letter of thanks which read, "As the peace prevailing throughout the land is indeed due to your loyalty and devotion, your descendants will never be treated with disrespect." Toshiaki handed it over to Kajiwara Heijūrō Kagenao and told him that with Lord Tadayuki and himself now called to Edo, Toshiaki felt that the fortunes of the Kuroda family were in great danger, and that it might be necessary for Kajiwara to take the document to Edo and bring it to the attention of the shogun's senior retainers—Kii, Doi, Sakai, and the others.

Kajiwara Kagenao himself was a man with a special relationship to the

Kuroda family. His legal father, Kanzō Kagetsugu, was the son of Suruga no kami Kagenori, lord of the castle of Takasago in Harima and Akaishi, the younger sister of the mother of Kuroda Yoshitaka. This Kagetsugu had married a woman named Onoe, and Kagenao was her son. Onoe's father Yasuemon, however, was himself the husband of the younger sister of Kuroda Yoshitaka. After he was killed in battle and his wife had retired from the world and become a nun, Onoe became a lady-in-waiting to Kushibashi, the wife of Kuroda Yoshitaka, and she became pregnant by Yoshitaka. Kagetsugu was married to her by the order of his lord and brought up Kagenao as his own son. Thus in reality, Kagenao was the illegitimate child of Yoshitaka, the younger brother of Nagamasa, and the uncle of Lord Tadayuki.

As it was, the document was not needed. Eventually it was returned to Lord Tadayuki's descendant, Kuroda Tsugutaka, by the Kajiwara family in Meiwa five [1768], more than a hundred years later.

At the time when Lord Tadayuki was called to Edo, Toshiaki took refuge in the official residence of Takenaka in Hida; it was Takenaka who had taken him to Edo just before the investigation of Lord Tadayuki began.

When Toshiaki left for Morioka, he took his first son, Daikichi, with him. Accompanying him were two of his own former personal retainers, Senkoku Kakuemon and Zaitsu Ōemon, as well as quite a number of other liege vassals. Toshiaki's wife and son Kichijirō, who had served in the mansion of Kuroda Hyōdo, were later given a stipend of five hundred *koku*.

Toshiaki began his service in Morioka when he was forty-four years old. He was full of strength and vigor. He took a second wife, Uchiyama, and she later gave birth to a girl.

In the winter of 1641, when Tadayuki was given his position at Nagasaki, a certain Inoue, the governor of some territories of the shogun not far from Morioka, heard of Toshiaki's extraordinary character and personal qualities and requested an interview. Toshiaki sent him the following answer. ''As I am, actually speaking, without a proper master, I feel that it would be improper of me to accept your kind invitation. However, since I am leading a quiet and retired life, it would be a great pleasure if you would come and visit with me.''

Inoue came to visit the mansion on the main thoroughfare. When he entered, he saw Toshiaki, wearing a loose work cap, bending over the hearth. Toshiaki lifted his head and made an informal greeting, without any usual show of deference to a man of Inoue's rank. Toshiaki was then fifty-one, but his complexion was still that of a man in his prime.

Inoue felt that, considering his position as a direct representative of the shogun, the greeting was rather inappropriate. He waited to see how Toshi-aki would continue to conduct himself. Nothing else was said, however, that could be interpreted as rude. He exchanged a few words with Toshiaki and returned home.

Afterward, Inoue began to puzzle over Toshiaki's attitude. Why had he been greeted in such a negligent fashion? The problem remained on Inoue's mind even after he returned home. He could make nothing of the whole situation and so decided to go and talk to Toshiaki again in order to ascertain his real attitude.

The second time as well, Toshiaki greeted Inoue in the same way and with the same seemingly careless attitude. Inoue immediately spoke out very strongly. He had come twice, he began, because he heard that Toshiaki was no ordinary person. He had been looking forward to discussing things together, and he even thought that on certain matters he might like to ask Toshiaki for some advice. Yet from all appearances, there was nothing extraordinary about him at all. He was rather disappointed, Inoue concluded.

Toshiaki replied that, indeed, he was nothing out of the ordinary. He did feel, however, that the only proper way to judge a person's wisdom and moral sense was to engage in a serious discussion.

Then, said Inoue, he wanted to bring up a question at once. Whatever his own personal qualities, he continued, he was a direct personal representative of the shogun. Thus he was unable to understand Toshiaki's motives in greeting him in such an obviously off-handed manner.

Toshiaki replied by suggesting to Inoue that perhaps he had not thought through his own reaction with sufficient care. After all, he reminded him, when he, Toshiaki, had been in Chikuzen, he had been in charge of the castle at Matera, with a territory yielding twenty-five thousand *koku*. True enough, after the battle of Osaka, Matera, like all other outlying fortifications, had been destroyed.[40] But he still retained the domains as before. Then again, as a chief retainer of the Kuroda family, he had been privy to responsibilities to administer a territory with an income of more than five hundred thousand *koku*, and he had been in charge of more than fifty thousand soldiers. Indeed the actions of a family with the prominence of the Kuroda were closely aligned to the welfare of the entire nation. At the time of the battle of Sekigahara, the Tokugawa family had been able to unite the country because Nagamasa and Yoshitaka served Ieyasu as faithful allies. There was certainly no reason, Toshiaki finished, why he should bend his knee to an official with an income worth some three or four hundred bags of rice.

Inoue recognized immediately the truth of what Toshiaki told him, apologized for his lack of perceptivity, and began to discuss a variety of matters on a most friendly and intimate basis.

When Inoue asked Toshiaki about the virtues and failings of different types of military strategy, Toshiaki explained his ideas as follows. The art of government requires a judicious mixture of civilian and military elements. The civilian aspects suggest moderation, the military, fierceness and strength. But "military" does not mean merely the use of weapons. It is only an aggressive and vainglorious rule that consistently depends on military might. Indeed no more than one aspect of military strategy depends on the force of arms. Various contemporary theories on the military arts are useless; outside of the Seven Books,[41] there are no other works of note to study. Have strong and brave men close by you, scrutinize the enemy's movements, and you will win. The question of strategy is always to be considered. If strategy is only conceived of in terms of numbers of men and how they are outfitted, there will be little chance to gain the final victory.

Inoue asked Toshiaki about the proper function of a castle. He replied that a castle should serve as a storehouse in times of trouble, so that families, provisions, and implements might be placed there for safe keeping. In a sense, a castle resembles the storehouse of a farmer or merchant. A fine general will not place too much importance on his citadel. Loyal retainers are the most important element in a strong castle. Those who have the status of daimyo should fear no one under the emperor. The training of good subordinates must always be kept in mind. Situations must always be watched as they develop, so that a lord's holdings may be enlarged whenever the occasion presents itself.

Inoue asked Toshiaki about the aspirations that samurai should cultivate. He replied that a samurai's aspiration must be high. If one were born in China, he should dream of becoming emperor. If born in Japan, one should aspire to become the shogun. Yet in order to accomplish his ambition, a samurai must always act prudently and treat others with genuine respect. When one has gained control over the provinces, he must make use of others with discretion and good judgment. Of ten men who can be of service, he should praise six and criticize four; if he praised all ten, he could only be weak and servile. Finally, the question of timing must always be carefully considered. At the right moment, decisive action is always required. To seize is against propriety; to protect is the proper order of things. Should you become aware of some misdemeanor, make sure you will not suffer from any misstep you make yourself, then make your decision and carry it out.

Toshiaki died at the age of sixty-two, on the first day of the third month of the First year of Jōō [1652], the year after Tokugawa Iemitsu was succeeded by Ietsuna. Toshiaki's grave and a large memorial tablet still remain on a hillside near the remains of the Hōrinji on Atagoyama at the village of Yonai in Iwate prefecture of the Tōhaku region. A young man named Uchiyama Zenkichi was adopted as heir for Toshiaki's family and married his daughter. He was in the service of the Nambu family with a stipend of two hundred *koku*. Toshiaki had decided to drop his own name, Kuriyama, since he felt it might remind people of the unfortunate incident of his earlier lord's misconduct. He purposely had the family adopt the surname of their maternal relative. Toshiaki's own retainers Kakuemon and Ōemon were called into service by the Nambu family and each received a stipend of fifty *koku*. Toshiaki's first son Rishū declined a similiar invitation from the Kuroda family and ended his days as a private gentleman.

September 1915

SUGINOHARA SHINA

"SHINA OF SUGINOHARA" is a popular story in Japan, yet an English-speaking reader may be puzzled at the attraction it has sustained. The narrative is broken up by the enumeration of small details that eventually seem to overwhelm the flow of events completely. In fact, however, the historical incidents with which the story deals are among the most famous in the history of the Tokugawa period. The quarrel of the Date family in Sendai over succession rights eventually involved the shogunate and cast into question many of the political principles on which the Tokugawa hegemony was constructed.* The incident was dramatized in a 1777 kabuki play *Meiboku Sendai hagi* that dominated the repertoire for several generations and is still performed with some frequency today. A Japanese reader, in other words, comes to the story with the necessary background, and interest, to follow the details of Ōgai's arguments.

In this perspective, Ōgai's accomplishments are considerable. He penetrates the myths surrounding the story of Tsunamune (who, according to popular accounts, was merely a dissolute) in order to discover his true temperament and character. Ōgai also locates with unerring precision the area of greatest potential interest for a writer: the psychological attitude of Tsunamune in exile, forced to watch passively the events that swirled around him. Ōgai, who often described himself as a "bystander" in his own earlier work, was no doubt naturally attracted to the character and situation of Tsunamune.

In addition, Ōgai provides a trenchant example of his dictum that ". . . the relations between the sexes are inscrutable . . ." in his sketch of the relations between Hatsuko and Shina, for whom the story is named. Shina, like several other women who figure in the historical narratives, represents a complex of virtues that, for Ōgai, make her altogether exceptional.

Ōgai's account falls short of fiction. As he himself points out in the course of his narrative, his regard for the historical facts, obtained through painstaking research, required a fidelity that precluded the creation of any new set of legends. We are left then with a web of facts and conjectures; read with understanding, they can exert a considerable appeal.

 I WAS ABOUT to set off for Kyoto to participate in the succession ceremony of the emperor one day, when a magazine of a certain society of which I was a member arrived.[1] Glancing through it in the midst of more pressing business, I noticed a story claiming that the descendants of a geisha named Takao were living in Sendai. I knew some rather comprehensive and ruthless evidence by Ōtsuki Fumihiko[2] that disproved this legend. As I wondered why this mistaken view was now being circulated anew, I realized, after pondering the matter more carefully, that a good reason existed.

Every writer has entertained the same question in his mind, I suppose; namely, how many people really read his work? Once a work is published, the possibility is born of its being read. However, the number of persons who actually do read it are few indeed. And not only are there comparatively few readers among the great masses of people—even among avid and learned readers their powers of reading are limited. They cannot read all the books that come out; hence even persons interested in such history as appears in the magazine I mentioned are not necessarily aware of the painstaking research of Ōtsuki Fumihiko.

The facts of the article were based on the "Ōshūbanashi" [Tale of Ōshū],[3] written by a certain Ayako,[4] the daughter of Kudō Heisuke of Sendai who became the wife of Tadano Iga. Ayako's claim to fame was her acquaintance with Takizawa Bakin. However, Ōtsuki Fumihiko also knew of the tale and demolished its credibility.

According to Ayako, the daimyo Date Tsunamune[5] had ransomed a geisha named Takao of the Shinyoshiwara district in Edo and brought her back to Sendai, where she died at a ripe old age; she says Takao's grave is in the Butsugenji temple in Aramichi and her descendants are the Suginohara family.

This account was completely erroneous. Date Tsunamune succeeded his father, Tadamune,[6] who died in the first year of Manji [1658]. On the first day of the second month of the third year of Manji [1660], Tsunamune was ordered by the Bakufu to direct the dredging of a canal in Koishikawa in Edo. He came to Edo from Sendai in the third month and commenced operations. The project extended from Sujikaebashi, the present-day Manseibashi, to Ushigome-dobashi. Therefore Tsunamune moved his headquarters to a temporary residence within the precincts behind Kichijōji temple. Kichijōji was a temple in present-day Komagome and at that time was still at the north foot of Suidōbashi, on the east side. Tsunamune first visited the li-

TRANSLATED BY DAVID DILWORTH

censed quarters at Yoshiwara at this time. This was not unusual for daimyos then, but the fact that his conduct was exaggerated and so quickly brought to the attention of the Bakufu seems to have been due to the connivance of certain people out to disgrace him. On the ground of misconduct, Tsunamune was ordered under house confinement and moved from the mansion at Shibahama to Shinagawa. The Shibahama mansion was apparently right in the middle of present-day Shimbashi Station. On the twenty-fifth day of the eighth month, his first son, Kamechiyo,[7] succeeded to the head of the Date house. At this time Tsunamune was twenty and Kamechiyo scarcely two. The dredging project was continued under the supervision of the Date family, and was completed in the following year.

Now, the Yoshiwara personage Tsunamune visited seems to have been a certain Kaoru of the Yamamoto-ya in Kyōmachi. In proof that she could not have been the Takao of the Miura-ya, it has been established that there was no geisha named Takao in the Miura-ya between the third and seventh months of the second year of Manji [1659]. There being no Takao for Tsunamune to visit, he could not have ransomed her either. Moreover, Tsunamune never went back to Sendai after being put under house arrest in the mansion in Shinagawa. At the age of forty-four in the third year of Tenna [1683], he became a monk and took the name Kashin. He died at seventy-two on the sixth day of the sixth month of the first year of Shōtoku [1711]. Even if there were a geisha Tsunamune ransomed, he could not have taken her back to Sendai.

Ayako, wanting to refute the popular version of the story that Tsunamune had ransomed Takao and then sailed off with her and killed her at Mitsumata, had Takao accompany him to Sendai and bear him sons there. She simply replaced one erroneous version of the story with another.

Whose grave, therefore, is in the Butsugenji temple mentioned in the "Ōshūbanashi"? It is that of a mistress of Tsunamune named Shina, whose descendants have the name of Suginohara since she was originally from that family. Shina was neither a Yoshiwara geisha nor the person named Takao.

What kind of person was this Shina? I myself was planning to write a story centering around Tsunamune in Shinagawa, and worked on the historical background of the plot for quite a long time. Tsunamune was no ordinary daimyo. He was a gifted poet, calligrapher, and painter. He succeeded to the head of the Date house at the age of nineteen. He had been daimyo of the six hundred twenty thousand *koku* fief for barely two years when he was placed under house arrest for being involved in an intrigue centering around his uncle, Date Hyōbu Shōyū Munekatsu.[8] From then until he became a monk at the age of forty-four, Tsunamune was never permitted to see his son Kamechiyo, later named Tsunamura. Kamechiyo became Sōjirō Tsunamoto at the age of eleven in the ninth year of Kambun [1669]; two years later he became the nominal father-in-law of Ichi no kami Muneoki,[9] the heir of Munekatsu. Because in that year there occurred the incident in which Harada Kai cut down Date Aki in the mansion of Sakai Uta no kami Tadakiyo, patron of Munekatsu, Kamechiyo could set his mind at rest concerning the domain he thought himself about to lose.[10] In the fifth year of Empō [1677], at the age of nineteen, he changed his name to Tsunamura. Munekatsu, his secret enemy, died two years later—four years before the reunion of Tsunamune and Tsunamura. On the scrolls he did during those lonely years under domiciliary confinement, Tsunamune often used the seal *chika hikkai*, which means "When one perceives his faults, he must correct them." Tsunamune's artistic talents were not confined to calligraphy and poetry. He worked in gold-lacquer ware, made pottery, and also forged swords. I find it of particular interest that Tsunamune rechanneled politically inexpressible energies in the direction of art. It is also interesting that Tsunamune's spirits did not dampen under house arrest. In the sliding door of the Shinagawa mansion he inlaid more than four hundred glass tiles, a material still rare at that time. It is said that the larger tiles sold for seventy *ryō* each. Does this not bear witness to his indomitable spirit? His mistress Shina, who served this magnificent personality Tsunamune into his late years, was surely no ordinary woman either.

Tsunamune did not have a legal wife. The two main women who lived with him were Misawa Hatsuko,[11] the mother of Kamechiyo, and this Shina.[12] Hatsuko was born in the eleventh year of Kan'ei [1639]. She was the same age as Tsunamune, while Shina seems to have been one year older. Of the two women, Hatsuko came from a good family and was well-sponsored. When he took her in, Tsunamune went through a formal marriage ceremony, but it was never registered with the Bakufu. It was held when Tsunamune and Hatsuko were both sixteen, three years before he succeeded as the head of the family. Four years later, on the eighth day of the third month of the second year of Manji [1659], Kamechiyo was born. This was the year prior to the assignment of the canal project. Shina came to serve at the age of twenty-one in their Hama mansion in the year that Hatsuko gave birth to Kamechiyo. She apparently caught Tsunamune's eye immediately and began receiving his favors about the time of Hatsuko's delivery.

Hatsuko, who served Tsunamune before Shina, was a person of excellent lineage. Iijima Saburō Hirotada, the eighth-generation grandson of Mutsu

no kami Mankai, who was in turn the fourth son of Rokusonnō Tsune-
moto,[13] was lord of Misawa in Izumo; Hirotada's great-grandchild was Misa-
wa Rokurō Tamenaga. The tenth-generation grandson of Tamenaga, one
Sakyonosuke Tametora, had moved to Fuchū in Nagato, serving first under
Amako Yoshihisa,[14] later under Mōri Terumoto.[15] Tametora's eldest son,
Tanomonosuke Tamemoto, had a dispute with his father and fled to Ōmi.
This Tamemoto had a son and a daughter. The older brother Gonnosuke
Kiyonaga[16] became the adopted son of Ujiie Hirosada, lord of the castle of
Ōgaki in Mino; because of the outcome of the battle of Sekigahara, he and
Hirosada were placed under the custody of Hosokawa Tadaoki.[17] The younger sister, Kii, through the sponsorship of Tadaoki served in the inner court
of Edo castle, and became the lady-in-waiting of Tokugawa Ieyasu's adopted
daughter, Furihime.[18] Since Furihime became the wife of Date Masamune
in the third year of Genna [1617] while Kii was serving her in the inner
court, Kii also accompanied the bride to Sendai. During this time Kii's
older brother, Kiyonaga, wandered about and ended up in Tottori in Inaba,
where Hatsuko was born to him and a daughter of Kutsuki Nobutsuna. Hatsuko was taken away by her aunt Kii to serve in the ladies' quarters of the
Date family.

Furihime was actually the child of Ikeda Terumasa;[19] her mother was
Ieyasu's second daughter, Kōhime. Ieyasu adopted her and married her to
Tadamune. Date Tsunamune was born to Kaihime,[20] a concubine of Tada-
mune, but was later adopted by Furihime and registered as a legitimate son.
Kaihime was a daughter of Kushige Sachūjō Takamune,[21] and the younger
sister of Mikushige no Tsubone, the mother of Emperor Gosai-in.[22]

Three years before his death, Tadamune became fond of the beautiful
and clever little Hatsuko whom he used to see in the company of Kii. He
told Kii that he wished Hatsuko to become his son's concubine. But Kii,
reeling off the lineage of their own house, refused. Therefore Tsunamune
and Hatsuko's marriage ceremony took place in the Hama mansion in the
first month of the first year of Meireki [1655].

Hatsuko's beauty can be surmised even from a wooden image of her that
survives. Specimens of her accomplished calligraphy remain in the poems
written on long strips of paper, some letters, and a copy of the *Lotus Sutra*
by her own hand. She was also well-versed in poetry. She seems to have been
a beautiful and refined woman. Probably for these reasons Tadamune chose
this niece of his wife's lady-in-waiting for his own son Tsunamune, even per-
mitting their marriage.

The relations between the sexes are inscrutable, of course, but for Shina,
who herself came only obliquely into the picture, to have gained Tsuna-

mune's affection precisely at the time that Hatsuko was bearing him an heir, would seem to have been impossible without some special attraction in her personality. Therefore, not only for the sake of again emphasizing that Shina was not Takao—proven beyond question by Ōtsuki Fumihiko long ago—I should here like to present Shina of Suginohara on her own merits.

What was Shina's family lineage? One member of the Akamatsu family of Harima was Suginohara Iga no kami Tatamori. Later he shaved his head and became the monk Sōi. The name Suginohara was based on the name of a region in Harima. One of Katamori's descendants was a person named Shinzaemon Morinori. Tradition says Morinori became a *rōnin* at the time of the destruction of the Akamatsu clan and went off to Edo, where he died from injury in the great fire of the third year of Meireki [1657]. The time of the destruction of the Akamatsu clan seems to mean the time when Akamatsu Norifusa,[23] holding a ten thousand *koku* fief in Awa, cast his lot in with Osaka at the battle of Sekigahara, and was killed as he fled from the battlefield. If that is true, then even if Morinori was a youth of fifteen at the time, he must have been fifty-three when Shina was born in 1639. At any rate, Shina seems to have been born to Morinori in his later years after he became a *rōnin*. Also in view of the record which says that Morinori's wife, who bore Shina, was the daughter of a Nichiren priest named Nichidō of the Seitaiji temple in Azabu, we can surmise that Morinori was married while a *rōnin* in Edo. Morinori had two children, Shina and a younger son named Unenosuke who died in infancy. Thus when Morinori died, the nineteen-year-old Shina was his only descendant and was taken to live in the Seitaiji temple.

Two years later, in the second year of Manji [1659], Shina was received as a servant in the Hama mansion, and seems immediately to have become Tsunamune's mistress. An incident only obliquely reported suggests that Tsunamune bestowed great affection upon her afterward. When Tsunamune was charged with intrigue and moved to domiciliary confinement in the mansion of Shinagawa in the third year of Manji [1660], Shina, who went with him, requested a day's leave during which she hurriedly met her grandfather, Nichidō, and relatives and old friends in Edo to bid them farewell forever. This signified that she was cutting all relations with society to devote her life to Tsunamune in his adversity. Tsunamune is reported to have been very pleased with this and to have given Shina one of the emblems of the Date family, the *yukisusuki*[24] emblem.

Shina never went back on her commitment to Tsunamune. She served him loyally from the day they fell in love when Tsunamune was twenty until he was an old man of seventy-two. When Tsunamune died she became the nun Jōkyū-In and moved to Sendai. She died at seventy-eight in the first year of Kyōhō [1716].

During these years, Tsunamune shaved his head when Shina was forty-five; Hatsuko died three years later. It seems safe to say that Tsunamune, now the lay monk Kashin, lived the long stretch of the next twenty-five years together with Shina. This cannot be proven, but I cannot help seeing Shina, who gave her love to this Kashin who bore his misfortune with indomitable spirit, as not only a loyal concubine but a companion of exceptional spirit and vitality.

In her later years, Shina adopted Ishi, a daughter of Nakatsuka Jube Shigebumi, and married her to Kumagai Itsuki Naokiyo; therefore Shina's line was continued by Naokiyo's second son, Tsunenosuke. The present Suginohara family derives from this Suginohara Tsunenosuke.

After Tsunamune was moved to the Shinagawa mansion on the twenty-sixth day of the seventh month of the third year of Manji [1660], the so-called Sendai disturbances broke out over his sentence, climaxing on the twenty-seventh day of the third month in the eleventh year of Kambun [1671] when Harada Kai cut down Date Aki[25] in the mansion of Sakai Tadakiyo.[26] Tsunamune had to watch these disturbances as a passive spectator. The mansion of Minamioi-mura in Shinagawa was a residence of modest dimensions which had been built by clearing away a temple and farm houses. Tsunamune lived there with one retainer put in his service. At that time his brother-in-law, Tachibana Tadashige,[27] wrote him a secret letter politely begging him not to try anything, saying "As far as I am concerned, you may walk about the mansion, but so as not to draw attention." At a time when his youthful and exuberant nature was so cooped up that he found it difficult even to walk with due composure within the mansion, Tsunamune now had the added burden of anxiety over the safety of the young Kamechiyo and the political situation in Sendai. His retainer at that time, Ōmachi Bizen, seems to have been a person of no great merit, which left only Hatsuko—and no doubt Shina—to share his depression.

Kamechiyo, who appeared so often in Tsunamune's anxious dreams, lived in the Hama mansion from the third year of Manji [1660] until the second month of the eighth year of Kambun [1668]. In fires of that month the Hama mansion was burned down together with the main mansion in Atagoshita. In the Date house, the main mansion seems to have been used only on special occasions. In Tsunamune's day the main mansion was in Sakurada, located just at the northeast corner of present-day Hibiya Park. At such times as Tsunamune received orders from the shogun, he would come from the Hama mansion to the main mansion. At the time of the fires, Kamechiyo moved to Shirokanedai in Azabu. This was a substitute location which they received when Sakurada was confiscated by the Bakufu in the first year of Manji [1658]. Atagoshita, which to that time functioned as an intermediate residence between the Sakurada and Hama mansions, became the main mansion of the Date family. But it too was burned down together with the Hama mansion. Repairs of the main mansion in Atagoshita were completed thereafter in the twelfth month of the year of the fires, and Kamechiyo moved in there. From that time on, the Date family always lived in the main mansion.

During this time Kamechiyo succeeded to the head of the Date house when he was two, in the eighth month of the third year of Manji [1660]; he had an audience with Tokugawa Ietsuna[28] when he was six, in the sixth month of the fourth year of Kambun [1664]; and after he moved to the residence in Atagoshita, when he came of age at eleven in the second month of the ninth year of Kambun [1669], his name became Sōjirō Tsunamoto, later changed to Tsunamura in the first month of the fifth year of Empō [1677].

In the shadows of this public career, there lurked dangers which proved Tsunamune's anxieties over Kamechiyo to be well warranted. These dangers surfaced in two poisoning attempts.

The first incident occurred on the twenty-seventh day of the eleventh month of the sixth year of Kambun [1666], when Kamechiyo was eight. Prior to this there had been no untoward incidents other than Kamechiyo coming down with smallpox in the ninth month of the second year of Kambun [1662]. In his attendance there were many retainers serving as bodyguards, but as he was under ten at the time, he was probably cared for by female servants. The chief of these women seems to have been a servant named Toba.[29] She was the daughter of the Edo *rōnin* Sakakida Rokuzaemon Shigeyoshi, and had been the attendant first of Furihime, then of Hatsuko, and finally of Kamechiyo. She turned forty-seven that year.

The meals set before Kamechiyo at the time were customarily pretasted by close vassals called *oni banshū*.[30] On one occasion a few of them died, among them being Yoneyama Heizaemon and Senda Heizō. Then they gave the food to a lower vassal and two dogs, and they also died. When Kamechiyo's guardian, Date Hyōbu Shōyū, received the report, he had a man named Kumada Jihē brought to the Hama mansion and executed together with the doctor Kōno Dōen and his three sons. The report says about seven or eight of the male servants from the cook on down and about ten female servants were also killed. Since Toba had been in the presence of the food, she was sent to Sendai and put under the custody of Daijō Gemba.

Since there were such facts as Toba having been once entertained by Dōen on a boat, if Dōen had actually prepared the poison, then Toba is not beyond suspicion. But as she later received a generous fief in Sendai, we reach the end of the thread suggesting her possible participation in the crime. And if Munekatsu, who had Dōen killed, had himself ordered the poisoning, what might his motive have been? Even if Kamechiyo died, since there was a younger brother born to Hatsuko, the authority of the main family could not have been handed down to Hyōbu's son, Ichi no kami. Did Munekatsu do it, then, simply to diminish the fief of the main house and increase the stipend of his own house? This poisoning incident took place when Kamechiyo was eight years old.

The second poisoning attempt occurred in the Shirokanedai mansion in the eighth year of Kambun [1668]. It took place in the interval between the fire incident at the Hama mansion and Kamechiyo's entering the newly repaired mansion in Atagoshita. On a certain day in the eighth month, a certain Shiozawa Tanzaburō, who had become a page through the good offices of Harada Kai, poisoned a serving of sea bass and died after eating it himself. He had poisoned the fish at Harada Kai's order, but had eaten it himself when he could not bear to present it to his lord. It is reported that since Tanzaburō had revealed this plot to his mother the night before, she also killed herself by falling forward on a sword. Kamechiyo was now ten. Just as there was no one named Takao in the alleged Yoshiwara affair of Tsunamune, so too in this poisoning incident there was no woman corresponding to the Asaoka of the popular legend.

Seeing the danger surrounding Kamechiyo both Hatsuko and Shina probably wanted to act as personal guardians—Hatsuko for the sake of her own son, Shina for the sake of her lord. There are indeed hints of Hatsuko's visits to Kamechiyo's mansion, but unfortunately no visitation is actually reported.

Next, what about the political situation in Sendai which made Tsunamune so anxious? The central person on this end of the Sendai trouble was Tsunamune's uncle, Date Hyōbu Shōyū, the guardian of Kamechiyo. Since it was said that if a person were in league with Hyōbu he would be rewarded even if undistinguished, but if he opposed Hyōbu, would be punished even if he were blameless, it seems that his administration of government was totally irresponsible. The leader of the Sendai administration was Watanabe

Kimbē, who came to exercise power irresponsibly in his office of Han Censor from around the third year of Kambun [1663]; after becoming Head Page the next year he became increasingly despotic. The oppressive policies of the Watanabe faction were underlined later when Date Aki enumerated one hundred twenty persons given capital sentences by them. The most conspicuous among those punished were Date Aki and Itō Uneme.[31] Itō Uneme was the adopted son of Itō Shinzaemon,[32] who died of illness right after becoming Han Elder in the third year of Kambun [1663]. His death in domiciliary confinement started a struggle over the ranking of seats in the *han* government. When the shogunate's Censor was entertained in the seventh year of Kambun [1667], the greetings of the *han* officials were made in the order of Han Elders, Councillors, Master of Ceremonies, Head of the Garrison, Civil and Financial Commander, Head of the Pages, and Censors. When their winecups were poured, Uneme, whose office was that of Master of Ceremonies, was made to wait until after the Censors. Harada Kai instigated this at the prompting of the Watanabe Kimbē faction.

Date Aki had jurisdiction over Tōdagōri and lived in Wakuya. Toyomagōri, which bordered on the north, was ruled over by Date Shikibu[33] in Teraike. However, a border dispute arose between Osatomura on the northern border of Tōdagōri and Akōzumura of Toyomagōri. On this occasion, Aki ceded the territory in dispute to Shikibu and there was no trouble. This was the fifth year of Kambun [1665]. Two years later, another border dispute arose between a detached territory under Shikibu's jurisdiction in southwest Momogōri and Aki's adjacent territory in Tōdagōri. A year later Aki lodged a complaint with the Han Elders, but the following year the *han* investigators decreed a new boundary extremely favorable to Shikibu. Incensed, Aki decided in Kambun eleven [1671] to press a legal suit at Edo even if it cost his life. Therefore these boundary disputes, like Uneme's over recognition of his rank, were arguments over essential rights, but both Uneme and Aki took these opportunities to resist the misgovernment of the Watanabe faction. Even in so doing Aki was primarily motivated by his desire to impeach the tyrannical retainers for the sake of his lord, and only secondarily by the legality of the border questions. For this reason he succeeded. Watanabe was placed under the custody of Date Kunai Shōyū[34] and died of self-inflicted starvation.

I contemplated writing a story about Tsunamune passively watching this trouble in Sendai. My interest focused upon his psychological state as an objective spectator completely powerless to act in these matters. I wanted to depict his life's companions, the refined and gentle Hatsuko and the intelligent and firm-willed Shina, and to construct a plot of tensions underlying the composure within this triangle. However, I abandoned this plan both from a lack of creative power and a habit of cherishing historical facts.

On fifth May last year [1915] I visited the Sendai grave of Hatsuko in the Kōshōji located in Shinterakoji. This is the grave people refer to when they talk of "visiting the grave of Asaoka." Within a time-worn old fence a new granite gravestone had been placed with the inscription "The grave of Misawa Hatsuko." It struck me as the grave of some school girl who had recently died.

I refrained from going to the grave of Shina in the Butsugenji.

January 1916

TOKŌ TAHEI

TOKŌ TAHEI is a short piece illustrating the virtues of resoluteness and fidelity in the Tokugawa system of values. As in other similar accounts by Ōgai, the reader is given characters who are not famous men themselves but who are involved in some way with extraordinary figures in history, in this case, with Miyamoto Musashi, a legendary swordsman and student of Zen. The period and events described seem all the more real when related not to some unusual personage but to a plain and simple man much closer to the ordinary reader in outlook and psychology.

Ōgai charts Tokō Tahei's activities quite precisely and with enough detail to make him real and credible. For those interested in Ōgai's methods of composition, the story is especially revealing for the sections that show his methods of construction: he uses meticulous historical analysis combined with real psychological insight into the personality he is analyzing in order to construct a proper framework for his story. If the results do, as Ōgai puts it, lie somewhere between history and fiction, the end result is no less satisfying.

TOKŌ TAHEI was a retainer of the Hosokawa family: he served both Tadatoshi, the governor of Etchū, and Mitsuhisa, the governor of Higo.[1] Tahei's uncle, a lay priest named Tokō Mikawa, first served the Ōtomo family[2] in Bungo, but when Ōtomo Yoshimune was banished, the retainers of the Tokō family became *rōnin*. Mikawa's nephew Tahei was called to serve the Hosokawa family at the time when Tadatoshi was still ruling over the province of Buzen, and was employed as an ordinary page.

When Hosokawa Tadatoshi's domains were transferred to Higo, Tahei accompanied him to Kumamoto.

At the time of the Shimabara Rebellion, Tahei served in Tadatoshi's forces.[3] For his valor in being "first to storm the citadel" during the attack on Hara castle, he was awarded a stipend of three hundred *koku*, and a company of ten riflemen was placed in his charge.

Later, while in the service of Hosokawa Mitsuhisa, Tahei was put in charge of a rifle company of thirty. However he asked that he might "respectfully decline those duties" because of his age, and instead he took a subordinate position and then retired in the first month of the second year of Empō [1647]. On the same day of the same month, his son, also named Tahei, became head of the Tokō house.

Such are the facts as officially set down in the records of the Tokō family.

Tahei had two or three extraordinary things happen to him in the course of his life, and mention of them turns up in various records. As these anecdotes seem to differ slightly from one account to another, I have been selective in what I have retained and in what I have passed over, according to my own judgment. Nevertheless I have managed to put down at least the general outlines of what happened, as a legacy for the future.

One of these anecdotes concerns the fact that Tahei's abilities were discovered by Miyamoto Musashi.[4] This anecdote has already found its way into a book about Musashi edited by a committee in Kumamoto, and so a certain number of people must by now be aware of the incident. In this volume, however, Tahei is referred to as Tokō Kimpei. A search of the Tokō family records reveals no one by that name, other than a certain Kimpei in the ninth generation, who lived at the time of the Meiji Restoration. But it is possible, I suppose, that the first-generation Tahei may have used the name Kimpei at a certain time during his life.

Indeed the book contains only the vaguest of references to the time when

TRANSLATED BY J. THOMAS RIMER

the affair took place. The entry begins, "One day, Musashi was by the side of Lord Tadatoshi," and says no more than that Musashi had an occasional audience with him and, further, that the incident took place at one of them.

In one record the same event is mentioned in connection with Musashi's first interview with Tadatoshi. This possibility strikes me as likely.

However, it is by no means clear as to precisely when Musashi had his first audience with Tadatoshi. Musashi left Kyoto for Kokura in Buzen in the fourth month of Keichō seventeen [1612]. At that time, the head of the Hosokawa family was still Tadaoki,[5] the father of Tadatoshi. Musashi went to Kokura hoping to test his skill against Sasaki Kojirō,[6] a swordsman in the employ of Tadaoki. The man who served as a mediator for the swordsmen was a disciple of Musashi's father, the swordsman Shimmen Munisai,[7] who now served under a retainer of Tadaoki. His name was Nagaoka Sado Okinaga. The match between Musashi and Kojirō is popularly referred to as the Match at Ganryū Island.[8]

After the match, Musashi is supposed to have left immediately for Shimonoseki. It has been suggested that he then returned a second time to Kokura, but I find no mention of any meeting with Tadaoki.

Later Musashi was patronized by Tadaoki's heir Tadatoshi in the eighth month of Kan'ei seventeen [1640]. These two events are separated by twenty-eight years. During that interval, the Osaka Winter and Summer Campaigns were waged,[9] the Shimabara Rebellion was put down, and the Hosokawa family changed its lord and its territory.

Taking this well-known period of history as a large hill standing as a marker on the road of time, I have tried to be as precise about the meeting between Musashi and Tokō Tahei as I can.

In order to understand the significance of their meeting, it is necessary to look not at the career of Musashi but at the historical facts concerning Tahei. Tahei was taken into service by Hosokawa Tadatoshi in Buzen sometime after Genna seven [1621], that is, after Sansai Tadaoki retired, but before his successor Tadatoshi was reissued lands in Higo in Kan'ei nine [1632]. Then again, Musashi must have discovered Tahei before he had risen to any position of eminence, that is to say, no later than the fall of Hara castle during the Shimabara Rebellion on the twenty-seventh day of the second month of Kan'ei fifteen [1638].

Therefore the two must have met at some time between Genna seven [1621] and Kan'ei nine [1632].

Let me again make some observations on Musashi's career. Previously I mentioned only the occasion when Musashi received a stipend from Tadatoshi, but now I wish to consider the occasion of their first meeting. It is not certain that both events occurred at the same time. Indeed it strikes me that two separate occasions were involved. This is because if Musashi's service with Tadatoshi began after the fall of Hara castle, then Tahei would not have been an unproven person whose abilities Musashi first noticed. Guessing from the known facts, it seems quite likely that Tadatoshi had an interview with Musashi before taking him into his service. Thus Tadatoshi, after receiving his new territory in 1621, saw Musashi before the swordsman was appointed to his service in 1640. It must have been on such a prior occasion that Tahei received Musashi's praise.

However the twenty-year period between 1621 and 1640 seems too long. Indeed if we look at the career of Tahei after his meeting with Musashi and subtract the three years after the fall of Hara castle in 1638, we make no significant progress in terms of an understanding of his careeer as a whole.

I would like to be as precise as possible in delineating the exact amount of time involved. My own analysis is as follows. Musashi, after he served with the Hideyoshi forces at the battle of Osaka, reportedly traveled through quite a number of provinces. However there is no record of his having been in Kyushu again until Kan'ei eleven [1634], when he came to Kokura in Buzen with his adopted child Iori as a guest of Ogasawara Ukyōdaiyū Tadazane,[10] who had been assigned the territory after the transfer of the Hosokawa family. Was it not perhaps during this visit to Kyushu that he visited Tadatoshi in Kumamoto? If so, it was within five years of the fall of Hara castle; at some point during those years, Tadatoshi probably met Musashi, and Musashi recognized Tahei's merits. At least I would like to think so. If I were writing a novel, I could merely write that it was so and not waste words in the fashion I have.

I have here exposed to view the conventional sort of mechanisms brought to bear on what is usually termed the historical novel.

Historians, seeing what I have written, will no doubt criticize me for my willfulness. Novelists, on the other hand, will laugh at my persistence. There is a Western proverb about sleeping between two beds. Looking at my own work, it seems that this proverb can be applied to me.

There is some discrepancy in the records concerning the meeting between Miyamoto Musashi and Tokō Tahei. Based on the reasoning I have outlined above, I have selected and discarded information at will, but I think the event was surely something like what follows here.

Musashi arrived at the castle town of Kokura, bringing Iori with him. This Iori was supposedly the orphan of an acquaintance Musashi knew from a family at Shōhōjigahara in the province of Dewa. I have tried to locate the place name of Shōhōji, but without success. When I made inquiries later I learned that there is reportedly such a place next to Kowakubino in the district of Senbaku in the province of Ugo. This might have been Iori's original home. After arriving in Kokura, Musashi remained a guest of Ogasawara, but Iori went into his direct employ and was given a very responsible position. His descendants still bear his name. When I myself went to Kokura I was shown at their home various objects bequeathed to the family by Musashi. One thing I still remember seeing there was a wooden sword with the luster of a mirror. And there was an unsigned picture of Bodhidharma.[11] I thought to call on the current Mr. Iori and inquired about him. According to what I was told, he is a farmer living in the country near Dairi in Fukuoka. Deterred by government business, I was unable to visit him. In any case, it is not about Iori that I now wish to write.

Musashi did not seek to serve any daimyo in an official position. Yet he seems to have selected some place in Kyushu to live out his days. Hosokawa Tadatoshi was learning swordsmanship of the Yagyū school;[12] thus he thought he would like to have a look at Musashi. It was no doubt because of the desire on the part of both men that Musashi had his audience with Tadatoshi.

It must have been some time after Musashi first arrived in Kokura, probably just before the uprisings at Shimabara—thus between Kan'ei eleven [1634] and Kan'ei fourteen [1637]. I imagine the interview took place in 1635 or 1636, during the time when Tadatoshi was in residence there.

I suppose they met at the Hanabatake mansion in Kumamoto. For the retainers who were serving at the mansion, the appearance of the matchless Shimmen Miyamoto Musashi was awaited as a sensational event.

Among them was Tokō Tahei. At that time he had worked for the Hosokawa family for no more than sixteen years and no less than four, depending on whether he joined Tadatoshi's service just after Tadatoshi assumed his position as head of the Hosokawa family, or only after the lands were transferred. Tahei held the rank of Ordinary Page and he was a man of no apparent talents. Tahei, seeing everyone so excited, knit his brows and muttered to himself, "Who is this Musashi? . . . just some nondescript retainer . . . It is quite unwarranted to summon him and give him an audience like this. There is certainly no excuse for all this pretentious preparation." When Musashi arrived and came to the mansion, Tahei sat on the steps of the entrance and watched him come and go.

When the official interview was concluded according to proper ceremony, both host and guest changed their seats and continued talking informally.

In the course of their conversation, Tadatoshi asked Musashi a question: Among Tadatoshi's own retainers, were there any whose skill and valor in the martial arts were known to Musashi? Musashi replied, "Yes, I just now saw such a man." When asked who it was, he replied that he did not know the man's name. Tadatoshi called from among those in attendance all those known for skill in military tactics, archery, and riflery and had them sit in a row. Looking them over, Musashi replied, "I regret to say the person I mentioned to you is not among these men."

"If that is the case," Tadatoshi told him, "would you be kind enough to go out, find him, and bring him back to me?" Musashi agreed and rose to go; and within the space of a moment he returned from the official's waiting room with Tokō Tahei.

When Musashi brought Tokō Tahei before Hosokawa Tadatoshi, Tadatoshi said to Musashi, "I know the man, but what was it about him that attracted your attention?"

"If you question him concerning his state of continuous enlightenment, you will surely understand," Musashi replied.

"Is that so? Well then, Tokō, give me some indication about how enlightened you are." As Tadatoshi said this, all the men there looked at Tokō's face as if for the first time.

"Indeed," Tahei replied, "I haven't the kind of enlightenment you speak of."

Musashi interrupted. "Tokō, I have reported that I had an intuition of your military discipline. You need only explain your customary habits of mind and that will serve admirably."

Tahei thought for a moment, then spoke. He was not considering what he should answer but was thinking rather how to put into words what he knew he wanted to say.

"If you speak of the Way of the Warrior, I cannot claim to have accomplished a single thing. Let me rather give my opinion concerning what you referred to as my customary habits of mind. I would say that I suddenly thought of myself as a criminal whose head can be cut off to test a new sword, and I took this realization to heart and concentrated on it. A man who is like this can be destroyed at any time. And in fact he comes to accept destruction with a light heart. At first he is unlikely to forget his insignificance, and yet precisely because this thought is always with him, he ceases to be afraid of it. Eventually as he begins to concentrate on the idea, it becomes perfectly natural for him. I am sorry to offer such a poor explanation," Tahei concluded, and he prostrated himself on the ground before them.

Before Tadatoshi could say anything, Musashi spoke. "Did you hear what he said? That is truly the essence of military valor."

Tahei withdrew, having earned a great deal of respect he had never anticipated.

I would like to think that the Shimabara uprising took place a year or two after this. In the tenth month of that year, Kan'ei fourteen [1637], when the uprising began, Masuda Shirō Tokisada[13] arrived at Hara castle at the head of the rebellious forces, on the first day of the eleventh month. The castle fell the following year, on the twenty-seventh day of the second month.

Miyamoto Musashi left Kokura with the troops of Ogasawara Tadazane in the capacity of honorary military commander. Tahei served in the Hosokawa forces that set out from Kumamoto. It was during this campaign that he distinguished himself and received the stipend of three hundred *koku*. Then, two years later, Musashi made his decision to retire in Kumamoto, and the Hosokawa family made him an honorary retainer, with the position as Head of a Reserve Command. On the seventeenth day of the third month of the year following, Tadatoshi died. Musashi followed him four years later, on the nineteenth day of the fifth month of Shōhō two [1645]. Such constitutes the story of Musashi's "discovery" of Tahei.

Another incident is that of Tahei's work as a stone thief. The records do not indicate when the incident took place. The gist of it is as follows: when the Edo castle was under renovation, various daimyo were asked to contribute large stones for the purpose. Eventually stones from various provinces began to arrive in Edo, but the ship from Higo with its cargo of stones still did not arrive. Tokō Tahei was asked how the matter might be taken care of; he evidently promised to supply the stones as soon as possible, and, by means of a most unusual procedure, he did manage to obtain them. I would like to determine as precisely as possible when this incident took place.

Tokō Tahei made a promise to take these unusual steps in order to try to cover over an unfortunate situation. When did the incident occur? As the various daimyo had received orders to send stones to Edo and were in the midst of dispatching them, it would have been almost impossible for anyone to obtain any stones while himself in Edo. To have asked this difficult task of a retainer, the Hosokawa family would surely have chosen someone of more than average ability. If this is so, the one chosen would not be the Tahei who was merely an Ordinary Page and had not yet manifested any of his abilities, but rather the Tahei who had received a stipend for his brave conduct. It seems to me that the repairs to the Edo castle must thus have taken place after the fall of Shimabara castle in 1638.

I do not have at hand any detailed materials referring to the various changes made to the Edo castle. According to Tokugawa official records, the various gates at Edo castle were ordered to be repaired on the fifteenth day of the second month of Kan'ei sixteen [1639]. On the second day of the eighth month of the same year, repairs were ordered on the enclosures of the West Enceinte. However, on the eleventh day of the same month there was a fire in the castle, and another order for major repairs was issued on the sixteenth. This work took eight full months to complete. From this date until the death of Tokō Tahei in Shōō two [1653], there is no record of any further repairs being made to the castle.

It thus seems to me that Tahei probably obtained these stones for the repairs in Kan'ei sixteen [1639]. The only worrisome thing is that I do not have the necessary documents to tell me which daimyo were asked to contribute building materials. I have heard that documents appropriate for such research are now in the process of compilation by the Hosokawa family. It would no doubt be wise to use the information in these records to verify the incident.

The unusual methods Tahei employed to obtain the stones were extremely simple. According to the records, ''Taking day laborers with him, he removed the identifying marks on stones contributed by other daimyo and replaced them with marks bearing the name of his province, Higo. He finished this work in several days.''

Tahei was suspected of being the guilty party and was apprehended by the Tokugawa government. When questioned, he said he knew nothing. Then he was tortured. First he was forced to carry heavy stones. Then he was given a treatment that went by the name of ''bamboo massage.''

In a book entitled *Miyamoto Musashi*, the following description is provided: ''The small ends of hollow bamboo tubes are hollowed out very thin. These are pushed into the knee and rubbed about, so that the flesh enters the tubes. When the bamboo is then removed, there are small holes left in the knees, into which boiling soy sauce is poured as a torture.''

Saying that the jailor's methods were too lax, Tahei took the bamboo in his own hands and twisted it himself, then also poured in the soy himself. From the holes, bumps of raw flesh appeared, as big as wild peaches. It is said that the Tokō family will not eat that fruit even now.

Tahei was not the sort of man who would give in to torture. The Tokugawa officials had no other resort than to try to replace torture with trickery.

One day Tahei was dragged into court. The official in charge suddenly raised his voice and pronounced the following: ''Tokō Tahei, the stone thief, you are not to be punished. Rise.'' Tokō remained where he was, as if he had heard nothing.

Shortly, the official then declared: "Tokō Tahei. You have been cleared of the charge of stealing of the stones. Rise.'' Now Tahei rose slowly and withdrew from the court. His guard, flustered, followed him out. It had been decided beforehand to let him go free if the last trick didn't work.

In *Miyamoto Musashi* only the incident of Tokō's discovery by Musashi and the incident of the prison sentence for stealing the stones are recorded.

As for the next incident, in which Tokō Tahei was part of an undercover maneuver, the records are also incomplete. Nevertheless, in terms of Tahei's own career, the two most important incidents were, in a public sense, his meritorious service at the battle for Hara castle, and, in a personal sense, his efforts concerning the problem of the succession within his lord's family.

The year after Hosokawa Tadatoshi welcomed Miyamoto Musashi as a guest, the lord of Higo died in Kan'ei eighteen [1641], on the seventeenth day of the third month. On the fifth day of the fifth month of the same year, his son Mitsuhisa took over the rule of the house. On the nineteenth day of the twelfth month of Shōhō two [1645], Miyamoto Musashi himself died. On the second day of the twelfth month of the same year, Tadatoshi's father, the long-retired Sansai Tadaoki died as well. Mitsuhisa died in the third year of Keian [1649] on the twenty-seventh day of the first month.

At Mitsuhisa's death, his son Rokumaru[14] was only an infant. For the Hosokawa family, with properties of five hundred forty thousand *koku*, the assurance of Rokumaru's succession without difficulty was a question of life or death. The Han Elder Nagaoka Shikibu was placed in charge of this grave matter and dispatched to Edo, along with two retainers sent to accompany him. One was Umehara Kuhei[15] and the other was Tokō Tahei.

Umehara was on good terms with Sakai Uta no kami Tadakiyo.[16] In discussing the pending visit to Sakai's mansion at Ōtemae, Shikibu cautioned Kuhei, "If our request is not granted as a matter of course, do not simply retire but hold yourself in readiness." Shikibu also told him, "You must always discuss everything with Tokō frankly and work closely together with him for the sake of our lord." Tahei's duties were also extremely important.

Nagaoka Shikibu's mission obtained the goal desired. On the eighteenth day of the fourth month of Keian three [1650], Rokumaru was appointed without difficulty as lord of the Hosokawa domain. He later took the name Etchū no kami Tsunatoshi.

The attitude Tokō adopted throughout his life was extremely simple. In a word, it was precisely the conviction on his part to be prepared to face death. No matter what the issue, he approached it with a willingness to die if necessary. And when he could not accomplish his aim, he would not give in. No matter what means might be required, he never questioned them.

The Hosokawa family ruled over a large province, and those charged with the responsibility of the family's affairs were of course not lacking in subordinates of talent. But when any situation reached the stage where a solution seemed impossible, Tahei was sure to be called upon. I have not sketched in any detail the character of Umehara. When the problem of the succession came up, however, he was no doubt selected because of his intimacy with Sakai. Yet Tahei was sent with him. Was it not Tahei's duty to keep pressing Umehara?

To be willing to die is no doubt a straightfoward attitude of mind. Nevertheless, among samurai, those who had such a will, no matter during what period, in no matter what domain, were, it seems, not so easy to find.

Enterprise and the resolution to die are complementary virtues; in that sense there is a decisive difference between a mere adventurer and a "man of enterprise." In addition to the incidents already mentioned, there is still another anecdote that has been handed down about Tokō Tahei. But I do not think that the incident contributes much to any understanding of his significance as a human being. Indeed, as far as I am concerned, if there were any purpose served in bending the truth to protect him, then the whole affair might as well be passed over in silence.

The month and year of the incident are not recorded. Nor is the place mentioned. Surely Tahei would not have behaved in such a fashion, however, after being awarded his three hundred *koku* for his brave efforts at Shimabara. Indeed it seems unlikely that he would have become involved in such an affair after being taken on by the Hosokawa family as a mere page. The whole thing was surely a simple diversion during his early life when he was a *rōnin*.

One day Tokō Tahei was crossing a certain street. A group of people had collected in front of a house and were milling around shouting abusive language. When he asked what was going on, someone in the crowd explained that a man who looked like a *sumo* wrestler had killed someone and then run into the vacant house with his sword still drawn. Now he had locked the door from the inside.

"Isn't there anyone among you who could capture him?" Tahei asked.

"As you see, there are policemen here in front of the house, but there seems to be nothing they can do."

"Then I'll quiet him down for you. Do you have any kind of tool that will break down a wall? A big wooden pounder would do as well."

Someone or other hurried off and returned with a large pestle. Tahei took it and walked around to the back of the house. Then he began breaking through the wall of the house in an overly dramatic fashion. Eventually he knocked a hole in the wall large enough for someone to crawl through. Tahei hoisted up his clothes and went in backwards, buttocks first.

As the crowd watched in astonishment, Tahei soon came back out of the hole, dragging the offender with him. It seemed easier than pulling something out of a bag.

Later Tahei was asked how he had managed to accomplish this. He laughed as he answered. "There is nothing very complicated about it. When I went in by the wall, rather than the door, and buttocks-first instead of head-first, the man inside stopped to look at me, thinking the whole affair very strange. It was his moment of negligence that let me get a hold of him. Even if he had taken a swipe at my buttocks I have a little extra to spare."

Tokō Tahei's descendants have continued on in a direct line until the present. Tahei's son died in 1696, and his grandson, who was put in charge of twenty archers, died of illness in 1715. The Tokō of the fourth generation held a high position under a shogunal administrator; he resigned in 1756. Gennosuke, in the fifth generation, was placed in charge of ten riflemen in 1780; in the sixth generation, Kōgorō was appointed an assistant chief for a group of thirty riflemen in 1803. Heya (later called Hōsuke) in the seventh generation was placed in charge of ten riflemen in 1838. In the eighth generation, Fukuma (later called Kurosuke) was placed in charge of ten riflemen and died of illness in 1853; in the ninth generation, Kimpei (later called Sahei) was put in charge of thirty riflemen and resigned in 1867. In the tenth generation, Genzō was attached to the first group of reserve forces in the Kimamoto domain. The present head of the Tokō family, Tokō Chiaki, the oldest son of Genzō, became an employee of the Yatsushiro paper mill in the village of Matsukuma in the district of Yatsushiro in Kumamoto province.

January 1917

SAIKI KŌI

"EVALUATIONS of human life are so endlessly diversified and subjective," wrote Mori Ōgai toward the end of this complex account, and this phrase may well serve as the real justification for these investigations that took him into the extraordinary world, and underworld, represented in this absorbing re-creation of the last days of the Tokugawa gay quarters and its colorful inhabitants. Ōgai's curiosity over his reading of popular literature of the Edo period and the purchase by his father of a small house serve as double means to involve him in a search for those who lived in a special society that, although it existed up until a generation previous, seemed to Ōgai as remote —and as fascinating—as any novel by Saikaku. The reader too is pulled into this world and can follow with great interest the slow accumulation of detail with which Ōgai reconstructs the past.

Ōgai seldom if ever wrote on such subjects, but his detached tone and sharp sensibility are nowhere seen to better advantage than here, in an atmosphere of the theater, tea house, and drinking party. Such subject matter may be more typical of the novelist Nagai Kafū, who considered Ōgai his mentor, but the results are pure Ōgai, and worthy of comparison with his best work.

SAIKI KŌI[1] is also known under the names of Tsutō and Tsunokuniya Tōjirō.[2] It was in reference not to Kōi himself but his father Ryūchi[3] that I first came across the name of Tsutō. The name Tsunokuniya Tōjirō continued through two generations.

When I was young, I devoured the books of a lending library man who used to walk around with books stacked on his back in something like a monk's backpack. These books were mainly of three kinds: *yomihon*,[4] *kakihon*,[5] and *ninjōbon*, or popular love stories.[6] The *yomihon* consisted mainly of the works of Kyōden[7] and Bakin,[8] the *ninjōbon* of the works of Shunsui[9] and Kinsui;[10] the *kakihon* were what we now call scenarios for professional storytellers. After going through all of these I asked the booklender if he had any others I hadn't read, and he recommended that I try reading *zuihitsu*, or miscellaneous literary essays. If one can get through these too, even through the likes of the antiquarian writings of Ise Teijō,[11] he deserves a degree in lending library literature. I got this degree.

I was first addicted to Bakin, then came to like Kyōden more; but I always preferred Shunsui to Kinsui. I developed a similar partiality later on when I read German literature, always having a greater taste for Hauptmann[12] than Sudermann.[13]

In Shunsui's *ninjōbon*, a character named Tsutō-san often appears as a kind of deus ex machina. He is a good samaritan, a rich man who rescues the lovers from the jaws of fate. Usually this Tsutō-san is only mentioned in the dialogue, but does not appear in person. One exception to this is the character of Umegoyomi Chitō, also known as Chiba Tobē.[14]

At that time a certain connoisseur of letters and the arts, a member of a group which called itself the Kokurabakama, informed me: "It is said that Tsunokuniya Tōjirō was a real person." The literary term *modelle* had not yet been used in such a sense.

This Tsutō senior was the proprietor of a wineshop in Yamashiro-chō in Shimbashi of Edo. From this locality he acquired the name of the Master of Yamashiro Riverbank, and this was also abbreviated to simply Riverbank Master. His clan was Minamoto, his family name was Saiki, and his crest was the holly; because he had a triangular fish-scale shape dyed onto the shop curtain under the horizontal character for "one," he used the pen name of Ichirindō, meaning Hall of One Scale. He signed his calligraphy with Ryūchi, meaning Dragon Pond, and his *haiku* with Sen'u, meaning Wizard Castle; he sang *kyōka*[15] under the names of Tōkōen, Tsuru no To Hinakame, and later Minamoto no Yamahito.

TRANSLATED BY WILLIAM R. WILSON

Ryūchi's father was named Ihē. Ihē was a shopman of Ryūchi's grand-father; relying on his character, he made Ihē his adopted son. This original Ihē had built the earthen walls around the Tsunokuniya. He also built the first and later warehouses, increased the size of the property, and created the wealthy house identified with the Yamashiro Riverbank.

When he was approaching seventy, Ihē turned the shop over to Ryūchi and went into retirement, taking up residence in the inner quarters of the second floor of the Yamashiro Riverbank. Even after he retired he continued to be a model of industry. For example, he used to pick up discarded straw sandals on the streets, bring them home, wash and dry them in the sun, then chop them up himself to give to the plasterers who frequented the shop.[16] Ihē, however, was no miser. There is a story that one year as the anniversary of the forty-seven *rōnin* of Akō was being celebrated in the Senga-kuji of Shiba, an old man in cotton clothes visited the graves, contributed a hundred *ryō* in gold at the offering place, and departed without leaving his name. When a monk, thinking this strange, had him followed, the old man returned inside the curtain of the Yamashiro Riverbank Tsunokuniya.

After Ryūchi succeeded to the household, he closed the wineshop and made his chief business purveying to daimyo households with which the Tsunokuniya enjoyed ancestral ties. The principal residences were those of the Kaga Middle General in Hongō go-chōme, the Uesugi Chamberlain in Sakuradahori-dōri, and the Matsudaira Lower General in Sakurada Kasumi-gaseki. Maeda of Kaga was the lord of the castle in Kanagawa, Uesugi of the castle in Yonegawa, and Asano Matsudaira of the castle in Hiroshima.

Ryūchi was married in the first year of Bunsei [1818] while his father and mother were still living. He used to send his senior shopman Kimbē and others to solicit business from the noble residences, and on the three cere-monial days of each month he would himself also make the rounds of the mansions to offer his greetings. In the house of Kaga, it was just before Lord Hizen no kami Narinori was succeeded by his son Nariyasu. In the house of Uesugi, it was the generation of Lord Danjo-no-taihitsu Narisada; in the house of Asano, it was that of Lord Aki no kami Narikata.

His father Ihē had probably never written a character except in account books or on bills. Ryūchi, however, practiced calligraphy under Hata Sei-chi.[17] He studied *kyōka* under Hinamaro, the first generation of the house of Yayoi'an,[18] and was given the name Hinakame; in later years he was called Momonomoto Kakuro, and also Gensen. He also wrote *haikai*[19] under the pen name of Sen'u.

His father Ihē had probably never set foot in a place of entertainment.

Ryūchi, however, frequented the theaters and the gay quarters. After each visit to the Nakamura, Ichimura, and Morita theater houses,[20] he would invite the famous actors to teahouses and ply them with drink. He frequented the gay quarters in Fukagawa[21] and Yoshiwara, also in Shinagawa[22] and Naitō Shinjuku.[23] His favorite in Fukagawa was an old courtesan named Yamamoto no Kampachi. In the Yoshiwara, it was a principal courtesan of the Hisakimanjiya[24] called Akashi.

When Ryūchi went to the gay quarters his boon companions were such denizens of the Fukagawa district as Sakuragawa Yoshijirō,[25] Tobaya Kosanji, Masumi Wajū, Kenkonbō Ryōsai,[26] Iwakubo Hokkei,[27] Onomaru Kokane, Chikunai, Sanchiku, Kisai, and their like. Yoshijirō later moved to the Yoshiwara, and became the second-generation Zenkō. Wajū was a master chanter of *katōbushi*;[28] Ryōsai was a *rakugo* performer; Hokkei a painter of ukiyoe who left the Kano for the Hokusai school. Chikunai was a physician,[29] Sanchiku and Kisai were masseurs.

Ryūchi used to wrap ceremonial gifts of money in thick offering-paper, put paper decorations on them, and had them piled up on great offering-stands to be given away to those he patronized.

But Ryūchi had not the capacity for even one drop of wine. Even when he took a sake cup in hand, he only pretended to drink. Also, he never spent a night in a brothel.

While the *ninjōbon* writer Tamenaga Shunsui was still called Sanro and So Mabito,[30] he became acquainted with Ryūchi and was his companion in these amusements. This was the basis for Ryūchi's name coming to be enshrined in the *ninjōbon* romances.

Ryūchi was not averse to having his name broadcast about like this by Shunsui. Indeed, he himself wrote a pamphlet entitled "Famous Places of Tsunokuni," which he had printed and distributed to his friends. The pamphlet featured stories in which his own companions in amusement were likened to famous places in Japan, illustrated with Hokkei's ukiyoe drawings.

Ryūchi's wife gave birth to a boy in the fifth year of Bunsei [1822]. This boy, whom they called Nenosuke, was the heir to the Tsunokuniya. As that year was under the zodiacal sign of the horse, they followed the common custom of making a name of the seventh sign from that, called *ne*, the zodiacal sign of the rat. Kōi the Dilettante, who as the second-generation Tsutō achieved a fame verging on notoriety that exceeded that of his own father, was this Nenosuke.

I came across the name of Kōi around the time I first happened upon the name of Tsutō through those *ninjōbon*. Actually it may have been at the same time. The name came to my attention several times thereafter, but always as a fleeting impression that never sank in. Ryūchi and Kōi, father and son, were confused in my mind.

Some time afterward the name Kōi came to be constantly in my mind. This was after I moved into the house in Dangozaka[31] where I now live.

This house has a relationship to Kōi, and was discovered by my then living father. My father had been practicing medicine in Senju, but decided to give it up and live with me. So he started to walk around every day looking for a house. This house soon caught my father's eye as one commanding a fine view.

South from the top of Dangozaka there is a lane resembling a steep path which comes out at the back of the Nezu Gongen shrine.[32] They call this Yabushita Road. What are now called the Yabushita houses at that time occupied only the east side of this road, near the Nezu shrine. Contrary to this, in the area near Dangozaka, there were no houses on the east side of the road, which cut over the top of a declivity. The front part of the little house faced out over this cliff, which was separated from it by the lane. It was a little shingle-roofed house.

The top of the rise is a hill that ranges from Mukōgaoka to Ōji.[33] Separated from them by the gardens and rice fields beneath the cliff, the house faces out on the hills of Ueno across the way. If one stands in front of the house and looks out, he will see to the right a spur of the hills of Ueno; the space between this spur and Mukōgaoka opens expansively into a sea of houses reaching to the far-off horizon. The view I have from the platform on top of my present house in this direction is one of white sails off Shinagawa moving above the tops of the trees of the Hama Detached Palace.

My father set his eye on this little house and often went to the top of the cliff to look at it. In the house there was a window facing out over the cliff, and in the window there was always an old woman with her head shaven. "A pretty nun," my father used to say.

Consulting his map, my father deduced that the house of the pretty nun was located on what had originally been the compound of the Sezon-in temple.[34] This temple has now lost the greater half of its former compound, and is crowded into its western corner.

My father led me to the top of the cliff to show me the house. I had been aware of both the cliff and the house before, but had not yet looked at them with the interest that father had. The house itself was a perfect "retreat within the city's midst." And behind the bamboo grille sat the pretty nun. She seemed to be over fifty. If one can call an old woman beautiful, I should say that this nun was beautiful.

Having won my approval, my father now determined to buy the house, and so made inquiries about its owner. At that time there was a gardener named Senjuen who lived below Dangozaka. My father knew the man and asked him about the nun's house.

According to Senjuen, the little house on the rise was the property of the old woman we had seen. She was a certain Takagi Gin, and the relative of someone named Ogura.[35] Ogura was originally a pawnbroker, and after he retired had been a hanger-on of Kōi the Dilettante. He died in that house. The old woman, Senjuen concluded, would probably be amenable to an offer.

Through Senjuen's assistance the negotiations were concluded with unexpected ease. The property owned by Takagi Gin was originally a rather extensive angular piece, but since a corner of it had been sold off, the remainder, from the side on which the small house faced out over the cliff, was left in a hook shape on the side facing the street on the top of Dangozaka. There were two small houses on the parcel which faced the street. One, with both house and land owned by Takagi, was a rental shop, the other was a house built on the Takagi land by a fire chief named Ishida, who was living there. After we acquired title, Gin moved into the rental shop.

Father disposed of the big house in Senju and moved into this little house on the cliff-top. The Senju house had been the residence of a man named Okada, who said it had been used as a resting place when the Tokugawa shogun went out to the hawking fields. In it my father had enough equipment for a small hospital. As he moved into the smaller residence, he exclaimed: "I feel like I've put down a heavy load." I came from my rented house in Otanohara to join him there.

The little house had three rooms and a kitchen. The three rooms were, respectively, of six, three, and four and a half mats—the last in tearoom style. Later this tearoom came to be the place of my father's last hours.

In the three-mat room adjacent to the tearoom were two sliding door panels covered with old pieces of paper. The papers were a travel account in the *haibun* style of poetic prose, about half in characters and half in illustrations. On the first page there was a half-length portrait of Kōi the Dilettante. It was only a sketch in black brush strokes, but enough to suggest that Kōi had been a round-faced, fat man.

The little house on the cliff-top became dilapidated after father's death, and because it was difficult to repair, fell into decay. The paper screens also completely peeled away. When I think about it now, they seem to have been the rough copy of the travel account of Kōi's tour of Enoshima and Kamakura, which he made at the age of thirty-eight in the sixth year of Ansei [1859].

More than half of what is left of the little house on the cliff-top is now vacant ground. Since my mother requested that a room be built in place of her seventieth birthday celebration in Taishō four [1915], I ordered an estimate from a carpenter for a four-and-a-half mat room in accordance with her wish. Meanwhile she fell gravely ill. I hurried the work to get the room completed while she was still alive. The room was finished and the second coat of plaster added to the walls in March of 1916. Mother moved in her bed and was happy in that room, but she soon departed this world. The room is my present study; the walls have never been replastered. The room is the site of the kitchen of the little house on the cliff-top long ago.

From the time I moved in with my father and mother, I had the name of Kōi firmly in mind. I already knew that the former owner of the house, Ogura, was later called Zeami.[36] Kōi received a number of "-ami" pen names[37] from the Reverend Yūgyō, chief priest of the Shōjōkōji[38] in Fujisawa of Kōza county in Sagami. He styled himself Juami, but then gave this name to Kawatake Kisui[39] and became Bai'ami. He later changed to Hōami, and parceled out other Ami names to his followers. They say Zeami was one of these.

Kōi died on the tenth of September, the third year of Meiji [1870]. His relatives held the anniversary memorial service on the tenth of September of the following year. Afterward his followers gathered at the house of Ogura Zeami and held Buddhist services on the tenth of October of every year, and then visited Kōi's grave at the Gangyōji in Komagome.[40] The place of these observances was the little house on the cliff-top.

Kōi, that is, Nenosuke, in youth studied the Chinese classics with Kita Seiro[41] and calligraphy with Matsumoto Tōsai.[42] When Nenosuke was fourteen, Seiro had already reached seventy and was living in retirement in Takegawa-chō Nishiura-machi. It is said that Nenosuke had barely attained knowledge of the Chinese characters when he began to inquire into the Way of Lao Tzu and Chuang Tzu. Tōsai was a famous calligrapher who had achieved his name in the style of Tung Ch'i-ch'ang;[43] he resided in Honkoku-chō Shiogashi.

There are very few facts by which one can establish the chronology for the interval from Nenosuke's birth to his becoming a man. In Bunsei six [1823] Ryūchi's teacher, Hata Seichi, died at the age of sixty-one, when Nenosuke was two. His grandfather Ihē's wife died on the twenty-ninth day of the seventh month of 1825. Her name in the Buddha is Rinshoin Sōyo Geigetsu

Daishi. At this time Nenosuke was four. Nenosuke was seven when his father's friend So Mabito took the pen name of Kyokuntei Shunsui in 1828.

In addition to Shunsui, Ryōsai, and Hokkei, his father Ryūchi's friends at
this time included Katsuta Moromochi.[44] Succeeding Chikusa'an Kawaguchi Sōo,[45] the *kyōka* master of Suwa-chō,[46] Moromochi was called the
second-generation Chikusa'an. His name in the Itchūbushi school of
jōruri[47] is Miyako Ikkansai. Ikkansai later established a separate school,
changed his name to Uji Shibun[48] and lived in Ikenohata.[49] At this time,
Ryūchi had Hokkei do impromptu sketches at gatherings with his friends
and had Moromochi make block prints of them with *kyōka*; he amused
himself in the gay quarters accompanied by Shunsui, Ryōsai, and others.

From about his seventeenth year in 1838, Nenosuke began to frequent
the restaurants and riverside teahouses,[50] became the intimate of geisha, and
before long took his pleasures in the brothels of Naitō Shinjuku and Shinagawa.

It seems that Ryūchi and Kōi encountered one crisis after another around
1841. Ryūchi divorced his wife, the mother of Nenosuke and his elder sister,
about this time. Nenosuke's older sister served in the women's quarters of
the mansion of Uesugi Danjo no taihitsu Narinori[51] in Soto Sakuradahori-
dōri. Ryūchi took as his second wife Sumi, the elder sister of Mimura Seiki-
chi of the Tobaya in Takekawa-chō. This was a branch family of the house of
Mimura Seizaemon, a member of the Ten-Man Company of Money-
changers to the Shogunate,[52] who lived in Sanjikken-hori.[53] At the same
time he established a separate house in Sannō-chō and kept a mistress.

Before very long Ryūchi was on the point of being officially punished and
in fact only narrowly escaped. This was because a *Guide to Harlotry*[54] which
he had written, printed, and circulated among his friends and acquaintances
came to the attention of the Edo City Commissioners. Fortunately the headman in Kaga-chō, Tanaka Heishirō, got wind of it and secretly informed
Ryūchi. Ryūchi quickly sent money to various functionaries to patch things
up; he dismissed the mistress, sold the separate house, and stopped his own
visits to places of amusement. It was at that time that he made the
Uchiyama-chō house of the blind man, Middle Chanting Master Momo-
shima Kōtō, his place for diversion and gathered Moromochi and the others
there.

Nenosuke was placed under the charge of the Tobaya, the home establishment of his stepmother, in the last days of the last month of this year. This
was because he had run up debts in the appointment teahouses[55] in the
Shinjuku and Shinagawa gay quarters. Nenosuke was now twenty.

However, while Ryūchi had stopped frequenting the gay quarters, Neno-

suke did not. From about the third month of 1842, Nenosuke of the stylish-
ly cropped head began to leave the Tobaya accompanied by an apprentice
named Kanekichi on visits to the calligraphy master Matsumoto, the *kyōya*
master Umeya Kakuju,[56] and the like. But on his way home he would send
Kanekichi on ahead, while he himself stopped in at the theater and brothels. Kanekichi had the nickname of Toba-picture Boy.[57] He was probably so
named because he was an apprentice boy of the Tobaya and was funny-
looking. Later he became the famous Meiji writer, Kanagaki Robun.[58]

The theater was the Kawarasaki-za[59] in Kobiki-chō. The most popular ac-
tor was the eighth-generation Danjūrō.[60] He visited the playwright Katsu
Genzō in his room and made friends with him. Genzō later was the famous
Kawatake Shinshichi.[61]

The brothels chiefly were the Shimazaki Minatoya and the Dozō Sagami[62]
in Shinagawa; his favorite assignation teahouse was the Ōnoya Manji. He
had his longest affair with Osome of the Minatoya.

His companions included the playwright Iwai Shigyoku[63] of the
Kawarasaki-za, Takedaya Umahei, the master of the teahouse attached to
that theater, the Shinagawa male geisha Tomimoto Tona Taifu and Tomimoto Noshi Taifu, and Sakuragawa Zenjibō, as well as such characters as the
haikai master Maki Otsuga and the wrestler Ikioi Tōgo. Shigyoku was later
Harufuji, the founder of the Shōdenbushi[64] school of *jōruri*; Otsuga was the
later Tōei VI.

Ryūchi's congratulatory gifts were a pretty sight with their paper decorations, but what he spent on them did not come to very much. Nenosuke, on
the other hand, racked his brain for ingenious gifts, and was indifferent to
price. He piled up huge bills for pocketbooks and tobacco pouches at bag
shops like the Maruri, Marujō, Yamadaya. Once while he was behaving like
this, the date for seasonal change of attire came around. Nenosuke had an
unlined haori and lined kimono brought to the gay quarters and changed
into them. He gave away by lot to the male and female geisha the clothes he
had thrown off—a lined haori of imported taffeta,[65] a flat silk wadded garment, underclothes of Ryūkyū pongee, a singlet of silk crepe, and so forth.

When he learned that Nenosuke's dissipation was becoming worse and
that the Mimuras left him alone and took no heed of it, Ryūchi himself
stepped in to control him. It was the middle of the sixth month. While Nenosuke was in the Minatoya in Shinagawa, Ryūchi came flying in a two-man,
open sedan-chair to the Ōnoya. Then he sent the message in to Nenosuke,
"Urgent business! Come!"

Fearing his father, Nenosuke jumped down into the garden from a lower room of the Minatoya, crossed the shallows along the shore, and tried to make his escape; but he was discovered by the messenger and caught.

Ryūchi dragged Nenosuke home and put him under the charge of Sahē, an agent he had set up on land he owned in Saiwai-chō. He was about to take steps to disinherit him. Through the mediation of the shop people, however, Nenosuke returned to the Yamashiro Riverbank and came to accept his father's supervision.

Happily, Ryūchi did not use hypocritical methods to discipline his son. He made Nenosuke attend upon his own more conservative amusements, and accomplished his purpose to teach him about these things, even though "on the mats of women and wine," with an attitude in which he never lowered his own dignity. These events were in Nenosuke's twenty-first year.

The seventh-generation Danjūrō,[66] to whom Ryūchi had given his patronage, was banished from Edo on the twenty-second of the sixth month, and Ryūchi's close friend Tamenaga Shunsui died in prison on the thirteenth of the seventh month of this same year.[67] These incidents may also have been indirectly intermediary in making the father and son of the Yamashiro Riverbank feel the displeasure of the authorities.

Few noteworthy facts are recorded for the interval from this time up to 1856. In Tempō fourteen [1843], the Kawarasaki-za moved to Saruwaka-chō to join the Nakamura-za and Ichimura-za which had moved previously; Katsu Genzō became chief playwright[68] with the name of Shiba Shinsuke after his place of residence in Udagawa-chō in Shiba. He later succeeded to the name of Kawatake Shinshichi through the recommendation of the third-generation Sakurada Jisuke.[69] Nenosuke's grandfather Ihē died at more than seventy on the twenty-seventh of the sixth month of 1848. His name in the Buddha is Kenyo Hōju Tokushō Zenshi. His grave is in the family plot by the Gangyōji temple. Ryūchi's teacher Seiro died this same year at eighty-three. Juami Donchō[70] also died at this time. Juami was most likely an acquaintance of Ryūchi and his son, but the nature of their association is not clear. However, Nenosuke later received the Juami pen name from the Shōjōkōji and therefore indirectly succeeded to the -ami pen name identified with Mashiya. In 1850, Ryūchi's friend Moromochi left the Miyako school of *jōruri* and styled himself Uji Shibun. In 1854, the eighth-generation Danjūrō, of whom Ryūchi and his son had been patrons, committed suicide with a sword. The next year, 1855, was the year of the great earthquake.[71] The gay quarters of Edo fell upon unprecedentedly hard times; it is said that male geisha resorted to selling tempura in street stalls, and female geisha of the town[72] sold *oden* stew and hot sake in rush-mat–covered shacks. Not even the beneficent patronage of the Yamashiro Riverbank seems to have been enough to bail them out.

Ryūchi was laid low by illness in the summer of 1856. He died on the twentieth of the ninth month, and was also buried at the Gangyōji. His name in the Buddha is Hakuyō Ungai Ryūchi Zenshi. The employees of the firm, concerned about its future under the young master Nenosuke, favored his elder sister's husband, Tsunokuniya Isaburō, who kept a bookstore in Osaka-chō,[73] and tried to have him succeed as head of the house. Nenosuke's elder sister had left her employment in the women's quarters of the Uesugi mansion, married this Isaburō and founded a branch house. However, Nenosuke's stepmother Mimura Sumi refused the proposal of the employees, stating that if she subjected the rightful heir Nenosuke to the misfortune of disinheritance, she would be looked upon by society in a way damaging to her own position. Nenosuke ultimately succeeded as head of the main house of Yamashiro Riverbank. He was thirty-five at this time. I note in passing that Ryūchi's kyōka teacher, the first Yayoi'an Hinamaro, died in the same month of the same year as Ryūchi.

Nenosuke, who became the second Tōjirō after succeeding his father, was on his best behavior for a while out of deference to his stepmother Mimura Sumi, his other relatives, and the many employees, from Kimbē, the most senior, on down. But after the completion of the distribution of presents on the forty-ninth day of mourning, he resumed his visits to the gay quarters, and once his old habits were re-established, came to take no account of the opinion of those around him. He had taken a wife in the time before he inherited the Tsunokuniya and already had two children. Her family was that of Enshūya Taemon of Kiba in Fukagawa. However, both wife and father-in-law had no course other than to look on, powerless to interfere.

Just as royalty and aristocrats often patronize literary figures and make them instruments to promote their own prestige and decorate their presence, Tōjirō associated with haikai masters, kyōka teachers, kyōgen playwrights, calligraphers, woodcarvers, and painters. There was almost no difference between his treatment of the majority of these persons and of male geisha. His father Ryūchi always took pleasure in kyōka; in contrast, Tōjirō's preference ran toward the haikai. The places where he assembled his companions were the Umenoya in Hasegawa-chō and the Kashiwagitei in Yorozu-chō.[74]

As Nenosuke, Tōjirō had the pen name Rikaku which he wrote in two different ways; but after he inherited the Tsunokuniya he received the formal name of Umenomoto from Seki Izan.[75] He further received the character

Shin from Shin Eiki,[76] and named himself Kōi which he wrote with various characters. Occasionally when he wrote *kyōka*, he signed himself Naninoya.

In the theater, Kōi was the patron of Kawarasaki Gonjūrō, who was later the ninth-generation Danjūrō.[77] Kōi organized his company of favorites into a group he called the Araisoren[78] and had Katsuta Moromochi draw up its by-laws. The success of the ninth Danjūrō at a later time was due in large part to Kōi's patronage. Also, after the suicide of the eighth Danjūrō, Gonjūrō's real father Jukai Rōjin, who was the seventh Danjūrō, had returned to Edo, and so Kōi became his patron too. In addition to this father and son, other actors who enjoyed Kōi's patronage were Ichikawa Kodanji,[79] Nakamura Kōzō, Ichikawa Yonegorō, and Matsumoto Kunigorō.

As to brothels, Kōi first frequented the Tamaya Sansaburō in the Yoshiwara Edo-chō Itchome, later the Inamotorō in Sumi-chō.[80] In the Tamaya, his favorite was Komurasaki; in the Inamoto, it was the second-generation Koine. When he went to the Tamaya, his appointment teahouse was first the Ōmiya Hanshirō, later the Ōsakaya Chubē; when he went to the Inamoto, it was the Tsuruhiko in Nakanochō.[81]

Kōi's hangers-on were almost uncountable. Among them there were also persons to whom we should probably be doing injustice by ranking them as mere "hangers-on." However, it is not easy to draw the line, to make a distinction among them.

Among *haikai* masters, in addition to Izan and Eiki already mentioned, there were Torigoe Tōsai,[82] Harada Bainen,[83] Maki Tōei, and Nomura Shuitsu. Bainen was later the eighth-generation Setchūan. It is said the sequence in this school was Ransetsu,[84] Ritō,[85] Ryōta,[86] Kanrai, Taizan, and Bainen. The common name of Shuitsu was Shinzō; he was styled Kakuhoan.

Kōi's favorite *kyōka* masters included Katsuta Moromochi and his son Fukutarō,[87] Murota Kakuju, and Ishibashi Makuni.[88] Fukutarō had the nickname of Abura Tokuri (Oil Bottle). He later succeeded to his father's name in the Itchūbushi *jōruri* as the second-generation Shibun. Kakuju was called Umeya. His common name was Matabē; he ran an assignation teahouse in Hasegawa-chō. Makuni's common name was Shichibē.

His best friend among playwrights included Kawatake Shinshichi and Segawa Jokō.[89] Shinshichi originally was Shiba Shinsuke. Among his favorite woodcarvers there was a certain Ishiguro. As for artists, there were innumerable men among his favorites, but these included Matsumoto Kōzan,[90] Kanō Ansen,[91] Tsukioka Hōnen, Shibata Zeshin,[92] Torii Kiyomitsu,[93] Tsuji Kasetsu, Fukushima Chikaharu,[94] and Yomo Umehiko.[95] Among copyists, there was Miyagi Gengyō.

Merchants and those retired from commercial houses in Kōi's entourage included Ogura Asaru (later Zeami), the retired pawnbroker of Dangozaka; Ashin'an Zebutsu, who was the master of the Yanaka Mikawaya,[96] and Ōtsuya Koboku, the retired master of the Funayado;[97] and Kanaya Sennosuke (Chikusen),[98] a peddlar of kimono material in Takekawa-chō.

There was also a medical doctor, Ishikawa Hojun, a surgeon by profession who had the *haikai* pen name of Gango.

Among his favorite comic storytellers, there were Kenkonbō Ryōsai, Gomeirō Tamasuke,[99] Shumpūtei Ryūshi,[100] and Irifune Yonezō. Tamasuke was a later name of the *haiku* poet Bashō. Among professional storytellers, there were the second Bunsha, Momokawa Enkoku, and Matsubayashi Hakuen. Enkoku was the later Joen.

The professional male geisha of the town who at that time were frequently in the house of the Yamashiro Riverbank were Sakuragawa Zenkō, Ogie Chiyosaku, Miyako Senkoku,[101] and Sugano Nonko. Senkoku's first name was Ogie Rosuke; later he was called Senchū. He lived in Genyadana.[102] Also, those who were called when Kōi went to the Yoshiwara included Miyako Uchū, Miyako Gombē, Miyako Yonehachi, Kiyomoto Senzō, Kiyomoto Nakasuke, Sakuragawa Juroku, and Hanayagi Narusuke. Among these, Kōi particularly admired the ready wit of Uchū, and always had him at his side.

Four female geisha of the Yoshiwara were regularly engaged through the geisha business office[103] of Daikokuya Shōroku.[104] They were Kiwa, Gin, Haru, and Tsuru. Kiwa later became the wife of Hanayagi Jusuke.[105] Haru had at that time already become the wife of Miyako Gombē. Tsuru of the Surugaya soon became Kōi's mistress.

After visiting the Yoshiwara for a while, Kōi bought out the contract of Komurasaki of the Tamaya.[106] A poem-strip said to have been written by Komurasaki at that time was left in the Tamaya:

> Murasaki no
> Hatsumotoyui ni
> Yuikomeshi
> Chigiri wa chiyo no
> Katame narikeri

> The troth that Murasaki plighted
> With her first hair-paper
> Is a pledge firm
> To eternity.[107]

Kōi's original wife was sent back to Kiba on the grounds that she had made a poor adjustment to Komurasaki. Komurasaki now became his wife Kumi and then changed her name to Fusa. This was before Tsuru, his favorite of the geisha indentured to the appointment-teahouse Surugaya in Nakano-chō, was ransomed and made his mistress.

Kōi's daily life at home was not conspicuously luxurious. His food was usually ordered from the Isekan in Minaminabe-chō. He liked broiled eel, and the Owariya and Kitagawa[108] were always coming to the house. When he specially treated someone, he usually went to the Shimamura Hanshichi in Sukiya-chō. The sedan-chair firm which considered Kōi its best customer was a house called Hōkaku in Ginza Yokochō. In those days when there was no postal service, a two-man team was on duty every day at the Tsunokuniya as letter carriers.

Kōi's visits to the Yoshiwara did not stop even after Komurasaki came to live with him. One grown accustomed to the gay quarters cannot forget the charm of a seat on the mats with the lamps ranged about. His next favorite was Wakamurasaki of the same Tamaya.

On a certain day, Kōi visited Matsumoto Kōzan in the compound of the Tomigaoka Hachiman shrine in Fukagawa, where he saw Kōzan's painting of pine and bamboo on a pair of gold screens. Those screens had been ordered by someone to present to Senshu, a geisha indentured to Izumiya Heizaemon in Edo-chō Itchōme.

Kōi seized these screens and as payment sent Kōzan twenty-five *ryō* in silver in stacks like cut rice cakes, to which he added bean jam from the Tenshindō in Takekawa-chō. This was because at the time they called a packet of twenty-five *ryō* "cut rice cakes."[109] Kōzan was a nondrinker.

Kōi wrote down the story of how he lifted the screens and had it made up as a satirical print,[110] which he passed out among his friends and acquaintances. Then he sent the screens to Tamaya Sansaburō. However, he had a bond placed on Sansaburō to the effect that he must not stand these screens upon the bed of a prostitute.

In Ansei four [1857], tobacco pouches with silver chains were popular in Edo. Kōi placed an order with the Maruri company for some thirty or forty, and gave them to all his cronies. He did the same with a set of haori of imported taffeta of the same pattern at about this time.

In the spring of this year, a certain Mimura of Takekawa-chō sent Kōi a hanging scroll of a carp painted by Ōkyo. With this as a start, the thirty-six-year-old Kōi took it into his head to collect thirty-six carp scrolls by Ōkyo. Dealers in books, pictures, and curios searched as far as the Kyoto-Osaka area and assembled a number of scrolls. However, when he showed them to Kōzan and Shibata Zeshin, most of them turned out to be fakes. Enraged, Kōi proceeded to choose thirty-six living artists and commissioned each to paint a carp. Then in the eleventh month he summoned Eiki and put on a performance of linked verse about carp. For the volume of eighteen verses which he distributed at this time, Torii Kiyomitsu drew a carp cover picture, and Kōi did a preface modeled on the declamatory speech typical of *Shibaraku*.[111] The last part goes as follows:

> Ten naru gozare
> Sokuten ni,
> Suao no kaki no
> Hetanagara,
> Tachi no kireji ya
> Teniwoha wo,
> Tadashite ten wo
> Kakeeboshi,
> Waruku soshiraba
> Katappashi,
> Bō wo shiyotta
> Ageku no hate,
> Kono yo no nagori
> Shuhitsu no aragoto,
> Fude no sokkubi
> Hikkonuki,
> Suzuri no umi e
> Hafurikomu to,
> Hoho uyamatte mōsu

> If it is the mark of excellence,[112] let it be!
> On making the mark of judgment[113]
> *He*, persimmon colored like the warrior's robe,
> And like a persimmon's stem,[114]
> While I am unskilled,
> Like a sword cut, the poem's cutting word,
> Here, the case particles, *teniwoha-*
> Corrected, write the mark!
> The warrior's hat, without chin-cord tied,
> If one speaks ill of it, scathingly,
> By one end, the cudgel,
> The end when one has shouldered it,
> The last linked-verse ending,
> Like a leave-taking from this world,
> Writing it is rough,
> In writing, playing at violence,
> Grabbing and pulling back,
> On the neck of the writing brush,
> One throws it in—
> Into the sea of the ink-stone, thus,
> Hoho! I speak with all respect!

In the fall of this year, *Ami Moyō Tōro no Kikukiri* by Kawatake Shinshichi was performed at the Ichimura-za in Saruwaka-chō. The play conjoins

the story of Amiuchi Shichigorō with an episode in the life of the pleasure
woman Tamagiku[115] in the Kyōhō era [1716–1736]. Kōi gave Kawarasaki
Gonjūrō and Ichikawa Kodanji each one draw-curtain, and donated the costumes and properties for Ichikawa Yonegorō, who played the geisha Osan,
and for Nakamura Kōzō, who played Sakuragawa Zenkō. This was all in
patronage of Gonjūrō.

At about this time also, Kōi had an audience with the chief priest
Yūgyō[116] of the Nichirinji in Asakusa and received from him a number of
-ami names. Kōi styled himself Juami, but before long yielded this to Kawatake Shinshichi, and changed to Bai'ami. Kōi was now thirty-six.

In the third month of 1858, a *kyōgen* entitled *Edozakura Kiyomizu Sei-
gen*[117] was performed at the Ichimura-za. The scene is in front of an appointment teahouse in Nakanochō. The courtesan-maid[118] played by Gennosuke[119] is gripping the collar of the *haikai* master Tōei, played by Kichiroku. Tōei is about to have his eyebrows shaved off in accord with the law of
the licensed quarter for having committed the "crime of evil nature"[120] by
being unfaithful to his regular favorite, the apprentice courtesan Hanakawa.
The brothel pimp played by Shigizō Takesuke backs up Tōei and he goes inside the door-curtain. Next, Kunigorō, Yonegorō, Kohanji, Santarō, and
Shimazō, all samurai, come out on the *hanamichi*, and are guided by Shigizō inside the curtain. The father of the pleasure woman Agemaki, Oshi-
agemura Shimbē, played by Sanjūrō, comes out as a sake peddler. The samurai come out, drink sake, and enter onto the *hanamichi* without paying.
Sukeroku of the Blackhand Gang, played by Kodanji, twists the arm of one
of the samurai, and comes out on the *hanamichi* to chastise them. The samurai take flight up the *hanamichi*. At this point Kinokuniya Bunzaemon,
played by Gonjūrō, lifts the door-curtain and makes his entrance. He wears
a taffeta haori, a short sword in his girdle, and low wooden clogs. Behind
him follows Tōei, holding a paper umbrella with a wide circular band. As
musical accompaniment, the shamisen play Itchūbushi style. Bunzaemon
calls Sukeroku over and admonishes him. When the stage turns, it is Agemaki's room. Bunzaemon buys out Agemaki's contract, and marries her to
Sukeroku. Agemaki was first played by Eisaburō, later by Baikō.[121]

This character Bunzaemon was named after and represented Kōi (who was
called Ima Kibun at this time in the gay quarters). Tōei was Maki Tōei. The
costumes and properties of the two chief actors were entirely donated by
Kōi, and Bunzaemon's silver-fitted short sword was one which Kōi always
wore. The writer of this *kyōgen* was Kōi's crony, Kawatake Shinshichi. After
playing Tōei, Kichiroku had the stage name of Hissei Tōri; Tō commemo-
rated the role of Tōei, and Ri was taken from Kōi's pen name of Rikaku.

On the twenty-sixth of the eighth month of this year, Ichikawa Gonjūrō wrote out an actor's testament in which he vowed to be diligent in his art and never to turn his back on his supporters. He had his father, the old gentleman Jukai (the seventh Danjūrō), endorse it, and sent it to Kōi.

The brothel which Kōi frequented at this time was the Inamoto; his partner there was the second Koine. As a follower, his ever-present "shadow" was Tōei, and his favorite male geisha was Miyako Uchū.

Uchū was originally a cloth-print dyer and was not educated, even though he was well versed in the arts of entertainment. He therefore sought knowledge in borrowed books, and took greatest pleasure in the Chinese novel, *The Romance of the Three Kingdoms*. Kōi was amused at Uchū extolling "Kōmei" every time he opened his mouth, and gave him money to celebrate a "Kōmei" festival.[122] This was like rich men nowadays putting on a Nogi Festival. After that Uchū acquired the nickname of War Drum.

Kōi was now thirty-seven. This year saw him at perhaps the height of his fame. Katsuta Moromochi, one of his followers, died this year on the twenty-second of the second month at the age of sixty-eight. He may have been afflicted with cholera,[123] the same as the scholar Shibue Chūsai,[124] the calligrapher Ichikawa Beian,[125] the *kyōka* master Rokudaen Arai Gachō,[126] and the third-generation master of the Kiyomoto school, Enju Taifu.[127] Moromochi was the first Uji Shibun.

It seems that Kōi's fortunes began to decline somewhat in 1859. It is said that loans to such houses as the Maeda and the Uesugi were for the most part paid off, and the silver and gold laid up for years in the Tsunokuniya were nearly all drained off. Kōi's extravagant pleasures, however, continued unabated. In this year Kōi made a sightseeing tour of Enoshima, Kamakura, and Kanazawa, accompanied by such men as Izan, Tōsai, Eiki, and Chikusen. If the travel account consisting of the words and illustrations we found pasted on the sliding panels of the tearoom of Ogura Zeami did in fact describe this frolic, then two or three women also went along. As Uchū had promised to join them but was late for the departure, he rushed on to Kanagawadai by three-man sedan-chair; as a reward he received five *koban*, and the carriers also received two.

Kōi visited the Shōjōkōji temple in Fujisawa on the way, where he received nine more -ami names from the chief priest, Yūgyō Shōnin; he gave these out to his friends.

After this tour, Kōi went back to visiting the Inamoto as of old. His lover was Koine. At this time, however, the Inamoto had a courtesan of the highest rank named Hanatori. Hanatori had a fearsome history. Once after becoming someone's mistress, she had secret meetings with another lover;

when the day came to be discharged from the former, she extorted heart-balm money from him. On other occasions she took money in down payment to become the mistress of various nobles, only to deliberately urinate in bed and thus secure her dismissal.[128] She was voluptuously beautiful.

Every time Hanatori met Kōi in the corridor, she gave him amorous looks. One evening when Kōi was suffering with boredom alone as Koine was entertaining another customer, a little maid came with a message from Hanatori. Kōi thoughtlessly fell into Hanatori's trap.

It was a few days later. The night, after the closing of the stalls in the street, was dead still. Keeping his appointment, Kōi went in behind Hanatori's screens. Suddenly someone else roughly pulled the screens away and jumped inside. It was Toyohana, the apprentice geisha of Koine.

Kōi, dragged by Toyohana, went and sat in a sitting room. Tsuruhiko of the appointment teahouse was summoned by a fast messenger. Attracted by the shrill voice of Toyohana who was raised in the Fukagawa area of Edo, crude-mannered men and women gathered in the passage, and the papered doors to the adjoining rooms were pierced here and there by moistened fingertips.

The geisha Kiwa[129] appeared at this juncture as go-between. She went into the next room with Toyohana and Tsuruhiko, arrived at a settlement whereby Kōi would give a hundred *ryō* each of hush money to Koine and Hanatori, and conveyed this to him. Kōi, however, did not have two hundred *ryō* in ready money on him.

Kiwa had Toyohana wait while she rushed out of the Inamoto, made the rounds of gay quarters to find men like Uchū, Yonehachi, and Gombē, who were indebted to Kōi, and made them dig to the bottom of their purses; but their combined resources still fell short by fifty *ryō*. Kiwa then borrowed the rest at high interest.

Kōi withdrew to a teahouse under cover of darkness; he thanked Kiwa effusively; then took his leave with the words, "I'll be sending the money soon from the shop," and got into a two-pole sedan-chair and sped back to the Yamashiro Riverbank.

This episode occurred in Kōi's thirty-eighth year. In this year, his favorite actor, the old gentleman Jukai (the seventh Danjūrō) died in his house on Saruwaka-chō Itchōme on the twenty-third day of the third month. Kōi made arrangements with Kakuju and distributed memorial prints. The print was a portrait by Toyokuni[130] depicting Jukai in the role of Renshōbō. Among Kōi's memorial poems was one which read:

> Kaerimiru
> Haru no sugata ya
> Ebi no kara

> The form of spring
> Which I look back upon!
> A lobster shell.[131]

In the summer of 1861, Kōi had a temporary house in Fukagawa. Renewing old friendships, he invited Gengyo[132] and Robun to Shimamura Hanshichi's place in Sukiyachō. Uchū and Yonehachi came as entertainers. After the party they hired a boat at the Saya-chō riverbank and went to the Inamoto in Matsuichō.[133] Koine and Hanatori were no longer there. The one they called the third Koine was the apprentice Ukon of the earlier Koine. Kōi had Gengyo and Robun settle on partners, while he himself took his leave with Uchū and Yonehachi.

This year Kōi was forty. While he indulged in parties and pleasures as of old, he had finally come to know his own fate.

> Toshi shiju
> Tsuyu ni ki no tsuku
> Hanano kana

> Forty years,
> Aware of transience,
> The flowered plain.

The story about Mori Kien[134] scolding a man at a drinking party at the Yamashiro Riverbank seems also to date from about this time.

The Yamashiro Riverbank went bankrupt in 1862. Kōi handed the shop over to his stepmother, and after arranging to receive an allowance from the shop upon his retirement, gave his mistress Tsuru her dismissal. Kōi, accompanied by his wife Fusa and son Keijirō,[135] moved to the compound of the Sarudera temple[136] in Asakusa Umamichi. On the gate of a spare grass hut was hung the nameplate of Bai'ami.

After Kōi moved to the wretched abode in the Sarudera compound he sought to supplement his allowance from the Yamashiro Riverbank by the path of literary hack work. Through the introduction of Kawatake Shinshichi, he became a playwright of the Ichimura-za, and they listed his name of Bai'ami on the show bills. He did *haikai* wood-block prints under the seal of Umenomoto, and he did *kyōka* prints under the name of Naninoya. To order, he wrote handbills for shop openings. These activities, of course, had not begun at this time. His "*Kyōka* Twenty-Four Examples of Filial Piety in This Realm," "*Kyōka* Pitch Pipe," and the like on the listings of the Bun'endō publishing house had already been printed in Kaei six [1853]. It was only that this sort of work had now become an occupation. But it did not bring much gain.

Against this, his so-called humble abode became the pleasure haunt of his artist familiars of old. Among actors, such notables as Ichikawa Shinsha, Ichikawa Ichizō, Ichikawa Kyūzō, and Bandō Kakitsu[137] were his constant guests. Shinsha was the later Monnosuke, Kakitsu the later fifth-generation Kikugorō. Kōi, having now reached a position in life where he associated with these artists as an equal, no longer gave out "congratulatory gifts," but the trifling fees from his literary work could not cover the cost of the sake and food he served them. The time this began is unclear, but it is said that dining trays were always laid out without fail for guests in the house of Kōi—while the food did not exceed one or two side dishes of salted fish and the like to go with the rice, invariably, on one corner of the tray a small paper package was placed with two *bu* of money inside. Kōi, again pressed by debt, had to fall back further in retreat from his holding position at the Sarudera. Kōi was now forty-one.

In the spring of 1863, through the help of a certain relative, Kōi retired to Shirahata Hachimanmae in Samukawa, county of Chiba in the province of Shimofusa. Samukawa is a fishing village. No more than two or three villagers could read characters or had a knowledge of *haikai* and the like. Kōi had a banked ring made on the sandy beach, gathered the village children, and had them wrestle sumo-style. To the winners he gave prizes of one Tempō *sen*.[138]

However, boats carrying fish and shellfish plied back and forth between Samukawa and Nihonbashi in Edo. Kawatake Shinshichi, Eiki, Chikusen, and other old friends availed themselves of these to send Kōi letters of comfort. From time to time they also used available boats to visit him. It is said that at such times they were deeply moved at seeing Ofusa, the former Komurasaki, faithfully going about her work with the sleeves of her cotton kimono tucked back with a cord.

> Hari motte
> Yūjo oikeri
> Ame no tsuki

> Holding a needle
> The pleasure-woman has grown old—
> Moon in the rain.

This was a poem by Kōi about his actual circumstances.

One day when the weather was good and the sea calm, Kōi came out on the beach. A ship arrived there and from it emerged a crowd of sumo wrestlers from Edo. When Kōi out of curiosity inspected their faces, he saw some men he knew, wrestlers above the third rank. The wrestlers nodded to one another as soon as they recognized Kōi. Coming up to him and prostrating themselves on the sand, they said: "Well, well! Please come and see us on the first day of the tournament." The villagers who had come out to welcome the wrestlers all popped their eyes with astonishment. "It seems the retired master of Tsunokuniya is a famous man! See how the champion wrestlers kneel on the sand in respect," they could be heard whispering to one another. Kōi sent the sumo wrestlers a basket of various eatables, and in consequence had to economize for more than a month.

Kōi lived in Samukawa from 1863 to 1866, in all, four full years. This was from his forty-second to his forty-fifth year. In this interval Umeya Kakuju died in 1864 and Tsuji Kasetsu in 1865. Kasetsu is the man who began *kyōka* contests.

Kōi returned to the Yamashiro Riverbank in 1866. Now retired in the shop where the family business no longer prospered, few among his companions of old came there to visit him. There was at this time a resident of Shinbori named Gotō Shin'ichi; he was known in the gay quarters by the nickname of the Shinbori Lad, and took great pride in extravagant pleasures. When Gotō heard of Kōi's return to Edo, he took it into his head to entertain him as his senior, and in consultation with a certain Okada Ryūgin of Kiba, invited Kōi's old followers, such as Hōnen, Bainen, Shigyoku, and Chikusen, to a party for Kōi at a restaurant in Shimbashi. Kōi, as a "great one overthrown," took no pleasure in showing his face on this occasion, but reluctantly accepted the request of Gotō and the others.

To add to the entertainment at this party, the hosts, Gotō and his friends, had engaged Matsunoya Kazan, a male geisha popular at the time. Kazan had acquired a reputation for dancing naked. He danced stark naked without even a breechcloth. And not only that, naked as he was he also did things unfit to set down in writing. His engagement for this particular party was of course a case of being right in style. But one of the invited guests, Shigyoku, had abominated Kazan's conduct from a previous party, and was all set for him: "If he puts on his indecent performance before my eyes, I'll give him a lesson," he vowed.

Hōnen surmised Shigyoku's intention and forewarned Kazan, who applied to Chakō for help. Chakō was a so-called man of respect—a gangster type—who exercised power in the Shimbashi area, and Kazan was under his boss Chakō's patronage and protection.

Chakō accepted Kazan's petition. The location of the party is in my territory, he thought. My own protégé, Kazan, is about to go there alone and be humiliated. I can't very well fail to respond and help him out. However, how shall I help Kazan? So pondering the matter, Chakō took the simplest method of bribery. He gave congratulatory gifts to all of Gotō's guests.

Shigyoku threw his gift on the floor and cursed Chakō. Once the mood of Gotō's party was destroyed by this crude behavior, the guests dispersed.

Fearing that Gotō might possibly get into trouble as a result, Kōi called Shigyoku to his house the next day and admonished him. He tried to get Shigyoku to apologize to Chakō for his misconduct. Shigyoku, however, would not listen to him. To entertain through one's talents and art is the function of a male geisha, Shigyoku said. But to associate with one who has discarded all sense of shame for love of money is something I will never do. For Shigyoku's rejection of Kazan, the fault lay with Kazan. For Shigyoku's refusal of the gift, the fault lay with Chakō. Shigyoku held adamantly to this position, and would not listen.

Kōi, bowing to the inevitable, arranged an amicable settlement between Gotō and Chakō through an intermediary. They say the two met in a tea-shop in Kubo-chō and "patched things up." This occurred in Kōi's forty-fifth year. Gotō later changed his name to Shōkichi, and entered the rice-brokering business.

In 1867 a collection of silhouette pictures entitled *Kumanakikage* (Shadows without Shade) was published on the third annual memorial observance of Tsuji Kasetsu, and Kōi himself wrote the preface. On the picture of Kōi inside the book there is pasted a poem-strip with the "Holding a needle" verse which I have quoted above. A copy of this book which I have handled myself is in the collection of the Bun'endō publishing house.

The Yamashiro Riverbank shop was shut up in 1868. At the time, Saiki Isaburō, the husband of Kōi's elder sister, kept a bookstore in Sannō-chō. Sannō-chō is the present Sōjūrō-chō in Tokyo. Kōi, his wife Fusa, and his son Keijirō lived with this Isaburō. At the time he was forty-seven.

Kōi took to his bed in the ninth month of 1870, and died on the tenth day at the age of forty-nine. His name in Buddha is Baiyo Kōi Koji. He was laid to rest in the cemetery of his forefathers in the Gangyōji temple. Among the rough notes he left are these:

> Fuyugarete ita wa
> Kisama ka
> Ume no hana.
>
> Kōbai ni
> Yuki mo yokeredo
> Kagenmono.
>
> Tada asobu
> Ukikusa mo furu
> Tsukihi kana.

Tsugomori ya
Yoshi naki keshi no
Hana akari.

Nusumaremu
Negi mo tsukurite
Nochi no tsuki.

Matsu koto no
Arige ni nokoru
Nomi ka kana.

Ne no takai
Mizu ni suna haku
Shijimi kana.

Ji ni tsukanu
Uchi zo nodokeki
Mau konoha.

Hana ni uru
Ippon mono ya
Edo gatsuo.

Kiri harete
Mina kochira muku
Yama no nari.

Ajikiri no
Nibuku mo hikaru
Samusa kana.

Wabi nureba
Fugu wo misutete
Nadaikon.

Onore ni mo
Akite no ue ka
Yarebashō.

The winter-withered—
Was it you?
Plum blossom.

On the red plum
Snow would be good, but
"How much" is the problem.

Even for the floating weed
Who only plays
The months and days pass!

Last day of the month.
Glow from the flowers
Of the trivial poppies.

Having grown onions
Probably to be stolen,
A later moon.

As if they were waiting,
They remain—
The fleas and mosquitos.

High priced,
It spews out sand into the water—
Freshwater clam.

Serene, but only while
Still floating in the air
The dancing tree-leaves.

Self-Portrait
Sold at its season's height
An item worth a hundred coins
Edo bonito.

Self-Pride
After the mist has cleared
All face this way,
The mountain shapes.

Samukawa
So cold!
A little fish-knife glitters
Though it is dull.

A Thought
When poor,
One gives up blow-fish
For greens and radishes.

Maybe it's tired
Even of itself
The tattered banana-tree.

On the tenth day of the tenth month of 1871, after intentionally delaying
by one month after the first annual memorial service held by relatives, Kōi's

past beneficiaries assembled at the house of Ogura Zeami on Dangozaka; they reminisced about the old days, then together paid a visit to Kōi's grave. Moromochi, Kakuju, Kasetsu, Kōzan were already long dead and the writer Tōsai had passed away in the fourth month of the same year as Kōi. Kanō Ansen, Kawatake Shinshichi, Kikakudō Eiki, Chikusen, Shigyoku, and Zenkō were among this group that visited the grave.

> Kono haka no
> Ochiba mukashi no
> Koban kana

> On this grave
> The fallen leaves are gold coins
> Of yesteryear.

> Eiki

The years rolled on, gradually swallowing up Kōi's companions in pleasure. Isan died in 1878, Gengyo in 1880, Chikaharu in 1882, Tōsai in 1890, Zeshin in 1891, Ansen and Kiyomitsu in 1892, Eiki in 1904.

For Kōi's personal history I have mainly followed Kanagaki Robun's *Sairai Kibun kakkagai*.[139] I hear it is now entitled *Ima Kibun Kuruwa no hanamichi*. Because of my bad memory I made notes from the book which Suzuki Shumpō[140] loaned me with the suggestion there might be a story idea in it.

In addition I consulted Nemoto Tohō's *Daitsūjin Kōi*. However, Nemoto seems to have also relied on Robun's account. I also benefited from conversations of two artists, Matsuda Kōen and Kubota Beisen,[141] as recorded by Suzuki Shumpō, and from the book entitled *On*[142] published by Hashimoto Sokō, alias Chikusen, which was in the possession of my younger brother Junzaburō.

If you go along the wooden fence of the First Higher School in Tokyo and turn east, then on the next corner turning north is the Saikyōji temple. Passing the front gate of this temple, if you continue on looking to the right at a boarding house where paulownia flowers bloom at the side, there will be three or four shops in a row, then another temple. This is the Gangyōji.

The gate of the Gangyōji faces south at the inner end of an alleyway; across the road from the boarding house is the outer enclosure of the graveyard. This enclosure was originally a straggling hedge, over which grave stones of various shapes and sizes met the eye of passersby in the street. Now, both the Saikyōji and Gangyōji have been renovated, and the hedge has been replaced by a strong stone wall. Only the two or three old trees with dense foliage towering into the air and covering all this preserve a continuity with the past.

I decided one day to visit the grave site of Kōi's family, and entered the gate of the Gangyōji. A strapping fellow wearing a blue summer kimono with white splashes was waving iron dumbbells around in the stand of cedar trees inside the gate, and did not even glance up as I entered. I walked along looking at the grave stones arranged in a row, around by the east side of the main temple toward the north rear. The sun was already getting low, and the inscription I was looking for continued to elude me.

Suddenly I heard the voice of a baby laughing, and turned and looked. A beautiful woman was standing there holding the baby in her arms; she had been watching me as I was walking along reading the characters of the epitaphs.

I broke off my search and asked, "Are you connected with this temple?"

"Yes, I am, sir. Whose grave are you looking for?" Her voice as well as the color of her face was bright and cheerful, making a vivid contrast with the gloomy surroundings. "I'm looking for Tsunokuniya. Perhaps the family name is Saiki." In Robun's account, the name is read both Saiki and Hosoki, but I had thought that perhaps the typesetters had accidentally made it Hosoki, although Saiki was the correct reading.

"But one writes the character 'Hosoki,' I think," she replied. She obviously knew Chinese characters.

"That's so? Then you know it?"

"Yes, I know it. Those at the end there are the Tsunokuniya graves." The baby in her arms kept watching me all the while laughing and wiggling around. I thanked her and made my way to the gravesite. I somehow had the feeling I had been talking with the wife of a Protestant minister.

At the middle of the east side of the main temple building, there is a little lane that goes along straight out toward the stone wall. The tombstone stands at the end of it, facing west with the wall at its back.

Opposite, on the left side, a stone lantern has been erected, and on it is carved "Tsunokuniya."

The tomb is nearly square and in the stone of its rather wide face many posthumous Buddhahood names are carved on two levels, upper and lower; beneath each a death-day is recorded.

As the posthumous names are set down in order on the Tsunokuniya stone going back to the remote ancestors of the house, I could read the names in Buddha from Kōi's grandfather to Kōi himself in the left corner of the lower row.

On my way back after paying my respects to the grave, I had to again pass by the woman with the baby in her arms.

"Do relatives of the Tsunokuniya visit the tomb?" I asked her.

"Yes. One lady who married into another family is alive and comes here on death anniversaries. I'm sure she's the wife of a man named Niihara Motosaburō;[143] they say he is a charcoal dealer in Shiba. The temple priest knows her well, but right now he is away. If you like, you can ask the flower seller who lives between here and the Saikyōji."

I thanked her again and left the temple. Then I stopped in the street and looked for the flower seller.

The shops between the Saikyōji and the Gangyōji temples are all small and newly built. Hemmed in between them there is a house, so tiny and old it is almost impossible to call it a house at all, surrounded with reed screens. As I looked at it, I remembered I had previously noticed Chinese anise branches in front of it.

I went inside the reed screens. Inside the house it was already almost pitch dark. When I became accustomed to the dim light, I saw a decrepit old man and woman crouched down. The house and its people gave me the feeling they had been somehow left untouched by the march of civilization. I also felt as if the semidarkness was permeated by the atmosphere of a fairy tale.

When I said, "Hello there," the old man stood up and came to meet me. The old woman remained crouched down.

"Perhaps you know the Tsunokuniya tomb in the Gangyōji?" I inquired. However, they both were hard of hearing, and I had to gradually raise my voice and repeat this two or three times.

The old lady in the rear was the first to make out my words. "Do you mean Hosoki-san?" she said. From this I decided at first to read Kōi's family name Hosoki, and sent it to the printer with that reading. But when I found that Chikusen, who was Kōi's intimate friend, wrote it Saiki, I again decided that Saiki was correct.

I wished to ask the name of the woman in Shiba who was Kōi's descendant, and also to assure myself of the name of her husband; but neither of them seemed to know anything about them.

The old woman only said, "They say he was a very rich man. People said then, if only they could be left some money, because only a little would be enough—they always say this."

I handed a small silver coin to the old man and asked him to offer Chinese anise branches at Kōi's grave.

"Very good, sir," he replied. "It's late now, I'll do it tomorrow morning."

Without trying to visit the temple priest of the Gangyōji after that, I finally finished this manuscript as it now stands without going into the details of Kōi's living descendent. When I recently asked Takahashi Kunitarō, he told me that the writer, Akutagawa Ryūnosuke, is a relative of Kōi. I shall be happy if Mr. Akutagawa would correct any mistakes in this manuscript.

Several years ago I wrote my *Hyaku monogatari*[144] based on an anecdote of Kajiyama Seibē.[145] For the times in my writing when there was wording which treated Kajiyama in a somewhat eulogistic manner, a critic attacked me for my "presumptuousness." I have no detailed recollection of it now; but it's easy to find a copy of the criticism, and if you take the trouble to do so, you can get to the bottom of it.

Kajiyama was a "Big Spender." The inability of a hard-up scholar like me to investigate and know his circumstances is like the inability of a pauper to divine the interior of an emperor's palace. Hence the charge of presumptuousness.

Evaluations of human existence are endlessly subjective and diverse. When my father lived in northern Senju, there was a servant woman in the house. She was plump, fair-skinned, and agreeable; her manner also was refined. However, the stories she used to tell me and my brothers and sisters shocked us.

When she was a young girl this servant served in a great establishment in the Yoshiwara and was praised for her loyalty. She returned to her family's village of Senju after she had passed the age of twenty.

This servant considered the *oiran*—the highest-ranking courtesan—to be the noblest of human beings. Members of the nobility and high government officials were all, in her eyes, uncouth customers. The high towers and great pavilions of the brothel and the serving men and women, the underlings in it, she saw only as instruments to serve and adorn the *oiran*; even the brothel master, however he might prosper through sensuality or exercise his authority, was no more than the chief among these inferior creatures.

The thoughts and sentiments of this servant woman centered entirely upon the *oiran*. In her judgment, the Yoshiwara district was civilization, outside it was wilderness; the Yoshiwara was the center of culture, outside were the barbarians. This is because the Yoshiwara is the "residence" in which the *oiran* lives.

My younger brother would say, "Yoshi, tell us a story." Yoshi was the name of the servant woman.

"All right, come here, I'll tell you a story." Yoshi would seat herself quietly on the board-floor of the kitchen and draw my younger brother onto the round mound of her knees. Her voice was clear and melodious. "Once upon a time there was an *oiran*. This *oiran* was one-eyed. A customer came to her.

This customer was pockmarked. The next morning, when the customer was going home, the *oiran* came out to see him off, and said, *Yuzukinamasue* [a pun on words, at the same time meaning 'Please come again many times,' and 'Citron-flavored fish salad']. I suppose the pockmarked face looked like a citron. Then they say the customer replied, *Mekkachi yokkachi jibun ni wa koyo yo* [another pun, meaning alternately 'I'll come around nine or ten in the evening,' and 'I'll come around the one-eyed, ten o'clock at night']." In Yoshi's fairy tales only *oiran* and their customers appeared as characters.

Evaluations of human existence are endlessly subjective and diverse. One can consider either the Buddha or the devil as a king. If Kōi and Seibē are big-spender kings, then *parvenu* with all their riches, reduced to being pennypinchers, probably repent their sins. If an *oiran* is the model for a queen, then virtuous women and heroines, sagacious wives and good mothers, reduced to being maiden ladies ignorant of the facts of life, no doubt hang their heads in shame.

Just as some great and learned priest should be the king of practitioners of religion, so also there is probably one who should be a novelist king. And just as a great scholar of encyclopedic learning should be a philosopher king, so also there is probably one who should be a critic king, and probably one who should be a publisher king, and probably one who should be a newspaper publisher king. Evaluations of human existence are endlessly subjective and diverse.

After I wrote the biographies of Izawa Ranken and Shibue Chūsai, I happened by chance to write the biography of this Saiki Kōi. When one of so little talent as I presumes to write literature, then regardless of the fact that I have not questioned the nature of the object in my chosen topic and have insofar as possible avoided crossing over into criticism, the charge of presumptuousness is something I could not escape.

September 1917

As I wrote the manuscript of the above biography of Saiki Kōi in haste, I was not able to escape some errors. I wish to correct them here.

I noted at the end of the biography that Akutagawa Ryūnosuke was Kōi's relative. Happily Akutagawa sent me a letter and also came to visit me. This was not our first meeting. It was only that we hadn't seen each other for quite some time.

According to Akutagawa, Kōi had an older sister, whose husband was the bookseller Isaburō in Sannō-chō. Kōi passed his last years in their house.

Isaburō's daughter Tomo[146] married into the Akutagawa family. Tomo was Akutagawa's mother. There is a story "Hell of Solitude" in the collection of Akutagawa's short stories entitled *Rashōmon*. It is said that the material for it is something the author heard from his mother. Kojima Seijirō had told me this prior to my meeting with Akutagawa.

In Kōi's biography I also wrote about an old woman who made visits to the grave at the Gangyōji. I said this woman was the wife of a man named Niihara Genzaburō. When I inquired of Akutagawa, he told me the woman's name is Ei. Kōi's heir is Keisaburō, and Keisaburō's daughter is this Ei. The name of her husband was correct.

I wish to add a note to the matter of Ei's visit to the grave. It concerns the old couple who sold Chinese anise branches by the Gangyōji. This old couple, of whom I once inquired about Ei, have now passed away. The other day I walked north in the vicinity of the First Higher School and by chance noticed that the Chinese anise seller's shop was closed up, so I visited a second-hand bookstore nearby and asked how the old couple was getting along. The old man, they said, died first, around April, and the old lady followed him within a hundred days. I could not help feeling deeply moved. Just as I was writing this, a postcard came from Miyazaki Toranosuke[147] with the message: "Prayerful greetings. Friend Mori! What is it that looms way over there? It is death! The wisest man acknowledges death as certain! December seventh. Prayers."

Next I wish to set down two or three miscellaneous facts I heard from Akutagawa. Kōi's family name is correctly read Saiki. But Kōi had sometimes gone under the name of Hosoki only because so many other people called him by that name.

Akutagawa made known to me the poem Kōi composed on his death bed. Following Robun's account, I had cited the poem above:

> *Last Writing*
>
> Maybe it's tired
> Even of itself
> The tattered banana-tree.

However, it is said that the true death-bed poem was this one:

> Ume ga ka ya
> Chotto denaosu
> Kakitonari.

> Fragrance of plum[148]
> It comes again a bit
> Hedge neighbor.

This latter poem has a feeling of freedom and ease. I think it is better.

Akutagawa has in his possession a one-volume travel account of a tour of Kamakura, Enoshima, and Kanagawa made by Kōi's father. It is a beautiful volume, fair copied before it was engraved in wood-blocks for printing; it has some tens of illustrations by Kunitomo, a disciple of Ichiyūsai Kuniyoshi.[149]

This was a five-day excursion beginning from the sixth day of the fourth month of 1855, as indicated at the beginning of the book. Also, among the *kyōka* in the Chinese seven-character, ancient verse style of Liu Shan-yin appended at the end, there are verses such as:

> Four seas, Ansei *kinoto-u* year
> Lined kimono, fourth month, every day pleasurable
> Going and coming five days, on the road, serene.

Kinoto-u was the year of the Great Winter Earthquake.

The book records the names of twelve participants in the excursion: Sharakuō, Kunitomo, Senkaku, Sōri, Senro (Seikansai), Kyōei, Kosanji (Toba), Kunitomo, Enjō, Senka, Ryōko, and Ankō (Amma Kōsuke). Sharakuō is probably Ryūchi. It is said that Isaburō was among them, but his pen name is not known. The story is that Kōi declined, saying, "When I go along with the old man I have no say, so please excuse me."

Kōi, Gango (Ishikawa Hōjun), Yohei, Ihaku, and Shūu (Gengen Mabito) came to welcome them when the group returned.

> Su e modoru
> Oya matsu niho no
> Morone kana.

> The tearful notes
> Of the little grebe who waits
> His parent returning to the nest.

The epilogue Kōi himself drafted. Other than that, *tanka, haiku,* and *kyōka* in the old and new Chinese style by several others are also appended.

It occurs to me that *kinoto-u* was the year before Ryūchi died, when Kōi was thirty-four. This is about the extent of the information Akutagawa was able to give me.

In addition to Akutagawa, there were others who had information about Kōi. One acquaintance said to me, "In the first year of Meiji there was a geisha house named the Minatoya next to Imadobashi. The master was named Kōno; he was short and fat. His wife was a daughter named Minato of the assignation-teahouse Minatoya in the Yoshiwara; she was usually

called Miichan. This geisha house was named after the Minatoya in the Yoshiwara. About February of 1871, the employees of this house were Kanro-
ku, Bankichi, and Ryūhachi. I hear this Kōno was Kōi's son.'' I have not
been able to verify this story. Moreover, I have not tried to ask Akutagawa
about it. However, if Kōno were, after all, Kōi's son, would he not then be
the dregs to which Keijirō had been reduced in his later years?

I also obtained two or three reports about Kōi's friends. A certain Katō,
who was known as Kokai'an of the Onoe school of kabuki, told me: "In
Kōi's biography you mention Kōi's friend, Shin Eiki; I don't think you were
right in recording his death year as 1904. Both the father and grandfather of
the present Ki'ichi were known as Eiki. Kōi's friend was probably the grandfather, and the one who died in 1904 was probably the father." Because I do
not know for certain the genealogy of Kikakudō, I may have made such a
mistake. So I made inquiry about it to the owner of the Bun'endō in Asakusa. His letter in reply was to the effect: "Kōi's friend Eiki had a close association with both Ichikawa Danjūrō IX and Onoe Kikugorō V. Danjūrō's
handwriting was exactly like Eiki's. This Eiki lived in Kikakudō in the precincts of the Misono shrine of Mukōjima around the first year of Meiji; later
he moved to the vicinity of Maruyama in Shiba and died there. The day of
his death was January 10, 1904, and his age was eighty-two. His temple is
the Nihon Enoki Jōgyōji, the same as Kikaku's.'' If we agree with this account there seems to be no mistake in my date. It should be looked into further.

My near neighbor Umemoto Takasada told me something about some of
Kōi's other friends. "In the biography you say Kōi's friend Ashin'an Zebutsu was the master of the Yanaka Mikawaya; Zebutsu's ordinary name was
Saitō Gonuemon," he informed me. From this I learned for the first time
that Zebutsu was the real father of Kariya Noriyuki. Saitō Gonuemon had
three sons. The eldest, Gonnosuke, was the fourth-generation Kiyomoto
master named Enju. In some books his ordinary name is recorded as Gennosuke, but he may have changed to that name later. The middle son, Sabue-
mon Noriyuki, was the adopted son of Kariya Sampei Yasuyuki, who was
the natural son of Ekisai Mochiyuki. The youngest, Gonuemon, succeeded
to his father's name; he is said to have become a master of a pawn shop.

Mr. Umemoto spoke of one more of Kōi's friends, Ogura Zeami. "Zeami
was of the Takagi family; Ogura was his business name. He had a pawnbroker business on the top of Dangozaka, just as you say in the biography. Zeami's wife was named Gin, and their child was called Sahei. Sahei had a son
Shintarō and a daughter Kei. However, both Sahei and the two children
died, leaving the widow Gin. She was the mistress of the house on the cliff-

top." Through this I learned that my father had bought my present house from Zeami's widow.

Finally, facts about two other friends of Kōi were related to me by the owner of the Bun'endō. They concern Ishibashi Makuni and Shibata Zeshin. "Ishibashi Makuni left numerous unpublished manuscripts on linguistics. They are now in the possession of Mr. Matsui Kanji.[150] Among the so-called light reading in this collection, there is one entitled *Inri no ki* [An account of the secret villages].[151] It is a study of the development of gay quarters outside of the Yoshiwara, that is, the *Oka-basho*. Makuni wrote splendidly in a T'ang-style hand. He was the master of a teashop in the area of the Edo City Commissioner's Office. Shibata Zeshin was a man with a sharp temperament. He was very friendly with Kōi, and among the things Kōi had printed there are many which include Zeshin's pictures. The following is typical of the anecdotes about him. Once Zeshin took his son and a number of his pupils to the Yoshiwara, where he entertained them with comic interludes. He had food and drink served to feast them. When he noticed, however, that one of the pupils had relaxed his formal sitting posture, he thundered and scolded at him. Zeshin had no qualms about setting foot in the gay quarter; he was no stickler, but he had a streak of sternness in him."

1917

NOTES

THE SIGNIFICANCE OF OGAI'S HISTORICAL LITERATURE

1. Fukuzawa Yukichi, *Outline of a Theory of Civilization*, translated by David A. Dilworth and G. Cameron Hurst (Tokyo: Sophia University Press, 1973), p. 1.

2. Martin Heidegger, *Being and Time*, translated by John Macquarrie and Edward Robinson (New York: Harper and Row, 1962), p. 436.

3. Nakano Shigeharu, *Ōgai: sono sokumen* (Tokyo: Chikuma Shobo, 1972) pp. 209–212.

4. Ibid., pp. 263–267. Some estimate of the importance of Ōgai can be gained from the comprehensive bibliography of secondary source material on Ōgai in Japanese. A recent compilation of this scholarly literature runs to fifty pages of small print. See *Mori Ōgai zenshū*, 9 vols., (Tokyo: Chikuma Shobo, 1971), vol. 9, pp. 349–398.

5. See Katō Shūichi, "Japanese Writers and Modernization," in *Changing Japanese Attitudes toward Modernization*, edited by Marius Jansen (Princeton: Princeton University Press, 1965), pp. 425–444.

6. Watsuji's "Nihon bunka no jūsōsei" first appeared in his *Guzō saikō*, 1918; it is found in the *Watsuji Tetsurō zenshū*, 20 vols. (Tokyo: Iwanami Shoten, 1963), vol. 17.

7. See Kōsaka Masaaki, ed., *Japanese Thought in the Meiji Era*, translated by David Abosch (Tokyo: Toyo Bunko, 1958), Part 6, 1, "Natsume Sōseki, Mori Ōgai, and Naturalism," pp. 392–470; and Okazaki Yoshie, ed., *Japanese Literature in the Meiji Era*, translated and adapted by V. H. Viglielmo (Tokyo: Toyo Bunko, 1955), especially "The Idealistic Romantic School," pp. 163–178, and "The Dawning Light of Neo-Idealism and Humanism," pp. 300–316.

8. For example, see Mishima Yukio, in Tanizaki Jun'ichirō et al., ed., *Nihon no bungaku: A Treasury of Japanese Literature, 3: Mori Ōgai* (Tokyo: Chūō Kōronsha, 1967), vol. 1, pp. 532–534, and Edward Seidensticker, *Kafū the Scribbler: The Life and Writings of Nagai Kafū, 1879–1959*, (Stanford: Stanford University Press, 1965), p. 28. See also note 24 below.

9. John Dower, "Mori Ōgai: *Tsuina, Hebi*, and *Sakazuki*," *Monumenta Nipponica* 26 (1971):116–117.

10. Hasegawa Izumi, "Mori Ōgai," *Japan Quarterly* 12 (April-June 1965): 239. Cf. Karen Brazell, "Mori Ōgai in Germany: A Translation of *Fumizukai* and Excerpts from *Doitsu nikki*," *Monumenta Nipponica* 26(1971):77–114.

11. Hasegawa, ibid. *Suikōden* refers to *The Water Margin*, a famous Chinese novel.

12. Ibid., p. 238.

13. The early influence of Goethe's *Faust* on Ōgai's literary and philosophical sensibilities has been documented by Thomas E. Swann, "*Mori Ōgai no Utakata no ki*," in *Ōgai* 9 (June 1971):105–137.

14. For example, Ōgai's "Gojiingahara no katakiuchi," "Suginohara Shina,"

and "Saiki Kōi." On Takizawa Bakin(1767–1858), Santō Kyōden(1761–1816), and other late Tokugawa era writers, see Leon Zolbrod, *Takizawa Bakin*. (New York: Twayne Publishers, 1962).

15. See James Morita, "Shigarami-zōshi," *Monumenta Nipponica* 24(1969): 47–59.

16. Ōgai completed his still standard translation of Goethe's *Faust* in 1911–1912 while he was Surgeon General of the Japanese army and, as noted below, in the midst of a prolific period of creative writing. Among other things, he translated Ibsen's *Ghosts* in 1912, Ibsen's *Doll House* and Shakespeare's *Macbeth* in 1913, and Strindberg's *Storm Weather* in 1914. The full list of items translated by Ōgai between 1912 and 1917 runs to over fifty-five titles, mostly novels and short stories, including the works of Verhaeren, Schnitzler, Dostoevski, Tolstoi, and Gorki. He translated over 100 items between 1900 and 1911.

17. Okazaki Yoshie has argued that Ōgai's greatest impact upon the Meiji literary world before the Russo-Japanese War was in this area. See Okazaki, *Ōgai to teinen* (Tokyo: Hobunkan, 1969), pp. 615–616. See also Okazaki's "Ōgai to Shōyō to no ronsō," in *Mori Ōgai zenshū*, vol. 9, pp. 86–97.

18. Hasegawa Izumi, "Mori Ōgai," *Japan Quarterly* 12(April-June 1965):241.

19. Ibid., pp. 242–243.

20. See Ivan Morris, ed., *Modern Japanese Stories: An Anthology* (Tokyo and Vermont: Charles A. Tuttle, 1962), p. 15. Ōgai's *Maihime* (1890) and *Utakata no ki* (1890) gave birth to the Romantic novel in modern Japanese literature. They did so three years prior to the inaugural issue of *Bungakkai*, a literary journal published by Kitamura Tōkoku and Shimazaki Tōson in 1892, which later became the mainstay of the Romantic movement in Japan.

21. Ōgai continued to do careful research until his death by either atrophy of the kidney, or pulmonary tuberculosis, in July 1922. He published *Hyōjun Nihon otogi bumpō* [Standard Japanese Fairy Tales] in 1920, and *Teishi kō* [A Study of Imperial Posthumous Names] and *Gengo kō* [A Study of Reign Names] in 1921.

22. Examples of this are "Ka no yō ni," "Chinmoku no tō," "Shokudō," "Fujidana," and *Ōshio Heihachirō*. See Katō Shūichi, "Japanese Writers and Modernization," p. 428, and note 5 above.

23. Ibid., pp. 433–444. See also John Dower, "Mori Ōgai: Meiji Japan's Eminent Bystander," *Harvard Papers on Japan*, vol. 2, 1963.

24. Katō Shūichi distinguishes the Meiji "compromise" literature of such writers as Ōgai and Sōseki from the "contemporary" postwar scene. In this context he writes: "The influence exerted on the Impressionists by the ukiyoe of Edo period Japan was a triumph for the Impressionists, not for Japanese art. The influence of German literature on Mori Ōgai was a result of Ōgai's own greatness rather than the grace of German literature. The level of traditional Japanese culture, however—as Nagai Kafū, among others, pointed out—has declined steadily ever since Meiji times. It is for precisely this reason that literature since Mori Ōgai and Natsume Sōseki has never been able to attain the heights of that Meiji 'compromise' achieved in those artists." See Katō Shūichi, *Form, Style, Tradition: Reflections on Japanese Art and Society*, translated by John Bester (Berkeley: University of California Press, 1971), p. 176. In another context, in reference to literary style, Katō observes: "The second approach, which resists the general tendency for the literary and colloquial

languages to come close together, was first evolved by Mori Ōgai. However, the lowering of the public's ability to appreciate literary classics since Ogai's time has been so marked, that there is little hope of a contemporary writer producing work of Ōgai's standard. Ōgai could write in *kambun*. . . . His public could at least read it, if not write it. Today, even the writer cannot write *kambun*, and can only read it with the greatest difficulty. As for his public, the majority cannot even read it." (Ibid., pp. 190–191)

25. Okazaki, *Ōgai to teinen*, pp. 624, 632, 638.

26. See Ōoka Shōhei, in Tanizaki Jun'ichirō et al., ed., *Nihon no bungaku: A Treasury of Japanese Literature, 3: Mori Ōgai*, (Tokyo: Chūō Kōronsha, 1967), vol. 2, p. 549.

27. Mori Ōgai, *Vita Sexualis*, translated by Kazuji Ninomiya and Sanford Goldstein (Tokyo and Vermont: Charles A. Tuttle, 1972). See also Hasegawa Izumi, *Mori Ōgai: Vita Sexualis kō* (Tokyo: Meiji Shoin, 1967).

28. Two decisive events in the development of modern Japanese literature were the Treason Trial of Kōtoku Shūsui and other alleged anarchists in 1910, and the death of the Emperor Meiji and the *junshi* of General Nogi and his wife in 1912. In both cases, the Japanese literary world seems to have followed the lead of Ōgai's initial reactions. For example, as noted by Fred Notehelfer in *Kōtoku Shūsui: Portrait of a Japanese Radical* (Cambridge: Cambridge University Press, 1971, pp. 1–2, 203), such literary figures as Tokutomi Rōka, Nagai Kafū, and Ishikawa Takuboku reacted to the 1910 incident. But Tokutomi's often-quoted speech on Kōtoku Shūsui delivered at the First Higher School in Tokyo was made in February 1911. Ōgai's "Shokudō" and "Chinmoku no to" had already appeared in the November and December issues of *Mita Bungaku* in 1910, and the trial did not take place until December 10 of that year. Kafū's "Hanabi," which dealt with the same events, was written in 1919. (Notehelfer, incidentally, does not even mention Ōgai.) As another example, Sōseki's *Kokoro*, which concludes with an important reference to the *junshi* of General Nogi, came out in 1914, and hence followed Ōgai's immediate reaction to the same *junshi* in "Okitsu Yagoemon no isho" (completed in the five-day interval between General Nogi's death and funeral in 1912), and in "Abe ichizoku," written in 1913.

29. Okazaki Yoshie, *Ōgai to teinen*, p. 5.

30. *Mori Ōgai zenshū*, vol. 7, p. 99.

31. Okazaki, *Ōgai to teinen*, pp. 297–298; Kōsaka, ed., *Japanese Thought in the Meiji Era*, p. 455.

32. For background to "Hanako," see Donald Keene, *Landscapes and Portraits: Appreciation of Japanese Culture* (Tokyo: Kodansha, 1971), pp. 250–258.

33. Okazaki, *Ōgai to teinen*, p. 338.

34. *Mōsō*, translated by John Dower, *Monumenta Nipponica* 25(1970):418.

35. Dower writes: "The bystander [in *Mōsō*] presents himself also as the 'eternal malcontent' and it becomes apparent that his dilemma transcends the Meiji scene. It is rooted in larger philosophical and existential questions relating to life and death, art and science, genius and mediocrity, and the meaning of progress." (Ibid., pp. 415–416)

36. Mori Ōgai, "As If," translated by Gregg M. Sinclair and Kazo Suita, in *Tokyo People*, edited by R. McKinnon (Tokyo: Hokuseido, 1957), pp. 61–115.

37. Ōgai's *Gan* is translated as *The Wild Geese* by Kingo Ochiai and Sanford Goldstein (Tokyo and Vermont: Charles A. Tuttle, 1959).

38. See Okazaki Yoshie, ed., *Japanese Literature in the Meiji Era*, "Romanticism and Idealism around Sōseki," pp. 268–284, and "The Dawning Light of Neo-Idealism and Humanism," pp. 300–316. The *Shirakaba* (White Birch) group of writers were heirs to this tradition from the Taisho period on. See also Katō Shūichi, *Form, Style, Tradition: Reflections on Japanese Art and Society*, p. 186.

39. Donald Richie, *Japanese Cinema* (New York: Doubleday, 1971), p. 64.

40. Ibid., p. 69.

41. Cited in *Vita Sexualis*, "Introduction," p. 15.

42. Cited in Kōsaka, ed., *Japanese Thought in the Meiji Era*, p. 463.

43. Okazaki, *Ōgai to teinen*, p. 476.

44. Donald Keene, "Mori Ōgai," in *Encyclopaedia Britannica*, vol. 15, p. 841 (Chicago: Encyclopaedia Britannica, Inc., 1973).

45. See Natsume Sōseki, *Kokoro*, translated by Edwin McClellan (Tokyo: Charles A. Tuttle, 1971).

46. Okazaki, *Ōgai to teinen*, pp. 484, 486, 488.

47. Ibid., p. 494.

48. Ibid., pp. 514–515.

49. Mori Ōgai, *Hebi-Tsuina-Sakazuki*, translated by John Dower, *Monumenta Nipponica* 26(1971):134.

50. Okazaki, *Ōgai to teinen*, pp. 563–564.

51. Ibid., p. 569.

52. *Vita Sexualis*, p. 24.

SAHASHI JINGORŌ

1. Sōtsushima no kami Yoshitoshi (1568–1615).

2. Ieyasu (1542–1616), the first Tokugawa shogun.

3. Tokugawa Hidetada (1579–1623), Ieyasu's son, who followed him as shogun in 1610.

4. Honda Masazumi (1565–1637), one of Ieyasu's closest retainers since his youth.

5. In 1570, thirty-seven years before the first section of the story.

6. Nobuyasu (1559–1579), son of Ieyasu and elder brother of Hidetada. In 1567 he was married to a daughter of Oda Nobunaga (1534–1582). He later incurred Nobunaga's wrath and was ordered to commit suicide in 1579, as indicated in the story.

7. Takeda Katsuyori (1546–1582) was involved with Ieyasu in several battles over territorial and clan rights. After several defeats he eventually committed suicide and so ended the activities of his important clan.

8. Uesugi Kenshi (1530–1578) and Takeda Shingen (1521–1573), two of the most brilliant warriors in the period prior to the reunification of Japan under Tokugawa Ieyasu. Accounts of the battles between these two rivals for power are well known in popular Japanese historical literature.

9. Ogimaru (1574–1607).

10. On a false charge that he and his mother, Lady Tsukiyama, were plotting with Takeda Katsuyori against Ieyasu. For a full account of the incident, see A. L. Sadler, *The Maker of Modern Japan* (London: Allen and Unwin, 1937), pp. 92–96.

11. Fukumatsumaru (1580–1607).

12. Akechi Mitsuhide (1528–1582) was a retainer of Oda Nobunaga, the first great general of the Sengoku period. He suddenly revolted and killed Nobunaga, throwing into disaster the whole military campaign mounted by Nobunaga to unify the country. Ieyasu and Hideyoshi, allies of Nobunaga, were forced to change their plans in order to put down Mitsuhide's forces. Hideyoshi quickly made peace with his enemies in southern Japan, the Mōri family, so that he could return north as quickly as possible.

13. Honda Tadakatsu (1528–1610) was a warrior who fought with Ieyasu in more than fifty battles. Ieyasu always praised his valor. Chaya Shirōjirō (1542–1596) was a retainer of Ieyasu who later became a trader and, with permission from Hideyoshi, traded with Annam. He was later purveyor to the Tokugawa family. On this particular incident concerning Ieyasu's attempt to attack Mitsuhide, Sadler writes that ". . . they went on by the country roads, Honda Tadakatsu brandishing his halberd 'Dragon-fly Cutter' in the faces of the rustics with a view to eliciting reliable information about the route, and Chaya Shirōjirō distributing money generously with the same purpose. Both were apparently effective in their fashion." (*The Maker of Modern Japan*, pp. 114–115).

14. Hōjō Ujinao (1562–1591) was the head of his clan in Odawara. Taking advantage of the political confusion brought about by the death of Oda Nobunaga, he tried to extend his power but was put down by Ieyasu, with whom he reached a compromise by marrying one of Ieyasu's daughters. (This incident also figures in the present story.) Ujinao's later schemes against Hideyoshi are of equal historical interest, but are not taken up by Ōgai in the present narrative.

15. Mizuno Katsunari (1563–1651) was the son of Mizuno Tadashige (1541–1600), a warrior who served Hideyoshi in several important capacities. Katsunari himself was much favored by Tokugawa Ieyasu later in life.

16. The book referred to here by Ōgai has not been properly identified by later editors. There are, however, a number of similar accounts in historical records of the period.

17. The Ikkō sect of Jōdo Shinshū Buddhism was involved in a series of armed uprisings at the time of the events taking place in this story. The stronghold of the sect was in Osaka.

18. A collection of historical essays and stories written in 1821.

19. Kakehi Matazō (1526–1560).

20. The *Kanshirai heiki* was a record of diplomatic exchanges between Japan and Korea compiled by Hayashi Shunsai (1618–1680), a distinguished Confucian scholar and the third son of Hayashi Razan (1538–1657), the well-known Confucian advisor to Tokugawa Ieyasu.

YASUI FUJIN

*Kafū quotes this old Tokugawa text in his short novel *A Strange Tale from East of the River*, translated in Edwin Seidensticker's *Kafu the Scribbler* (Stanford: Stanford University Press, 1965).

1. Shinozaki Shōchiku (1781–1851) was a scholar of the school of Ogyū Sorai, the eighteenth-century Confucian philosopher. Shinozaki ran a private school in Osaka in the early nineteenth century that attracted a variety of talented pupils. He was

noted also for his Chinese poetry and calligraphy. Chūhei's father Sōshū (1767–1835) had studied in the Sorai school.

2. The Shōheikō was the official Confucian college of the shogunate in Edo.

3. Koga Tōan (1788–1837) was another Confucian scholar in Edo.

4. Matsuzaki Kōdō (1771–1844) was an expert on the Confucian classics and wrote commentaries on the Analects of Confucius. He was a student of Hayashi Jitsuzai (see note 5, below) and later served the lord of Kakegawa as an advisor.

5. Hayashi Jitsuzai (1768–1841) was appointed head of the Confucian college and compiler of the history of the Tokugawa family at the request of the shogun, Tokugawa Ienari (1773–1841).

6. A joking reference to Ono no Komachi, the famous ninth-century beauty and poetess.

7. These dolls represent an old man and old woman who symbolize long life and supposedly the spirits of the pine forest of Takasago. Their story is told in a Noh play of that name.

8. Shionoya Tōin (1809–1867) was a Confucian scholar who studied at the Edo Confucian college and later served the lord of Hamamatsu.

9. The Sankei Juku was Yasui Sokken's private school. The name, literally "Three Plans School," derives from Yasui's dictum that one must plan the day's work in the morning, the year's work during the New Year period, and one's life work when a young man.

10. Kajimaya Seibē was a wealthy sake dealer in the Shinagawa area of Edo; he studied with Nishijima Ran'en, a noted scholar. He was reputed to have amassed a large library.

11. The Master of Ceremonies (*Sōsha*) had as his office the duty to announce the family lineage and the gifts presented by the various feudal lords paying formal homage to the shogun in the Edo castle. He also took charge of the coming-of-age ceremonies and other similar official functions for the shogun.

12. The Recording Secretary (*Oshiaikata*) had as his office the duty to record the visitations of the various feudal lords to Edo castle.

13. The *Chin-wên shang-shu* is a compilation of ancient Chinese documents said to have been revised by Confucius. The collection survived the burning of the books by the first emperor of the Ch'in dynasty about 200 B.C. and was written in the new ideographic characters formalized in the Han dynasty.

14. Fujita Tōko (1806–1855) was a Confucian scholar in charge of compiling the Mito clan history of Japan. He was killed in an earthquake in Edo in 1855. He was an advisor to Tokugawa Nariaki (see note 15, below).

15. A reference to Tokugawa Nariaki (1800–1861), lord of Mito, one of the most prominent figures in politics at the time of Perry's visit to Japan; he was closely involved in events leading to the Meiji Restoration.

16. Ii Naosuke (1815–1860), the lord of Hikone, supported the shogun against the resurgence of the emperor's forces. He was assassinated at the Sakurada Gate of the shogun's castle in Edo by imperialist samurai from Mito.

17. Nakamura Teitarō (1827–1861) was involved in various plots with the insurrectionist and politician Kiyokawa Hachirō (1830–1863) in a plot to overthrow the government. Both were eventually executed.

18. Kumoi Tatsuo (1844–1870) was a disciple of Yasui Sokken who tried to de-

fend the shogunate against the Imperial Court. At the time of the restoration he plotted to try to separate the imperialist alliance between the clans of Satsuma and Chōshū. He managed to raise troops and fought the government's army at Utsunomiya. He was betrayed by one of his own men in 1869 and was executed in 1870.

19. The *Tso Chuan* [Tso commentary] is a famous Chinese historical classic that purports to explain the Spring and Autumn Annals of Confucius. It was written in the third century B.C.

TSUGE SHIRŌZAEMON

*In his essay "Rekishi sono mama to rekishibanare," in *The Incident at Sakai and Other Stories*, volume 1 of The Historical Literature of Mori Ōgai, edited by David Dilworth and J. Thomas Rimer (Honolulu: The University Press of Hawaii, 1977).

1. Yokoi Heishirō (1809–1869), scholar and statesman of the late Tokugawa period. Shōnan was another of Yokoi's names. Tsuge Shirōzaemon's dates are 1848–1870.

2. "The men of wisdom" refers to such men as Shimazu Hisamatsu (1817–1887), Shimazu Nariakira (1809–1858), Yoshida Shōin (1831–1859), and Arima Shinshichi (1826–1862).

3. Motoda Eifū (1818–1891), a scholar of Chinese classics and Confucianism; later the tutor to the Meiji emperor.

4. Ikebe Keita (1798–1868) and Takashima Shūhan (1798–1866) were arrested on the charge that they criticized the shogunate's closed-door policy and imprisoned in 1842; Ikebe stayed in prison for five years, Takashima eleven years.

5. Euphimi Vasilievich Putiatin (1803–1883).

6. Yoshida Shōin (1831–1859) was later imprisoned in 1854 for attempting to board an American ship in order to sail overseas and learn firsthand the situation abroad.

7. Katsu Yoshikuni (1823–1899) studied naval warfare under Dutch instructors, was commander of the *Kanrin maru* on its trip to America, later was appointed commander-in-chief of the armed forces, in 1872 was Minister of the Navy, and in 1873 became Member of the Senate and Privy Councillor, and was given the title of viscount.

8. Saheita (1845–1875) traveled to America twice; his first trip was from 1866 to 1872. Tahei (1850–1871) curtailed his trip because of tuberculosis and returned to Japan in 1869; he died within two years, while establishing an English school in Kumamoto. Both men changed their names because overseas trips were then still legally forbidden.

9. Inoue Kowashi (1843–1895). Iwakura Tomomi (1825–1883) and Tamamatsu Misao (1810–1872) together plotted restoration of the imperial regime. Inoue and Iwakura were prominent statesmen around the time of the Meiji Restoration. Goin was a pen name of Inoue; *Goin zankō* is a posthumous collection of Inoue's manuscripts, letters, diaries, and so forth.

10. Iwakura-mura, the residence of Iwakura Tomomi in present-day Sakyō-ku in Kyoto. A steady stream of visitors passed through the secret back door.

11. Iki Wakasa (1818–1886), better known as Iki Tadazumi, was so respected for his military expertise that, when Perry landed at Uraga, Iki was entrusted with the

defense of strategic points on the land. After the Meiji Restoration he declined a request that he join the Meiji government, preferring to maintain law and order in his own Okayama clan.

12. Ukita Naoie (1529–1581), a warlord of the Sengoku period.

13. The Ikeda were the hereditary daimyo of the Okayama *han* with holdings worth 520,000 *koku* annually. That Chiyo was privileged to ride a palanquin indicates her high status with the Ikeda.

14. The Chinese official Ch'in Kuai of the Southern Sung dynasty, through whom the celebrated patriot Yüan Fei was executed; considered a traitor for having worked for peace with the Tartars, who had invaded Chinese territory.

15. Abe Morie (1846–1907), one of the most renowned swordmasters in his day.

16. The Japanese did not adopt the Western calendar until 1872; in this translation, all dates prior to the change are given as here: "the second month," which does not necessarily correspond to February.

17. Tokugawa Keiki (1837–1913), the fifteenth and last shogun.

18. Kagawa Keizō (1839–1915), Kawada Sakuma (1829–1897), and Katsura Kogorō (1834–1877) were all staunch imperial loyalists. Katsura was later known as Kido Takayoshi (Kōin).

19. Matsumoto Minosuke: dates unknown.

20. Noro Katsunoshin: dates unknown.

21. Itakura Katsukiyo (1822–1889), lord of the Matsuyama *han* and defender of the shogunate cause; eventually defeated by imperial forces, he was imprisoned, later pardoned, and finally allowed to become a priest at the Tōshōgū Shrine in Nikkō.

22. Fujishima Masanoshin: dates unknown.

23. Iki Takumi: dates unknown.

24. Ueda Tatsuo (1830–1870), second son of a rural samurai in Iwami province; an imperial loyalist.

25. *Banki-isshin*, literally "complete renewal of the entire government," a slogan of the imperial restorationists.

26. *Chōshi*: term used to designate those outstanding men who in 1868 were specially selected by the Cabinet (see no. 39 below) to serve as councillors or bureau heads.

27. Bureau of Institutions: an organ set up to study and reorganize government institutions.

28. Matsudaira Yoshinaga (1828–1890), also called Shungaku, lord of Fukui *han* and patron of Yokoi.

29. Ōkubo Kaname (1798–1859), steward of Tsuchiya Tomonao. The incident mentioned here is conjectured to have taken place in the fifth month of 1851.

30. Warden of Osaka castle, Tsuchiya Tomonao; he held this position from late 1850 until late 1858.

31. Fujita Seinoshin (1806–1855), also known by his pen name, Tōko.

32. Mito Nariaki (1800–1860), a member of the Tokugawa family and lord of the Mito domain; he was a staunch imperial loyalist who figured prominently in pre-Restoration politics.

33. Tsuzuki Shirō, Yoshida Heinosuke: retainers of the Hosokawa domain, dates unknown.

34. Yanagida Tokuzō (1845–1869); correct name is Chokuzō.

35. Kashima Matanojō (1846–1870).

36. Maeoka Rikio (1844–1870); Nakai Toneo (dates unknown), conjectured to have been twenty-four or twenty-five at this time.

37. Miyake Tenzen (1818–1882), rabidly antiforeign and pro-emperor, he finally was sentenced to life imprisonment in 1871.

38. The "seven" includes Miyake, at whose house the other six were staying.

39. This translates dajōkan, the highest government organ in the land, set up in 1868 and abolished in 1885.

40. Teramachi, Goryōsha; the former designates a street, the latter a shrine, both of which are still to be found in Kyoto.

41. Yokoyama Sukenojō, Shimotsu Shikanosuke: dates unknown.

42. Ueno Yūjirō, Matsumura Kinzaburō: dates unknown.

43. Miyake Sakon (Sahei): dates unknown. Saga is the northern part of Ukyō-ku, present-day Kyoto.

44. Naka Zuiunsai: dates unknown.

45. Kanamoto Kenzō, etc.: little is known about these men, except for Kanamoto (1829–1871), who was sentenced to strict confinement for three years and died in prison.

46. Kaima Jūrōzaemon (1818–1873), whose zeal for the imperial cause ultimately led to excesses that earned him imprisonment.

47. "The popular lampoons" refer to anonymous satirical poems making the rounds then; for example, one went: "*Massugu ni ikeba ii no ni, Heishirō Yokoi iku kara kubi ga korori to*" ("It would be better to go straight, yet Heishirō goes to the side, so his head bites the dust")—there is a pun on Yokoi and *yoko e* (to the side).

48. Referring to the famous assassination by Mito clansmen of Ii Naosuke at the Sakurada gate of Edo castle in 1860.

49. The Danjodai, established in 1869. It was merged with the Ministry of Justice in 1871.

50. Kondō Jūbē: dates unknown.

51. Tokura Sazen, Saitō Naohiko: dates unknown.

52. Nihoko (1835–1881): more details about her will appear in the material appended by Ōgai to his original story.

53. Niwa Hiroo, Suzuki Muin: dates unknown.

54. Sugi Magoshichirō (1835–1920), Aoki Umesaburō (1873–?), Nakaoka Moku (1848–?), Tokutomi Iichirō (1863–1957), Shimizu Koichirō (1854–1932), Yamabe Takeo (1851–1920).

55. "Imperial Bodyguards Affair" refers to the attempt in 1868 to form a band of men who would protect the emperor's person; Naka Zuiunsai and Totsugawa samurai formed the majority of the band. Yokoi was instrumental in thwarting their efforts.

56. The Negoro family was descended from the Fujiwara clan; their ancestors had served under Tokugawa Ieyasu, and became *hatamoto* of the shogun.

57. Miya Taichū (dates unknown), a Confucian doctor. Kamihira Chikara (1824–1891) was given special pardon in 1878 because of his medical services to the island's inhabitants.

58. Ichinose Tonomo: dates unknown.

59. Kanda Kōhei (1830–1899), scholar of Dutch learning and later politician and baron.

60. Nakai Hiroshi (1838–1894), a learned politician and prolific writer.

61. Koga Jūrō (date unknown), head of the police in the Justice Department.

62. Minami Jun'ichi; both he and the work mentioned here are now unknown.

63. Osatake Takeshi (1880–1946), historian of Meiji times and culture.

64. Arakawa Jinsaku (1840–1901); Wakae Shuridaibu (1812–1872).

65. Tanaka Fujimaro (1846–1909), politician with a long record for distinguished service, for which he was made a viscount.

66. Niwa Juntarō (1846–1922), another high-ranking politician in Meiji times.

67. Matsuyama Yoshine: dates unknown.

68. Yashirō Rokurō (1860–1930).

69. Tsuji Shinji (1842–1915), scholar of Dutch learning and of Buddhism; nothing is known about Gotō Kenkichi.

70. The Kaisei Gakkō was formerly the Bakufu's *Bansho shirabe sho* ("Translation Bureau of Foreign Books"); it later was incorporated as Tokyo Imperial University in 1877.

71. Mimaki Motoyoshi: dates unknown.

72. Empress Shōken (1850–1914), wife of the Meiji emperor.

73. Honda Tatsujirō: dates unknown.

74. This is the Shoryō-ryō, a part of the old Imperial Household Agency. Its function was the maintenance and care of imperial tombs, and the surveying of sites thought to be imperial tombs.

75. Shiba Katsushige (1880–1955), member of the Imperial Household Agency.

76. *Jige-kaden*: a book in thirty-three volumes completed in 1844, it gives the family histories of those of fourth rank and below.

77. Tanimori Tanematsu (1817–1911).

78. Suzuki Katsunori: dates unknown.

79. Toda Tadayoshi (1832–1899).

80. Hashimoto Saneyoshi (dates unknown), a fanatical imperial loyalist.

81. Ueda Keiji's biography of Empress Shōken appeared in 1914.

KURIYAMA DAIZEN

1. Kuroda Tadayuki (1602–1654); he inherited his father Nagamasa's domain evaluated at 520,000 *koku* in 1623.

2. Kuriyama Daizen Toshiaki (1591–1652) was a high retainer of the Kuroda family with a stipend of 23,000 *koku*. He was forty-two at this time.

3. Takenaka Unemenoshō Shigeyoshi (?–1634), daimyo of Bingo.

4. Inoue Yukifusa (1554–1634).

5. Kuroda Mimasaku (1571–1656).

6. Kuroda Nagamasa (1568–1623).

7. Hoshina (1585–1635).

8. Toku (1606–1625).

9. Inuman (1610–1665).

10. Mankichi (1612–1639).

11. Kurimoto Toshiyasu (1549–1631).

12. Kuroda Yoshitaka (1546–1604).

13. Araki Murashige (?–1586), a powerful warrior, was an early ally of Oda Nobunaga and aided him in unifying the country. In 1578, however, he had a falling out with Oda, who attacked his castle at Itami and massacred most of his followers. Araki escaped and lived in retirement as a priest. Later, after Oda's death, he was befriended by Oda's successor, Toyotomi Hideyoshi.

14. Takikawa Kazumasu (1525–1586) was a celebrated military strategist who served Oda Nobunaga in a variety of battles such as the one for the castle of Arioka. Later he served Hideyoshi and upheld his claims against those of the Tokugawa family; when Hideyoshi's family forces were defeated he retired to a temple in Kyoto.

15. Akechi Mitsuhide (1528–1582) killed Oda Nobunaga in the Honnōji temple in Kyoto; fleeing, he was killed himself in an ambush shortly after. Akechi had been a retainer of some importance to Oda, and his deed had profound implications for the history of Japan, since he indirectly brought about the rise of Hideyoshi and Tokugawa Ieyasu.

16. Uesugi Kagekatsu (1555–1622) was one of the major advisors of Hideyoshi. In the battle of Sekigahara (1600) in which Tokugawa Ieyasu emerged victorious, those who supported forces loyal to Hideyoshi's family were defeated and Japan was finally united under the Tokugawa family. Uesugi, who sided with Hideyoshi's family, was defeated by Ieyasu, subsequent to the battle at Aizu, and was sent into retirement with a much-reduced stipend.

17. Ishida Mitsunari (1560–1600) sided with Uesugi Kagekatsu against Tokugawa Ieyasu. He was also defeated at the battle of Sekigahara, then beheaded. Thus the friendly daimyo are those who stood against the Tokugawa family, and supported the forces of the family of Hideyoshi.

18. Kushibashi (1553–1627).

19. Tōjō Nagayori (1577–1631).

20. An ally of Tokugawa Ieyasu.

21. Hosokawa Tadaoki (1563–1645) sided with the Tokugawa forces after the death of Hideyoshi in 1598. Thus the forces fighting for the family of Hideyoshi want to take his wife Gracia (one of the most well-known of the early Christian converts) a prisoner as well. As Ōgai relates, she refused and committed suicide. The incident is a famous one, but Ōgai does not dwell on the details.

22. Akechi Gracia (1564–1600); see note 21.

23. Katō Kiyomasa (1562–1611) was another famous general who, after Hideyoshi's death, sided with the Tokugawa forces.

24. The fall of Osaka castle during the summer campaign marked the end of the power of the family of Hideyoshi. Hideyori, Hideyoshi's son and heir, committed suicide and the family was extinguished. Ieyasu was now undisputed ruler of Japan.

25. Kame (1616–1646).

26. Ukiyo Matabē (1578–1650).

27. Doi Toshikatsu (1573–1644) was a distinguished member of the Tokugawa government, who served Tokugawa Hidetada and Tokugawa Iemitsu. He was considered one of the finest men in the public life of his time.

28. Muroga Masatoshi (1610–1681).

29. Katō Tadahiro (1598–1653) was the son of a celebrated warrior and ally of To-

yotomi Hideyoshi, Katō Kiyomasa, who was made lord of Kumano castle in 1600. Tadahiro took over his father's estates while still a young man and allowed a series of quarrels to develop among his retainers. He was officially reprimanded by the shogun, then later called to Edo and exiled. At this point he allegedly tried to take a young son out of Edo illegally, with the results indicated in the story.

30. Abe Shigetsugu (1598–1651).

31. Naruse Masatora (1594–1663).

32. Andō Tatewaki Naotsugu (1554–1635).

33. Takiguchi: dates unknown.

34. Ōgai provides a long list of fortifications and the names of those who planned to man them. The information is impressive in that it shows the extent of the preparations made, but it has not been translated.

35. Ōgai has provided a list of all the high officials in attendance. The names of those who feature in the story are later translated and identified, but the list is not reproduced here.

36. Inoue Awaji no kami Mochina (1593–1642).

37. Sakai Tadakatsu (1587–1662), like Andō, Ii, Doi, and the others, was a principal retainer of the Tokugawa family.

38. Nambu Shigenao was the daimyo of the important northern province of Iwate (Mutsu); his family had served both Hideyoshi and Ieyasu with great distinction. His ancestor Nambu Nobunao (1546–1599) helped secure the northern provinces for Hideyoshi.

39. The famous battle caused by the misrule of the lord of the Shimabara clan, Matsukura Shigemasa. The final results involved the merciless persecution of the Christians all over Japan.

40. At the orders of the Tokugawa shogunate, to prevent any possible fortifications that could be used as rallying points for future rebellions.

41. The so-called Seven Military Classics from ancient China, written by (or attributed to) such important figures in the early dynasties as Sun Tzu, Ch'i Wei-liao, Huang Shih-kung, T'ai Kung, and others.

SUGINOHARA SHINA

*For a fairly complete and accessible account of the main historical events involved, see Sir George Sansom, *A History of Japan*, (Stanford: Stanford University Press, 1959), vol. 3, pp. 63–67.

1. The ceremony to which Ōgai was invited took place in November 1915. "Suginohara Shina" was published only two months later, in January 1916.

2. Ōtsuki Fumihiko (1847–1928), a scholar of Japanese linguistics. Ōgai based this story on Ōtsuki's *Date sōdō jitsuroku* [Record of the Date disturbances].

3. "Ōshūbanashi" [Tale of Ōshū], date uncertain. An 1832 revision by Takizawa Bakin (1767–1848), the late Tokugawa novelist, was included in his *Onchi gyōsho*, a collection of strange tales and ghost stories of Ōshū, under the title of "Takao ga koto."

4. Ayako (1765–1825) gained a reputation for a time as a student of Japanese literature and a poetess.

5. Date Tsunamune (1640–1711), third lord of the Sendai domain.

6. Date Tadamune (1589–1658), second lord of Sendai.

7. Kamechiyo (1659–1719).

8. Date Munekatsu (1621–1679), the younger brother of Lord Tadamune.

9. Ichi no kami Muneoki (1649–1702).

10. Harada Kai (1617–1671), a high retainer in the Sendai domain, was involved in a plot with Tsunamune's uncle, Date Munekatsu, to have the young Tsunamune put under domiciliary confinement and to have his heir, Kamechiyo, inherit the Sendai domain, with the idea of taking it over. Date Aki pressed a legal suit against Harada Kai with the Tokugawa shogunate in Edo in 1671. When confronted by Aki in the mansion of the shogunate councillor, Sakai Tadakiyo (1623–1681), Kai cut down Aki with his sword, and was himself killed by the Edo City Magistrate, Shimada Tadamasa.

11. Misawa Hatsuko (1640–1689).

12. Shina (1639–1716).

13. Rokusonnō Tsunemoto (917–961), the progenitor of the Seiwa Genji family.

14. Amako Yoshihisa (?–1610), a warlord of the Sengoku period.

15. Mōri Terumoto (1553–1625), a famous warlord of Kyushu who had clashed in battle with Oda Nobunaga and Toyotomi Hideyoshi; he later was reconciled with Hideyoshi and distinguished himself in the Korean campaigns.

16. Gonnosuke Kiyonaga (1598–1651).

17. Hosokawa Tadaoki (1564–1645), general of the Azuchi-Momoyama period; he served both Nobunaga and Hideyoshi, but later joined forces with Tokugawa Ieyasu at the battle of Sekigahara in 1600, and, as a consequence, was enfeoffed with the provinces of Hizen and Higo. He figures in Ōgai's "Abe ichizoku," "Kuriyama Daizen," and "Tokō Tahei."

18. Furihime (1607–1659).

19. Ikeda Terumasa (1564–1613), a warlord of the Azuchi-Momoyama period. He served both Nobunaga and Hideyoshi, later joined with Ieyasu at the battle of Sekigahara, and became the lord of Himeji castle.

20. Kaihime (1612–1642).

21. Kushige Takamune (1582–1613), a court aristocrat of the Shijō line of the northern Fujiwara family. He received the name Kushige when he became the maternal grandfather of Emperor Gosai.

22. Emperor Gosai-in (1637–1685), the one hundred eleventh Japanese emperor, who reigned 1656–1663. His name was formally ruled to be Gosai tennō in 1916. Mikushige no Tsubone (1604–1685) was a Fujiwara.

23. Akamatsu Norifusa (?–1600).

24. *Yukisusuki*, a kind of pampas grass.

25. Date Aki (1615–1671); see note 10 above.

26. See note 10 above.

27. Tachibana Tadashige (1612–1675), lord of the castle at Yanagigawa in Chikugo.

28. Tokugawa Ietsuna (1641–1680), the fourth shogun.

29. Toba (1620–1684); also called Biwako.

30. *Onibanshū*, literally, vassals who protect the lord against the devils (that is, poisoning).

31. Itō Uneme (1650–1669).

32. Itō Shinzaemon (1631–1663).

33. Date Shikibu (1640–1670).

34. Date Kunai Shōyū, who was Date Munesumi, the fourth son of Hidemune, the heir of Date Masamune.

TOKŌ TAHEI

1. The Hosokawa family, a clan prominent in Japan since the Muromachi period, was closely allied with the forces of Tokugawa Ieyasu in the battle of Sekigahara in 1600. Their territories were in Kyushu. Tadatoshi (1586–1641) and his son Mitsuhisa (1619–1649) appear in the opening pages of Ōgai's "Abe ichizoku."

2. The Ōtomo family was another clan located in Kyushu that held great power at the time of Toyotomi Hideyoshi. Ōtomo Yoshimune (1558–1605), mentioned in the text, fought in the Korean campaigns with Hideyoshi but through an act of cowardice was exiled and died in disgrace, in 1605.

3. The Shimabara Rebellion (1637–1638) was a famous insurrection over local misrule in which Japanese Christians were implicated. The Christians in the area of Shimabara in the province of Hizen revolted and were eventually driven into the abandoned Hara castle. Hosokawa Tadatoshi's forces led the attack against the castle. The insurrection was put down, Christianity cruelly suppressed, and Japan's contact with the outside world was sharply cut down.

4. Miyamoto Musashi (1584–1645) was a famous fencing master, student of Zen, and painter. A legend in his own lifetime as well as in the modern Japanese cinema, he traveled throughout Japan engaging in various matches with other well-known swordsmen. A man of extremely independent character, he cared little for public office and devoted himself to the perfection of mental discipline. For the connection between Zen and swordsmanship, see D. T. Suzuki, *Zen and Japanese Culture* (New York: Pantheon Books, 1959).

5. Hosokawa Tadaoki (1563–1645) was a staunch supporter of the Toyotomi family, and, after the death of Hideyoshi, of Tokugawa Ieyasu, for whom he performed a variety of distinguished military exploits. The family rose to its pinnacle of political importance during his lifetime. Tadaoki (Sansai) was the father of Tadatoshi and the grandfather of Mitsuhisa (see note 1 above).

6. Sasaki Kojirō, also known as Sasaki Ganryū (active about 1600), was another famous swordsman who traveled about the country participating in fencing matches. The match he fought with Musashi, mentioned in the text, was such a celebrated one that the island where it took place was given Sasaki's name, Ganryū. Legend has it that Sasaki was killed by Musashi in another duel fought soon after that time.

7. Shimmen Munisai (active in the late sixteenth century), the father of Musashi, was another famous swordsman around whom many legends have clustered. He remains a prominent figure in modern popular fiction.

8. Ganryū Island is located on the coast of Hizen Province. See note 6 above.

9. The Osaka Winter and Summer Campaigns were waged by Tokugawa Ieyasu in 1614 and 1615 against the followers of the Toyotomi family. With the surrender of Osaka castle after a prolonged siege, Ieyasu emerged the undisputed ruler of Japan.

10. Ogasawara Tadazane (1596–1667), daimyo of Kokura.

11. Bodhidharma (sometimes abbreviated as Daruma) was an Indian mystic who came to China, according to tradition, in A.D. 520 and introduced there what is

known as Ch'an Buddhism (Zen in Japan). Pictures of him were often painted by Japanese Zen priests, and Ōgai is doubtless suggesting that Musashi painted the picture shown him by the Tokō family. A picture of Daruma painted by Musashi is reproduced in Suzuki's *Zen and Japanese Culture*.

12. The Yagyū school of swordsmanship, founded by Yagyū Muneyoshi in the late sixteenth century, was adopted by Tokugawa Ieyasu and his successors as the official method to be used in training government officials. Tadatoshi would of course have received training according to Yagyū precepts.

13. Masuda Tokisada (?–1638), also known as Amakusa Shirō, was a young warrior who was one of the leaders of the revolt at Hara castle. He was captured and beheaded by Tadatoshi's forces when the castle fell in 1638.

14. Rokumaru (1643–1714), later Tsunatoshi.

15. Umehara Kuhei (?–1673).

16. Sakai Tadakiyo (1624–1681) held high rank under several Tokugawa shoguns. He was a man of eccentric temperament who wielded tremendous power. Various stories of the difficulty of cajoling him to accept various policies or opinions have been recorded.

SAIKI KŌI

1. Saiki Kōi (1822–1870) gained a reputation as a *daitsūjin*, "a great man of taste," in the late Edo period. He was the intimate of champion sumo wrestlers, famous actors, *haikai* (*haiku* poetry) masters, and *kyōka* (comic verse) poets, and a generous patron in the gay quarters. One of his beneficiaries who appears in the story, Chikusen, published the book *On* [Gratitude] on Kōi in 1900 (in two volumes). Another friend, Eiki, published Kōi's collected poems, *Kōi Koji hokku*.

2. This was the *tsūshō*, or "ordinary name."

3. Ryūchi was a rich merchant who became a master of *kyōka* poetry (see note 15 below), and a patron of literary men and artists. In the popular book *Umegoyomi* [Plum calendar] published by Tamenaga Shunsui in 1832, Ryūchi is depicted in the character Chiba Tobē.

4. *Yomihon* were popular Edo books which emphasized texts for reading rather than pictures. They were generally printed in five- or six-volume sets on cheap paper, with a frontispiece and several illustrations.

5. *Kakihon* were texts in large characters for chanting narrative poems set to music (*jōruri*).

6. *Ninjōbon* were popular romances depicting the love life of the townsmen toward the end of the Edo period. Tamenaga Shunsui (see note 9 below) was a typical author.

7. Kyōden (1761–1816); his original name was Iwase Denzō. He gained a reputation as a writer of popular comic works called *sharebon* and *kibyōshi* until his punishment in 1791 in the course of the Kansei Reform, after which he devoted himself to topics acceptable to the government.

8. Bakin (1767–1848), whose original name was Takizawa Tokuru, got his start as a disciple of Kyōden; he then switched from *kibyōshi* to *yomihon*. His influence, gained through such works as *Satomi hakkenden* and *Chinsetsu yumiharizuki*, continued into the Meiji period.

9. Tamenaga Shunsui (1790–1843) was originally Echizenya Chōjirō. After work-

ing at various occupations, he became the disciple of Shikitei Samba. He achieved fame through his *Umegoyomi* [Plum calendar] in Tempō three (1832), and was styled the originator of the *ninjōbon* genre. He was punished in the Tempō Reform on the ground that his writings were contrary to public morality, and the blocks for his books were burned. He died the following year at the age of fifty-four.

10. Kinsui (1795–1862).

11. Ise Teijō (1717–1784) belonged to a house of hereditary experts in court etiquette. He was a scholar of encyclopedic learning and an authority on ancient practices. His pen name was Ansai.

12. Gerhart Hauptmann (1862–1946), the Nobel Prize winner in 1912, was particularly influential in the development of the modern theater, and the German Naturalist movement.

13. Hermann Sudermann (1857–1928), novelist and dramatist, was another leader in the German Naturalist movement.

14. See note 3. Tobē, modeled after Ryūchi, becomes the hero who sets things right at the end of this story of life in the gay quarters.

15. *Kyōka*, literally "mad poems," were verses in *tanka* form, but likely to be comic; in any case, they did not conform to poetic convention in either content or diction.

16. The chopped straw was mixed with plaster or clay for making walls.

17. Hata Seichi (1763–1823), a noted calligrapher; in his prime he was sought out as a pupil of the Chinese calligrapher Hu Chao-hsin in Nagasaki. Ryūchi appears to have received the second character of his pen name from him.

18. There were four generations of the Yayoi'an school. The dates of the founder are unknown; one theory places his death in Tempō one (1830).

19. *Haikai* is a style of linked verse composition that developed from the medieval linked verse (*renga*) tradition and gained its literary stature through the efforts of the great poet Matsuo Bashō (1644–1694). The *haiku* which he made so popular was originally the opening verse for a *haikai* sequence.

20. The "Three Theaters of Edo." The Nakamura-za was founded in 1704 and went out of business in 1893. The Ichimura-za was founded in 1635 and went out of business in 1930. The Morita-za was founded in 1660 and met its end in the Great Earthquake of 1923.

21. Fukagawa, a gay quarter outside the Yoshiwara, is said to have originated from the time teashops were permitted in front of the gate of the Tomigaoka Hachiman shrine in the Kan'ei era (1624–1644). It began to prosper in the late eighteenth century, and later rivaled the Yoshiwara gay quarter.

22. The Shinagawa gay quarter was known as one of the "four lodging places of Edo." In 1718 it was permitted to have two "waitresses" known as *meshimori* in each place of business; by 1764, the number had grown to five hundred. The courtesans here were reputed to be of higher quality than in the other three places.

23. Naitō Shinjuku was originally a posting station on the highway to the province of Kai, and called the Western Entrance to Edo. A mansion of the Naitō daimyo was erected there. Toward the end of the eighteenth century, it was permitted to employ one hundred fifty *meshimori*.

24. The Hisakimanjiya was one of the two highest-class houses (*ōmise*) in the Yoshiwara gay quarter.

25. Sakuragawa Yoshijirō (1809–1874) was a male geisha described in Tamenaga's *Umegoyomi*. He was a pupil of Zenkō, and became Zenkō the Second.

26. Kenkonbō Ryōsai's name was Umezawa Ryōsuke. He first ran a lending library; later he learned *rakugo* (the recitation of comic stories), and became a *gundanshi*, a reciter of warrior tales set to music.

27. Iwakubo Hokkei (1780–1850), an ukiyoe artist. His original work was as a fish dealer, so his artistic name became Totoya, literally "fish house." He is best known as a pupil of Hokusai, and left many prints, particularly with *kyōka*. He also painted pictures of famous places in Japan, and popular prints.

28. *Katōbushi* was a type of Edo *jōruri*. Katō refers to gay quarters east of the Sumida River, that is, Fukagawa; it was an offshoot of *handayūbushi*, which it replaced in popularity. It was originated by Masumi Katō, and is described as restrained in taste (*shibui*) and beautiful.

29. At the time, many male geisha were also doctors.

30. See notes 6 and 9. Sanro was the pen name given him as a disciple of Samba; he later became the second-generation So Mabito. Tamenaga took the name of Shunsui in Bunsei eleven (1828).

31. Ōgai moved into this house on 31 January 1902; it was located at 21 Sendagi-chō.

32. The shrine was located in Nezu Suga-chō in Bunkyō-ku until it burned down in World War II. The deity of this shrine was the guardian god of the sixth shogun, Tokugawa Ienobu, and its festival was one of the three great shrine festivals of Edo (with the Kanda and Sannō shrines).

33. Now in Bunkyō-ku. It was so named because it faces across from Ueno Shinobioka.

34. The temple is located in Sendagi-chō, and is of the Tendai sect.

35. Ogura was the "business name" of Takagi Sahei (1814–1879), whose original name was Tōyama. He served as a shopman for Ogura Shōsuke, who was a banker and purveyor for several *han*. He later opened a pawnbroker business in this location under the sign of Oguraya. Ogura had the *haikai* names of Hisako and Sōa.

36. Ogura did not actually have this pen name. See Doi Shigeyoshi, "Saiki Kōi Shūi," *Kokugo to kokubungaku*, 1946, no. 7.

37. The practice of adding the -ami suffix stemmed from such addition to posthumous "names in the Buddha" used in the Jōdo and Ji sects, identifying the recipient with Amitābha.

38. The principal seat (*honzan*) of the Jishū sect of Buddhism, whose founder Ippen Shōnin was also called Yūgyō Shōnin. Chief priests of this temple have since been designated by this title. *Yūgyō* implies a wandering or traveling by a preacher, as in the case of Ippen, but there may here be a homonymous relationship with *yūkyō*, merry-making.

39. The dramatist Kawatake Kisui was also known as Furukawa Mokuami (1816–1893).

40. The Gangyōji was a temple of the Jōdo sect.

41. Kita Seiro (1766–1848) was a scholar in the Japanese classics and a *kyōka* master.

42. Matsumoto Tōsai (?–1870), a calligrapher of the Bakumatsu period.

43. Tung Ch'i-ch'ang (1555–1636), a master of calligraphy, painting, and

Chinese poetry. He painted in the Southern Sung and Ming styles, and was widely studied by Confucian scholars in the Edo period.

44. Katsuta Moromichi (1791–1858) was also known as a *kyōka* master.

45. Chikusa'an Kawaguchi Sōo, (1761–1811), whose ordinary name was Yamanaka Yōsuke, lived in Asakusa and operated a book business, through which he published many *kyōka* collections.

46. The name currently survives in the Suwa shrine in Asakusa.

47. Itchūbushi takes its name from Miyako Itchū. The school was popular in the Osaka-Kyoto area in the late seventeenth century but declined in the late eighteenth century. The fifth-generation Itchū (1760–1822) refurbished the traditional tunes, and the school came to specialize in the so-called *zashiki-jōruri*, which was popular with the rich merchants in the Kuramae area.

48. Uji Shibun founded the Uji branch in 1849.

49. Ikenohata refers to Shinobazuike, a pond in the south part of Ueno Park. In the Edo period there were mercantile houses on the south edge; this was probably on the west side where city dwellers had cottages for retreat.

50. *Funayado*, literally, boat moorings. These were places along the Sumida River where boats could be hired to go to the Yoshiwara, Fukagawa, or Shinagawa gay quarters. In time such places became teashops for assignations.

51. Uesugi Narinori (1820–1889) was the daimyo of the Yonezawa domain.

52. *Jūninshū*, also known as *mikawase jūningumi*, administered the public funds of the Tokugawa shogunate.

53. Vicinity of present-day Ginza Itchōme in Chūō-ku, Tokyo.

54. *Jorō kai'annai* [Guide to harlotry] was published about the time of the Tempō Reforms. It contained names and locations of brothels, prostitutes, geisha, their fees and similar information.

55. *Hikite chaya* were teahouses where arrangements were made for visits to the brothels they served.

56. Umeya Kakuju (1801–1865), whose ordinary name was Murota Matabē, operated a *machiai*, assignation teahouse, named Umenoya in Nagayagawa-chō.

57. *Toba-e*, "Toba pictures," were comic pictures originated by Toba Sōjō, depicting animals and satirical in intent.

58. Kanagaki Robun (1829–1894), the Meiji-period writer. In his youth Robun studied *kyōka* and playwriting; he was well established as a writer of *kokkeibon* (comic books) by 1867. His ordinary name was Nozaki Bunzō. He is perhaps best remembered as the author of the satirical Meiji work, *Aguranabe* [The Beefeater].

59. The Kawarasaki-za was one of the "eighteen theaters of the Kantō," and functioned as the "stand-by" theater for the Morita-za. It was founded in 1648, lost its license in 1855, and reopened in 1873 under a different name.

60. The eighth-generation Danjūrō (1823–1854), the eldest son of the seventh Ichikawa Danjūrō. He was famous for several roles, such as that of Kirare Yōsa, in addition to those traditional in his house. He died by suicide in Osaka.

61. Katsu Genzō (1816–1893), whose original name was Yoshimura Shinshichi, became the second Kawatake Shinshichi, and used the pen name of Furukawa Mokuami. See note 39. He is credited with instilling new life into the kabuki theater of the late Edo period with his "new historical pieces" and "late *sewamono*."

62. Famous for its connection with a plot to attack foreigners in 1862. It has survived as the Sagami Hotel.

63. Iwai Shigyoku, whose pen name was Hajitsuan.

64. The Shōdenbushi school of *jōruri*, mainly popular in the Osaka-Kyoto area.

65. *Kowatari tōzan*, striped cloth from Sao Thome (San Tome) in India; later, as *wasan*, it was imitated in Kyoto.

66. The seventh Danjūrō (1791–1859) collected the *jūhachiban*, "eighteen best plays" performed by the Ichikawa family since the first Danjūrō. The copyright is in that family, and the plays can only be performed with its permission. Even when performed, the musicians, singers, and stage attendants must wear the Ichikawa *mon* and the brick-red formal costume of the family. Danjūrō VII was banished from Edo in the Tempō Reforms; he was later pardoned in 1849.

67. Tamenaga Shunsui was summoned to the City Commissioner's Office in Edo toward the end of the twelfth month of 1841; he was sentenced on the tenth of the sixth month of the following year. Two literary works place his death on the thirteenth of the seventh month, but the evidence is not clear. The correct date, the twenty-second of the twelfth month of 1843, is recorded on his grave at the Myōzenji temple in Tsukiji Hongwanji.

68. *Tatezakusha*: writing a play in the Edo period involved a cooperative effort. The chief playwright supervised, but he shared the work of writing with two other playwrights. Six or seven apprentices wrote the less important parts. All were employees of the theater, and were paid less than the actors.

69. Sakurada Jisuke (1802–1877) was a leading playwright in the late Edo and Bakumatsu periods. Most of his plays were revisions, but he wrote many original *jōruri*.

70. Juami Donchō (1769–1848) originally operated a cake business in Kanda. He then studied the Confucian classics and became a lay monk. His pen name was Juami, under which he wrote many *jōruri* and *nagauta*. See Mori Ōgai's "*Juami no tegami*," 1916, included in *Mori Ōgai Zenshū* (Tokyo: Chikumi Shōbō, 1971, vol. 4, pp. 194–230).

71. The earthquake occurred on the second of the tenth month of 1855, and affected the entire Kantō area. It is recorded that 16,000 dwellings were demolished, and more than 6,600 persons' obsequies were conducted at temples.

72. Geisha of the town were distinguished from those who operated only within licensed quarters.

73. The bookstore was located in the original Yoshiwara, as distinct from the "New Yoshiwara."

74. The Umenoya was the assignation teahouse operated by Kōi's *kyōka* master, Kakuju. Hasegawa-cho was in the vicinity of the Suitengu in present-day Chūō-ku, Tokyo; Yorozu-chō was near the Shirokiya in Nihonbashi Itchōme.

75. Seki Izan (1804–1879) was originally a plasterer to the shogunate; he became a typical *haiku* poet of his time after studying with Baishitsu. He wrote under the pen names of Tsukinomoto and Umenomoto.

76. Shin Eiki (1823–1904) studied *haikai* poetry under his father, who was the sixth-generation Kikakudō, and succeeded him as Kikakudō VII. He yielded the name to his pupil Ki'ichi in 1887.

77. The ninth Danjūrō (1838–1903) was the fifth son of the seventh Danjūrō. He entered the Ichimura-za in 1857 and became its head in 1869. He succeeded to the name of Danjūrō when he became head of the Kawarasaki-za after it reopened in Shiba.

78. The Araisoren ("Rough Coast League") took its name from the alternate crest

of the house of Danjūrō. *Araisogire* is a piece of woven material of dark blue background on which a design of a carp (*koi*) swimming among waves is woven in gold thread. The crest is described as *ryūmon no koi*, where *ryūmon*, literally "dragon gate," usually refers to a type of heavy white silk.

79. Ichikawa Kodanji (1812–1866).

80. The street still exists in Tokyo.

81. A "street" in the Yoshiwara passing through the center in a northeast-southwest direction, extending from the Great Gate to Kyō-machi; many appointment teahouses were lined up along it.

82. Torigoe Tōsai (1803–1896) was a *haiku* poet, originally from Osaka; he was ranked with Izan and Shunko in his day.

83. Harada Bainen (1825–1905), who was the eighth-generation Setchūan.

84. Ransetsu (1654–1707) was known, with Kikaku, as a principal disciple of Bashō. A *haiku* school stemming from him has persisted to the present.

85. Ritō (1681–1755) succeeded the second Setchūan.

86. Ryōta (1718–1787) became a disciple of Ritō about 1738 and later succeeded as the fourth Setchūan. All of these poets show the influence of Zen.

87. Katsuta Fukutarō (1821–1879) was Uji Shibunsai II. See notes 44 and 48 above. He originally had the pen name of Miyako Wajū.

88. Ishibashi Makuni (?–1855) gained a reputation for his erudition in linguistics; he was a master of a teashop in the Edo City Commissioner's Office area.

89. Segawa Jokō (1806–1881), the third of his name; his ordinary name was Kichibē. Along with Sakurada Jisuke III and Kawatake Shinshichi II (Mokuami), he was ranked as one of the "three famous playwrights" of the Bakumatsu period. He is noted for his *sewamono*, of which a representative work was his *Genyadana*.

90. Matsumoto Kōzan (1784–1866), whose family name was Kamijō, was originally a master of a teahouse in the precincts of Fukagawa Hachiman until he turned it over to a younger brother and lived in a separate house. Matsumoto was the business name. He studied under Tani Bunchō, and painted under the artistic names of Shichisōan and Kame Kōzan.

91. Kanō Ansen (1809–1892) was a disciple of Kanō Isen, and artist by appointment to the shogunate. During the Meiji period, he was active in educational matters for the government.

92. Shibata Zeshin (1807–1891) was a painter and artist in lacquerware.

93. Torii Kiyomitsu (1832–1892) was the eldest son of Kiyomitsu II, and styled Kiyomitsu III; he was a specialist in kabuki pictures (*shibai-e*).

94. Fukushima Chikaharu (1812–1882), whose ordinary name was Iseya Sahei, had the pen names of Kasho and Amenoya. After studying painting under Takashima Senshun and Ukita Ikkei, he specialized in noh and *kyōgen* pictures, and "popular pictures" in the ukiyoe style.

95. Yomo Umehiko (1822–1896) followed Mokuami as a dramatist, and was styled Takeshiba Hyōzō. He wrote for Kanagaki Robun's publication, called *Iroha Shimbun*, under the pen name of Shibagaki Kibun. He produced *yomihon* and *ninjōbon*, and in the Meiji period became associate editor of the *Kabuki Shimpō*.

96. Ashin'an Zebutsu (1816–1874) had the family name of Saitō, and the ordinary name of Gonuemon. His name as a *haiku* writer was Eiho. He became a lay monk, styling himself Zebutsu. He was a pawnbroker and also banker to various no-

ble houses, and earned a reputation as an exponent of the Omote Senke style of tea ceremony and as a painter and calligrapher.

97. Ōtsuya Koboku (1801–1879), whose ordinary name was Ōtsuya Chūemon, operated a brothel first in Fukagawa, later in the Yoshiwara. He studied *haiku* with Eiki, and wrote under the pen name of Koboku.

98. Kanaya Sennosuke (1823–1907), family name Hashimoto. He acquired the name Chikusen (bamboo immortal) because of his dwarfish stature.

99. Gomeirō Tamasuke (dates unknown) was a *rakugo* performer who became very popular during the period from 1830 to 1855.

100. Shumpūtei Ryūshi (?–1868).

101. Miyako Senkoku (1812–1865), family name Yoshida; a master of Itchūbushi, he lived in Genyadana. Uchū, mentioned below, was his disciple.

102. Genyadana was a quiet residential area located at Nihonbashi Ningyō-chō. Its old name was Shin Izumi-chō, Minamigawa, a small street off Sumiyoshi-chō in Edo. It had been formerly land granted to a medical official named Okamoto Genya Hōin by the Tokugawa shogunate.

103. *Kemban*: responsible for the supervision, appointments, and financial matters, including fees and their collection.

104. Daikokuya Shōroku was the operator of a famous *kemban* in the Yoshiwara. His family name was Kataoka; he wrote under the *haiku* names of Shūmin and Sankyūan. He was fond of noh and *kyōgen*, and was officially censured for holding noh performances with costumes forbidden to townsmen.

105. Hanayagi Jusuke (1821–1903) was the founder of the Hanayagi school of dance in 1849. His name was Hanayagi Yoshijirō.

106. According to the widow of Akutagawa, it was not Komurasaki but Wakamurasaki whom he brought into his home at this time.

107. An alternate nuance of the first two lines:

> The knot tied
> With the purple first hair-paper.

108. Both were in Owari-chō, and were numbered among the twelve famous eel restaurants in Edo.

109. Twenty-five *ryō*, made up of one hundred one *bu* silver pieces wrapped in a square paper parcel, to make *shiruko* ("bean soup") for a nondrinker.

110. *Akuzuri* were relatively small prints, *surimono*, which memorialized the failings of others, and which were first made about the Tempō era (1830–1844).

111. *Shibaraku no tsurane*. *Shibaraku* [Just a moment!] is one of the *jūhachiban* kabuki dramas of the Ichikawa family; it is considered the finest example of the *aragoto* style, and was first staged by Danjūrō I in 1697. It is performed as a *kaomise*, "face-showing," performance; as such, the hero Gongorō Kagemasa interrupts the action with this speech, full of references to the Ichikawa family, to tell why his role is important. It is revised for each performance, and appears to be a greeting made up on the spot. It always ends with the same line: "I speak with all respect."

112. *Ten*, or "mark." In *haikai* judging, an excellent verse was singled out by writing the sign pronounced *he* at the right.

113. *Sokuten*: making the mark of judgment on a verse as it is composed and set down.

114. *Suao no kaki no heta*: according to Robun, this should be read *kaki no suao no heta*, thus following a passage in the speech as given by Danjūrō IX: *mijuku mo kaeri mimasu no mon, kaki no suao mo heta no tane*, in which *mimasu no mon* is the three-rice-measure crest of the Ichikawa family, and the persimmon-colored robe is also characteristic of the role as they played it.

115. Tamagiku was skilled in the arts of the tea ceremony, flower arrangement, poetry, and as a samisen player in the Katōbushi style. She died of drink on the twenty-ninth of the third month, 1726. In the seventh month of that year at the time of the *Obon*, "Festival of the Dead," teashops hung up lanterns for her soul's repose. Tamagiku Lanterns thereafter became a yearly observance in the Yoshiwara.

116. *Yūgyō shōnin* designates the head priest of the Ji sect, of which the Nichirinji was one temple (also known as Yūgyōji). There is a homophone here with *yūkyō*, referring to amusement at restaurants and the like, and Asakusa was an entertainment center. See also note 38.

117. This was a first performance that took place in the third month of 1858. The play was written by Mokuami; the character Sukeroku is adapted from one of the Ichikawa family's *jūhachiban*—the *Sukeroku Yukari no Edozakura*.

118. *Bantō shinzō*: implies a younger courtesan who handles details and performs services for an "elder sister" courtesan.

119. Sawamura Gennosuke III (1804–1863) was a younger brother of Sōjūrō V, and a pupil of Danjūrō VIII.

120. *Shōaku*: customers were required by the custom of the gay quarters to be faithful to one courtesan.

121. Kikugorō IV (1808–1860); Baikō was his *haiku* name, which he also read in a variant, Baifu. His earlier names were Nakamura Tatsunosuke, Kachō, Kikugi, and Eisaburō.

122. Kōmei (Chinese: K'ung-ming) was a nickname for Chu-ko Liang, a major hero in the Chinese novel.

123. A cholera epidemic broke out from the end of the seventh month to the end of the ninth month of 1858, and reportedly left 28,000 dead.

124. Shibue Chūsai (1805–1858) was a doctor in the Hirosaki *han*, and a learned scholar in the Confucian classics; he was employed in the latter capacity by the Tokugawa shogunate. Ōgai had a great personal interest in Chūsai, and wrote a major historical novel-biography about him in 1916.

125. Ichikawa Beian (1779–1858).

126. Rokudaen Arai Gachō (?–1858), whose ordinary name was Tsuchiya Bunshirō, was a brother master in the Shinyoshiwara district. As a *kyōka* master, he was a judge at poetry contests.

127. Enju Taifu (1822–1858).

128. The historical record has it that beginning in the late eighteenth century certain mistresses, known as *shōbengumi* (the urine gang), used such means to secure their dismissal from their patrons without returning the down payments previously made to them.

129. Later the wife of Hanayagi Jusuke (see note 105).

130. Utagawa Toyokuni: it is not clear whether this refers to the third- or fourth-generation Toyokuni. The former, better known as Kunisada I (1786–1865), was the better artist and collaborated with Hiroshige in triptychs (Kunisada doing the landscapes, Hiroshige the figures); Kunisada II's dates are 1833–1880.

131. The idea of form, or shape (Japanese:*sugata*), of spring is that it is *character-istic* of spring—in this case, part of a New Year's door decoration. The second mean-ing is that its color is characteristic of the Ichikawa kimono color, particularly in *Shibaraku*. So Kōi is looking back with nostalgia at Danjūrō VII in his prime.

132. Miyagi Gengyo, mentioned earlier as a copyist.

133. The Inamoto moved here due to an extensive fire in the Yoshiwara in 1860.

134. Mori Kien (1807–1885), a medical doctor; his name was Yōchiku, his nick-name Tatsuo, his ordinary name was Yōshin. He originally served the Fukuyama *han*, but lost his employment in 1837. From 1854, he was a lecturer in the Sho-gunate Medical Institute; after the Meiji Restoration he was employed in the Minis-tries of Education and Finance.

135. This was the eldest son by his original wife, Taki, who took the second son home with her where both died before long. Keijirō became a disciple of Yoshitoshi and a block-print artist.

136. Sarudera was the common name of the Kyōzen'in, a branch temple of Asa-kusadera. It was located on the east side of Asakusa, on Umamichi ("Horse Road"), so named because patrons traveled on horseback to the Yoshiwara on this road. The temple was moved elsewhere in the Meiji period; its old location corresponds to the corner of Kita Umamichi 7-chōme in Tokyo.

137. Ichikawa Shinsha (1821–1878). Monnosuke VII was a famous *onnagata* of the Edo period; Danjūrō VII was his master. Ichizō (1833–1865) was a principal *on-nagata* in the Ansei-Bunkyū eras, 1854–1864. Kyūzō (1836–1911) later had the name of Danzō. Bandō Kakitsu (1844–1903) became famous after his performance of Benten Kozō in 1862; he received the name of Kikugorō V in 1868.

138. The Tempō *sen* was an oval copper coin minted from 1835 until just before the Meiji Restoration. Originally equivalent to one hundred *mon*, in the Meiji period it was worth eight *rin* (0.8 *sen*).

139. Literally, *The Red Light Quarters of Kibun, Revisited*; it is included in *Kinsei jitsuroku zensho*, eighteen volumes, under the title *Tsunokuniya Tobē*.

140. Suzuki Shumpō was Ōgai's stenographer.

141. Kubota Beisen (1852–1906) was an artist and man of letters in the Negishi School. He introduced a new style of news picture in the *Kokumin Shimbun*, but began to lose his sight about 1897, and had to give up illustrating. He was fond of poetry and drama.

142. *On* was published in 1900; see note 1 above.

143. Niihara Motosaburō was Akutagawa Ryūnosuke's uncle; his wife Ei was Kōi's granddaughter.

144. Ōgai's *Hyaku monogatari* was originally published in *Chūō Kōron* magazine in October 1911.

145. Kajiyama Seibē (1866–1924) became a famous photographer. He was born into a sake-brewing family in Hyōgo, then adopted into a branch of the same family in Tokyo. He lived extravagantly in the boom after the Russo-Japanese War, but was finally disowned because of his profligate ways. He went under the name of Ima Kibun, and continued his photographic activities until he was injured by a magne-sium explosion; he then became an expert flute performer for the Noh drama.

146. Tomo was actually the wife of Akutagawa's mother's elder brother, in whose house he was raised after his mother, Fuku, became insane.

147. Miyazaki Toranosuke (dates uncertain) was a self-styled messiah who pub-

lished his gospel in 1904 and built a church for Sunday services in the Kanda area of Tokyo in 1907. Ōgai also refers to him in the closing paragraph of his postscript to *"Kanzan Jittoku."*

148. "Fragrance" (Japanese: *ka*) is an allusion by Kōi to his own name.

149. Ichiyūsai Kuniyoshi (1797–1862) was Utagawa Kuniyoshi. He was a pupil of Toyokuni I, and had the pen name of Ichiyūsai. His work was influenced by foreign pictures, is characterized by realism, and has been compared with the later French Impressionists.

150. Matsui Kanji (1863–1945) was a scholar of Japanese literature. He graduated from Tokyo University and became professor at the Tokyo University of Science and Literature. He edited the dictionary, *Dainihon kokugo jiten*.

151. The *Inri no ki*, in two volumes, by Ishibashi Makuni, was published in 1844.

GLOSSARY

Bakufu. The government under the Tokugawa.

Chō. A linear measurement; about 120 yards.

Daimyō. The lord of a manor, or a feudal lord, usually the ruler of the area in which he resided.

Go. A game similar to checkers.

Haiku. A seventeen-syllable verse.

Hanamichi. A "flower way"; a stage passage through the audience in the kabuki theatre.

Haori. The traditional cloak or coat worn by men.

Hatamoto. A direct retainer of the shogun.

Junshi. Ritual suicide to follow one's lord to the grave.

Kimono. The traditional long-sleeved robe worn by both Japanese men and women.

Koban. A gold coin of late medieval Japan.

Koku. About five bushels (English) of rice. The *koku* was used as a measurement of weight and, during the Tokugawa period, as a measurement of currency, since standard yields for fixed acreage could be calculated.

Kyōgen. A type of comic play especially popular in the Tokugawa period.

Kyōka. A comic poem.

Mai. A gold coin used during the Tokugawa period; its value fluctuated considerably.

Noh. The medieval poetic drama.

Ri. A linear measure, about 2½ miles.

Rōnin. A masterless samurai.

Ryō. A gold coin of considerable value. An exact equivalent in modern currency is impossible to provide.

Sake. Rice wine.

Samisen. A three-stringed musical instrument often used to accompany singing.

Sarugaku. In the Tokugawa period, a comic farce with dancing.

Se. A square measure of land; about a quarter of an acre.

Seppuku. Ritual suicide by disembowelment, often referred to in the West as *hara-kiri*. After the person committing suicide cuts into his own abdomen, his Second beheads him.

Sewamono. A style of Kabuki drama dealing with contemporary life.

Shogun. The highest administrative title of the Bakufu, always held by a member of the Tokugawa family.

Shoji. Sliding screens covered with translucent white paper to let in light.

Tan. A square measure of land; Ten *se*, or about 2 ½ acres.